VARIETIES

OF

RELIGIOUS

PRESENCE

MISSION IN PUBLIC LIFE

David A. Roozen
William McKinney
Jackson W. Carroll

THE PILGRIM PRESS

NEW YORK

Library of Congress Cataloging in Publication Data

Roozen, David A.
  Varieties of religious presence.

  1. Hartford (Conn.)—Religious life and customs.
2. Hartford (Conn.)—Church history.   3. Sociology,
Christian—Connecticut—Hartford.   4. Religion and
sociology.   I. McKinney, William, 1946–
II. Carroll, Jackson W.   III. Title.
BL2525.R66   1984   261.1'09746'3   84-19075
ISBN 0-8298-0724-1 (pbk.)

The Pilgrim Press, 132 West 31 Street, New York, NY 10001

Contents

Preface

Two imposing towers rise from Hartford, Connecticut's Main Street. One is the steeple of the First Church of Christ, founded by the Rev. Thomas Hooker in 1636; the other is the home office of The Travelers Insurance Companies, one of the nation's major financial institutions. The two buildings are at the center of a metropolitan area of two dozen towns and nearly 700,000 people.

In a sense this book is about the two towers and thousands like them across the United States. Its subject is "religious presence," the myriad ways that religious institutions and religious values influence—consciously or unconsciously—the life of a metropolitan area and its people.

The setting is important. Hartford is not Milwaukee, or Atlanta, or Salt Lake City, or Los Angeles. It has its own history, culture, problems, and religious mix and climate. Religion is "present" in Hartford in distinctive ways. At the same time we believe that what is true of Hartford is true of many other areas as well: The relationship between the "two towers," between religious institutions and the communities of which they are a part, is less clear than it once was. In this book we look at Hartford and its religious institutions in some detail, but the subject transcends the middle-sized New England metropolitan area that is its focus.

We begin with an introduction to the problem itself—the relationship of religious institutions to public life—and to the concept of religious presence that informs our work. In chapter 2 we turn to congregations as institutional expressions of religious presence, outline a perspective on congregations, and introduce four "mission orientations," or ways in which congregations understand their relationship to public life. Chapters 3 and 4 deal with the setting of our study, tracing the role of religion in Hartford's history and looking at the region from varied perspectives.

Chapter 5 provides an overview of Hartford's congregations and introduces the case studies that constitute the main body of the book. Chapters 6 through 9 look at ten different congregations and the ways they understand and live out their relationship to the wider community. We take a comparative look at the cases in chapter 10 and sum up and discuss our major findings in chapter 11.

The study on which this book is based grows out of the commitment of Hartford Seminary and the United Church Board for Homeland Ministries to the application of social science research to mission issues. The project has been a cooperative effort throughout. We especially appreciate the support of officials and colleagues at our institutions over the course of the research.

The Lilly Endowment provided significant financial assistance for the project, for which we are particularly grateful.

Several persons assisted with the case studies and in other ways and in so doing contributed to our understanding of religion's role in the region and to this book. Special thanks to David Bromley, Alice Evans, Larry Feder, Thomas Hoyt Jr., Joanne Kidd, Douglass Lewis, Adair Lummis, Arlene Nickerson, Anne Puyo, Lucille R. Rios, Susan Carroll Rome, Melvin Williams, and Elliott Wright.

A substantial number of people gave of their time as Project Advisory Group members, and others completed survey questionnaires and talked with us about their faith and concern for public life. We especially single out Philip Amerson, William V. D'Antonio, Linda Davis, Carl S. Dudley, Theodore Erickson, Sidney Gardner, Clifford Greene, Barbara Hargrove, R. Alan Johnson, Fr. David MacDonald, Rudi Mitchell, Alfonso Roman, Donald Steinle, Robert Strommen, and Franklin Vilas.

Kathy Jansen, Mary Jane Ross, and Lynne Schechter provided able office assistance over the course of the project.

Above all, we thank the members and leaders of the congregations who opened themselves to us and let us learn from them. This book is dedicated to their continuing ministry and presence in the life of the region.

The order of the authors' names reflects a break from convention to allow the last alphabetically to be first. In the degree of contribution to the various aspects of research and writing, each author contributed equally.

VARIETIES
OF
RELIGIOUS
PRESENCE

CHAPTER 1
RELIGIOUS PRESENCE: AN INTRODUCTION

[Emily] climbed the tower of Riverside Church and looked out, turn-
ing around time after time like a dog unable to find its spot. Across
the Hudson, the high rises of New Jersey lurked behind a veil of smog.
Southward stretched the apartment buildings of Riverside Drive, in
their decaying, multi-windowed elegance. Inland lay brick row
houses and redevelopment projects. But even if she could have looked
in every direction at once, the city was too vast to take in. . . . It was
composed of hundreds of self-contained worlds. Getting a fix on it
was like trying to do a jigsaw puzzle with pieces from many different
puzzles. From the Castle Tree [a tree which Emily and her friends
climbed in their childhood in Newland, Tennessee] you could take in
all Newland at once. Most everyone you saw, you already knew. You
knew what church they went to and which dentist cleaned their teeth.
You knew which shop the clothes they were wearing came from and
how much they cost. You knew which movie they had seen last
weekend and with whom. You knew whose third cousin once removed
they were, and which three houses in town their family had previ-
ously occupied. And they knew all those things about you. You could
sit on the beach at a TVA lake with the ageless cliffs and perennial
falls behind you, and the billions of receding stars overhead—and
know exactly where you sit. Here in New York, she didn't have a
clue. . . .
    She put her head in her hands and cried.[1]

The disorientation and despair that Emily felt on her encounter with the
city may not be too different from that which pervades many urban

3

churches and synagogues. Despite the fact that Christianity began as an urban social movement, the Christian church's presence in the city has frequently been an uneasy one. More often than not it has been ineffective as church leaders, sharing Emily's disorientation and despair, have faced the complexities of urban life without many clues as to its character or strategies for responding to its challenges. Why has this been the case? Why is it that religious presence in urban life has been so difficult? Emily's difficulty provides some important clues. There are at least two reasons for the bewilderment and despair that Emily expressed as she gazed out on New York City from the tower of Riverside Church. First, there was the sheer complexity of the city that unfolded below her. She was unable to comprehend such a phenomenon. The second cause of her difficulty was that she was trying to see the city that surrounded her through the cultural lenses she had brought with her from Newland, Tennessee, and those lenses were inadequate for the task. We suggest that these two factors are at the heart of the problem of leaders and members of religious institutions as they face questions of institutional survival in the cities and seek meaningful individual and institutional expressions of religious presence today. The urban reality is complex, dynamic, and fluid. It is also difficult to comprehend. And the cultural lenses and social forms through which religious leaders and members have sought to understand their role in relation to urban reality and to develop meaningful strategies have not always been helpful or adequate. Each of these factors is discussed below.

church's goals

Characteristics of Urban Society

We do not intend to provide a comprehensive review of the factors that make modern urban society so complex; numerous excellent treatments of the topic are already available.[2] Rather, we discuss a few especially critical and enduring problems.

The first problem to be noted is that urban society includes both the central city and the surrounding suburbs that depend on the central city for jobs or various services. The Bureau of the Census uses the term Standard Metropolitan Statistical Area to refer to a central city of 50,000 or more and its contiguous counties (or towns in New England, where the town, not the county, is the meaningful political unit). Thus when we use the term urban we refer not only to a central city, but also to an entire metropolitan area. This is necessary because of the movement of people and industry out of the central cities into the surrounding suburbs. The movement of people to the suburbs is not a new phenomenon; the suburbanization of industry and other businesses is more recent. This development is a product of the improvement of the interstate highway system, dramatic changes in telecommunications, new shopping malls,

4

and industrial and office parks, which tax-hungry suburbs have recently encouraged. The movement of industry to the suburbs has meant a depletion of job opportunities in central cities and a change in the nature of the jobs that are available. Rather than being regional centers for retail shopping or manufacturing centers, the central cities have become administrative and financial centers, convention centers, and centers of cultural, health, and recreational opportunities for the metropolitan region. Thus the jobs available in the central cities are, for the most part, no longer in manufacturing, but in service, clerical, managerial, and professional occupations.

Second, the movement of people and jobs to the suburbs has been selective. Primarily, it has occurred among those who can afford to move—the middle- and upper-income families—leaving the central cities with heavy concentrations of minorities, new immigrants who have come looking for jobs, the elderly, and the less educated and extremely poor (regardless of age or ethnicity). Among these groups those who are able to work have traditionally found jobs in blue-collar industries. But these jobs have now migrated to the suburbs or, as is the case in some areas, have declined as high-technology industries have replaced heavy manufacturing. The result is a severe mismatch of people and jobs in central cities, exacerbating the poverty that was already high and increasing the unemployment rates of inner-city residents to more than twice the national average. The unemployment rates for black teenagers—the majority of whom are in the central cities—are especially high, exceeding 30 percent since 1970 and surpassing 50 percent in some reporting periods. These rates are caused not only by the mismatch of jobs and people in the central cities, but also by the continuing legacy of racism that has excluded minorities from equal opportunities in housing, education, and jobs. Although these problems are not new to the cities, they are persisting and, if anything, getting worse because of the changes that are occurring in the decentralization and deconcentration of people and jobs. A generally upbeat assessment of the next fifty years that appeared in *U.S. News and World Report* in 1983 foresaw most of the population living in "urban utopias." But the article included this caveat:

> *One problem for which no relief is forecast: In large, aging cities, vast neighborhoods housing the least mobile of Americans—the poor, the elderly and new immigrants from other lands—will continue to crumble. The residential parts of central cities "will be more a repository for those who have fallen off the train."*[3]

A third related characteristic of metropolitan areas, which follows from the first two, is the increasing financial problems faced by central city governments in particular and by some suburban towns. The erosion of

5

the central city's tax base through the migration of business, industry, and middle- and upper-income families to the suburbs or the Sun Belt has not been accompanied by a corresponding decline in the need for services. Indeed, the concentration of the elderly and the poor in the cities has increased the need for services. Additionally, the cities have continued to house services, such as hospitals, institutions of higher education, museums, and other cultural and recreational opportunities, for surrounding suburbs. Some of these services cost the city directly to provide; others cost indirectly because they are tax exempt. One study shows that the net public service subsidy of Detroit to its suburbs ranges from $1.73 per capita for one of its low-income industrial suburbs to $12.58 per capita for a high-income residential and commercial suburb.[4] The "new federalism" of the Reagan administration has contributed to these problems by drastically reducing federal funding to assist cities in providing human services. Also there is the domination of many state legislatures by suburban and small-town legislators, with little apparent interest in the plight faced by the cities. Unless considerable funding from state and federal sources is restored, it is highly likely that some central cities will not be able to make it financially.

The economic problems of the central cities reflect a fourth characteristic of metropolitan areas: the interdependence of central cities and suburbs. The character of urban society is such that it is impossible for central cities and suburbs to exist without each other. The problem is, however, that this interdependence is often not recognized, much less acknowledged or supported, by the actions of suburban residents and governments. Thus restrictive zoning codes and the refusal to allow low- and moderate-income housing to be built in many affluent suburbs have made it difficult, if not impossible, for many blue-collar central-city residents to move nearer to available jobs. Instead, they must commute out of the city, passing many suburban residents on their way to white-collar jobs in the central city. School busing, especially when it has involved crossing city-suburban political boundaries, has been among the most controversial and divisive issues of the latter half of this century. Furthermore, efforts at establishing regional governments to deal with issues of interdependence have generally met with great resistance. Regional planning units in some metropolitan areas, made up of representatives from the city and its suburbs, have made some progress toward affirming city-suburban interdependence, but they have little actual clout to enforce compliance with regional plans.

The political problems of regional planning commissions are indicative of a fifth characteristic of urban life. It is what might be called "enclave" politics. Both within the central cities, with their various groups—ethnic, racial, elderly, gay, straight, and so forth—and in suburbs there has been a growing polarization into class, race, ethnic, neighborhood, life-style, or

6

life-cycle interests. This political activism calls into question the often-stated assumption that urban mass society gives rise to anomie, apathy, and lack of involvement in community political issues on the part of its citizens. Much of the political involvement that does emerge is reactive and negative. There appears to be an inability or unwillingness to allow any vision of a common good to transcend or set limits on one's particularistic loyalties or group interests. As a result, urban politics are increasingly characterized by acrimonious conflict (although we do not mean to suggest that all conflict is negative). Those who are involved in city and suburban governments are subjected to criticism and abuse by special interest groups to the point where many potentially effective leaders are discouraged from entering electoral politics or government service.

The final characteristic of contemporary urban life that we will mention is *privatization*. This involves giving the concerns of an individual's private life and fulfillment precedence over a concern for public life and the public good, that which pertains to and affects the people as a whole. One's private life includes one's leisure activities, one's life with friends and family, and one's solitude. In contrast, public life, to use Parker Palmer's helpful definition, is "our life among strangers, strangers with whom our lot is cast, with whom we are interdependent whether we like it or not."[5] Both aspects of life are good and necessary for fully human life. ⎦ = ?? They are interdependent; each enriches and strengthens the other. Many observers of contemporary society, however, believe that there has been a growing tendency to give the private precedence over the public, to place personal fulfillment over the public good.[6] Perhaps it is a reaction to the complexity of the public sphere, which has come to be dominated by large-scale institutions—not only government, but corporations and other large-scale bureaucracies (including religious bureaucracies) as well. Also, like what we called enclave politics, perhaps it reflects the relative lack of any overarching beliefs and values that define the common good and promote a sense of solidarity.[7] Such beliefs and values historically have been the function of a society's religion, as in the *societas christiana* of the Middle Ages. But it is debatable whether any such solidarity-promoting values or vision of the *common* good exist in a society as religiously and culturally pluralistic as urban America. Thus, owing to the complexity of public life and the lack of beliefs and values to promote unity, society has come to exalt the private over the public and to ignore their interdependence. With considerable irony, columnist Ellen Goodman describes the conversion of a vacant church building in her Boston neighborhood into condominiums. She interprets it as a parable of privatization:

nice word choice

> It seemed to me that there was something too symbolic in this secular conversion. Another meeting place had been lost. Another private living space had been created.

worth"

7

public → private...

church = community amongst strangers
(in metro, t importance perhaps?)

very problematic

It looked like part of a pattern, away from the communal world to the private. A pattern in which people value what we share less than what we own. . . .

As our sense of community diminishes, we retreat to our private spaces. As we retreat, our sense of community diminishes. Public space becomes a burden on the private dweller, a white elephant on the market.

So we no longer meet on public ground but subdivide it. We sell the church and buy a living unit. We call this conversion.[8]

Suburbanization—whether it is cause, correlate, or consequence—has provided a most hospitable environment for the expression of privatization. It has enabled the separation of residence—the prime locale for the private sphere—from work and from the other institutions that make up the public sphere. It has enhanced the homogeneity of suburban residents by restrictive zoning, making it less likely that one encounter the "strangers" who are part of the larger public and more likely that one encounter those who are one's own "kind of people." Suburbanization has also provided an escape from the problems of the central cities. A town official in the suburb from which several of the case studies are drawn, described the town as a Shangri-la *into* which its citizens retreat from their jobs in the city. It is interesting to contrast the Shangri-la image with that of the ancient Greek cities into which the farmers and shepherds retreated to escape the dangers lurking outside the city walls. But there is some evidence that all is not well in Shangri-la either, that the "golden age" of the suburbs is beginning to tarnish. Declining birthrates, together with the inability of many young couples to afford single-family suburban housing, have led to a sharp decrease in school enrollments, an increase in school closings, and a graying population. Rising divorce rates and a higher incidence of violent crimes, juvenile delinquency, and drug abuse are cited by suburban police as significant social problems.[9]

The six characteristics of metropolitan areas described in this chapter constitute a complex and difficult situation that is sure to perplex any person or group wishing to work for a more humane and equitable urban environment. It is little wonder that religious leaders and members who want to make a difference in such a setting often end up despairing. The reader who is familiar with the urban situation in the 1960s will note, however, that many of the urban characteristics mentioned here were true in that period as well, or were beginning to be evident. And much of the literature on urban ministry of the 1960s bemoaned the churches' failure to address these issues significantly. The strong conviction expressed in many quarters was that the forms in which religious life was present in urban society were anachronistic, inappropriate, and unfaithful to the Judeo-Christian tradition. This leads to the second clue from Emily's experience on the tower of Riverside Church.

8

RELIGIOUS RESPONSES IN URBAN SOCIETY

As suggested earlier, another reason Emily was so disoriented and despairing from what she saw of the city stemmed from the cultural lenses through which she viewed the city—lenses brought with her from her small hometown. Like Emily, religious leaders have often tried to comprehend the urban reality and develop urban strategies using perceptions and organizational forms that are inadequate or inappropriate for such a complex situation.

Let us consider first the perceptual framework that the various religious groups bring to urban society. U.S. Protestantism is rooted deeply in rural and small-town America. Its beginnings in the towns and villages of New England and the colonies along the Eastern seaboard and later its missionary successes on the western frontier shaped its perceptions of the good society, even as Protestant values helped to shape the moral climate of the rural areas and small towns. As the cities began to grow rapidly in the latter half of the nineteenth century, and especially as they began to be peopled by immigrants who did not share a Protestant heritage, Protestants had difficulty comprehending and accepting the new reality. God made the country, it was said; man made the city. The implication was that the latter had not done a good job. This predilection for rural and small-town values was coupled with an individualistic interpretation of the gospel, what Martin Marty calls "private" Protestantism. "It accented individual salvation out of the world, personal moral life congruent with the ideals of the saved, and fulfillment, or its absence in the rewards or punishments in another world in a life to come."[10] Its opposite, "public" Protestantism, was social in orientation and found expression in the Social Gospel movement, in various forms of social service, and later, in what was called "social realism" in theology and ethics. But many Protestants, both in mainline and evangelical denominations, continue to have strong roots in the "private" Protestant camp—even as they have strong affinities with rural and small-town values—and they bring these perceptions to the urban reality.[11]

Related to this perceptual problem is that of organizational forms. The U.S. Protestant parish system was different from that in Europe and Great Britain, where established churches were the rule and had a virtual monopoly on religious life. On the U.S. scene, where disestablishment took place early—if it existed at all—congregations were voluntary associations. On the one hand, this organizational form tended toward homogeneity of members, especially in the rural areas and small towns, where the entire population was already homogeneous. Furthermore, when two or more congregations of different denominations existed in the same area, a "competitive parish" form developed in which the congregations competed for members. "The competitive parish meant that the

9

continued prosperity of any one church was not ensured because members and new residents had the option of going elsewhere."[12] Although this organizational form posed little problem in pre-Civil War times, it suffered greatly with the rapid growth of the cities. As Sidney E. Ahlstrom described it:

> *In the absence of denominational or interdenominational planning, like-minded groups simply organized congregations as best they could with little concern for other groups or for the needs of the city. Within each denomination, therefore, there were often a variety of churches for different areas of the city and different types of people, most of them following the predictable patterns of America's small towns and rural areas, except that social stratification often became more pronounced.*[13]

Additionally, as urban neighborhoods changed, either becoming business or industrial districts or experiencing an influx of immigrants who did not share the culture of earlier residents, many churches moved to join their members in their new residential neighborhoods or simply closed. As Ahlstrom points out, Josiah Strong, general secretary of the Evangelical Alliance around the turn of the century and a spokesperson for the Social Gospel, "compiled statistic on statistic to demonstrate the dramatic exodus of Protestant churches from the growing sections of American cities."[14] This exodus is perhaps not as great as in Strong's day (partly because so many have moved already or have closed), but some center-city and inner-city congregations are in serious trouble, with declining memberships and income, rising costs, and not too many clues as to how to respond to the changes taking place around them.

To be sure, some Protestant congregations and organizations have had significant ministries within the cities, many having been inspired by the Social Gospel and other expressions of "public" Protestantism. These have included congregations—often of black and other minority backgrounds—and para-congregational forms of the church, such as settlement houses, urban missions, the Salvation Army and similar groups, the YMCA, and the YWCA. When "private" Protestants engaged in urban mission it was typically to establish "rescue" missions, reflecting the belief that the Christian's major responsibility is to save individuals from the sinful world. In general, however, neither form of Protestantism has fared well in the central cities. It has been the suburbs—more nearly in tune with rural and small-town values—in which much of Protestantism has had its greatest recent successes.

The experience of Catholics in the cities has been different from that of Protestants. In contrast to the generally rural cast of U.S. Protestantism, U.S. Catholicism has always been predominantly urban, with approximately 80 percent of its members living in cities. Catholic parishes in the cities developed into strong communal bases for meeting the needs of various Catholic immigrant groups. Additionally, a host of Catholic institutions—schools, hospitals, newspapers, social clubs—were established to meet member needs. The parish structure and network of Catholic institutions created all-encompassing, religioethnic ghettos for many Catholics in the face of discrimination and persecution from the dominant Protestant culture. Although these urban institutions were strong, they, along with an otherworldly, liturgically centered doctrine, generally discouraged Catholic concern for the broader community and joint efforts with others for the common good. At the same time Catholic communalism provided a basis for the development of city politics along ethnic lines with special interests, a phenomenon reflected in enclave politics.[15]

By the midtwentieth century, with the success of the Americanization movement within the Catholic Church in the United States, capped by the election of John F. Kennedy as President; with the upward social mobility experienced by many Catholics, including "buying into" the postwar suburban dream; and with the change to a more this-worldly theological and ecclesiastical emphasis brought about by Vatican II, Catholicism had largely abandoned its ghetto stance and had moved more into the mainstream of U.S. life. This has included a concern for the welfare of the cities and making the Catholic institutional network of hospitals, schools, and welfare agencies broadly available to the urban populace. At the same time Catholics have experienced problems similar to their Protestant counterparts: declining participation in many urban parishes, expensive and difficult-to-maintain inner-city institutions and buildings, and resistance on the part of many suburban parishioners to involvement in broader issues of metropolitan mission.

The Jewish experience, much like the Catholic, has been predominantly urban, with even more Jews than Catholics living in the metropolitan areas. Judaism too has developed its own institutions in the cities and has tended to respond to threats to its existence, such as anti-Semitism and nativism, with a similar kind of ghettoization. At the same time Jews have differed significantly from Protestants and Catholics in their response to urban society. More so than either of the other groups, Jews have actively supported causes promoting social justice and civil liberties. Nathan Glazer has speculated as to whether this involvement reflects continuity with the Hebrew prophets' concern for justice, or whether it is more a reflection of the attraction to socialism that many immigrant Jews from Germany and Russia brought with them. He suggests that the latter is the case. Furthermore, he believes that

> *it is specious to say that American Jews express religious attitudes indirectly in their concern for social problems. Whatever the* origins

11

of this concern, it is now divorced from religion. . . . Indeed, it is one
of the most remarkable things about American Judaism, as distinct
from American Jews, that it is not particularly concerned with social
problems.[16]

Instead, the preoccupation of American Judaism, as a religion, has
been the preservation of Jewish identity, first in the Jewish ghettos of the
central cities and then in the suburbs, as upwardly mobile Jews joined the
exodus to suburbia.[17] Much like Protestants in their move to the suburbs,
Jewish congregations sold their buildings to new immigrant groups coming into the central cities and relocated to the suburbs.

Given the complexity of urban society and the perceptual and organizational characteristics of the three major faith groups—albeit different in
their particulars—it is not surprising that religious leaders and members
have had and continue to have difficulty relating to urban society. Indeed,
the coexistence of the three faith groups (along with the multiple subdivi-
sions that exist, especially within Protestantism) adds another level of
complexity to their efforts at responding to urban issues and problems.
Their coexistence under norms that acknowledge religious pluralism and
enjoin tolerance makes it difficult for any single religious group to make
exclusivistic claims for itself or attempt to influence public policy in ways
that appear to foster its own particular interests or point of view. Although
some religious groups continue to do so, their behavior is considered to
be in bad taste, violating the norms of religious pluralism that sociologist
John Murray Cuddihy calls "the de facto 'established' religion in
America." It is, he says, basically a "religion of civility."[18] A recent study of
present-day Protestant evangelicalism notes how even evangelicals, who
continue to hold a monopolistic claim on religious truth, have "culturally
edited it to give it the qualities of sociability and gentility. It has acquired
a civility that proclaims loudly, 'No offense, I am an Evangelical.' "[19] Thus
religious pluralism adds to the complexity of urban life and to the
difficulties that religious groups have in relating to it.

Perceiving these difficulties as essentially moral failures, a number of
authors have been strongly critical of churches and synagogues for their
inability or unwillingness to make a difference in urban life. This literature includes such telling titles as *The Suburban Captivity of the
Churches* by Gibson Winter, Peter Berger's *The Noise of Solemn Assemblies,* and Pierre Berton's *The Comfortable Pew.* In these and other books
like them, American religious bodies—especially mainline Protestants—
are taken to task for abandoning their moral responsibility to urban society by developing exclusivistic, homogeneous, white middle-class
suburban enclaves. The critics argue that Protestantism in particular has
so accommodated itself to American culture that its major social function
is as legitimator of the status quo. They also point to the increasing

privatization of American life and charge that churches and synagogues, by their sellout to the suburbs, have become institutions of the private sphere, no longer able to influence decision making in the public sphere.

Out of this criticism has grown a concern to develop new forms of church life—new missionary structures—appropriate to the kind of urban society that is emerging. A major effort in this regard was made by the World Council of Churches in a study entitled "The Missionary Structure of the Congregation." Some participants in the study believe that the new urban society can be served by renewing existing congregations; others believe that new structures are needed. George W. Webber describes an encounter between advocates of the two strategies. Robert Raines, then pastor of First Methodist Church of Germantown, Pennsylvania, was concerned to find ways of reshaping the structures of existing congregations to make them faithful vehicles for authentic mission. Howard Moody, pastor of Judson Church in Greenwich Village, bluntly told Raines, "If we could renew all the traditional churches like First Methodist, we still wouldn't begin to have the new forms of missionary presence which will be required for faithful witness in the cities of our day."[20] Another strong advocate of the latter position was Gibson Winter, who followed up *The Suburban Captivity of the Churches* with another book, *The New Creation as Metropolis*. The thesis of the latter title is "that the world is radically changed; a wholly new relationship of the Church to the world is called for in our time. This new relationship can be described as the servanthood of the laity."[21] Both strategies were tried with some success during the 1960s and early 1970s.[22] Such efforts were costly, however, especially the various new forms that were developed, including inner-city ministries, metropolitan missioners, and industrial chaplaincies. Unless the new forms developed their own base of continuing support, they were not likely to survive. National denominational support, which had been crucial, dwindled as leaders became preoccupied with declining memberships.

The denomination's preoccupation with stemming membership declines in the 1970s (continuing down to the present) signals a more general shift in emphasis. From a heavy critique of congregational structures as anachronistic and needing to be replaced or radically restructured, a new emphasis on congregational revitalization, on discovering and releasing the potency present in existing congregational structures, has developed. Organizational development techniques—assessment and planning, leadership training, improved communication, conflict management—have been applied to congregational life in an effort to make it come alive. Additionally, insights from cultural anthropology and from overseas mission experience have formed the basis of a "scientific" approach to church growth. In an interesting use of images, James Hopewell sees the emphases of the 1960s and 1970s as reflecting the difference between ghost stories (in which the spirit is all important and only needs to be released from an inadequate body) and monster stories (in which a body is brought to life by scientific techniques and then develops uncommon size or proportions).[23]

While mainline religious groups were focusing on revitalization and stemming the loss of members, the evangelical movement was again coming to prominence. Conservative churches were growing, not declining. Evangelical organizations moved to prime-time television and established their own media networks. And while many mainline groups and members seemed to have pulled back from the political concerns of the late 1960s and early 1970s, conservative Christianity was finding its political voice—a voice that spoke the language of "private" Protestantism.

What, then, can be made of these changes? What do they imply for the presence and role of religion in a metropolitan area? As suggested earlier, religious leaders' confusion about urban ministry stemmed not only from the complexity of contemporary urban society, but also from the inadequate or inappropriate perceptual lenses and organizational structures that they brought to such a ministry. These included the inadequacies of an individualistic theology, more attuned to rural and small-town life, and the inadequacies of the competitive parish structure that accompanied it. But is this not where religion finds itself again? Was the critique wrong? Or is it still appropriate? And what does this mean for the 1960s' critiques of individualism and competitive (and homogeneous) parishes and their appeal for new missionary structures? Were they correct? Because the critics seem not to have succeeded in realizing their agenda, were they wrong? Are there yet other ways of viewing religion's presence in urban society, both perceptually and structurally?

This book and the research that lies behind it address these questions. We, the authors, would be less than candid if we did not admit that our religious affinities are more closely akin to the 1960s critics who called for a serious engagement with urban society on the basis of what might be called a public theology. Nevertheless, we are struck by the plurality of religious responses that are present in an urban area like Hartford, Connecticut—and we do not believe that Hartford is atypical in this regard. Some individuals and congregations in urban areas share the perspectives of the "missionary structures" and public theology approach, but there are also clear and thriving examples of the more "private," or individualistic, approach. And these two approaches do not exhaust the options that are possible.

Clearly, all religious groups in urban America are not playing by the same rules. Reflecting the religiously pluralistic situation, there are different understandings of what it means for religion to relate to public life. We believe that it is important to take seriously these different understandings of religious presence. In this book we present new information about urban ministry. We hope that the insights our research provides into the varieties of religious presence will enhance the quality of life in urban society. Arnold Toynbee expresses this well in commenting on urban planning:

> Aristotle maintains that cities were brought into existence originally to make life possible, but that the ultimate purpose of them is to make life worth living. This dictum reads ironically today, when Megalopolis is the city in which we are going to have to live. Yet, Aristotle is surely right. Mere existence on the defensive cannot satisfy human beings; so we have to make life worth living, even in Megalopolis, and this means making spiritual room, in Megalopolis, for the inner life of human feelings, ideas, ideals and purposes. Since this field of life is a spiritual one, each human soul has to find salvation in it for himself. But, here again, the town-planner, if he has the imagination and the skill, can help the citizens of Megalopolis to win their spiritual battle. He can help by providing them, in inspiring visible forms, with material symbols of these invisible spiritual treasures.[24]

Toynbee's comments about town planning are not inappropriate when applied to religious institutions and their presence and role in urban society.

Religious Presence, Its Definition and History

The term religious presence has been chosen deliberately as the focus of inquiry. On the one hand, it is relatively general and can encompass the diverse religious expressions existing in contemporary urban society. On the other hand, it has long been used both in the history of religion in general and in twentieth-century Christian missions in particular. By religious presence is meant quite simply the ways in which religion or the religious is manifest or present in a society. Although this clearly can include a sense of the direct presence of God or the sacred, this book focuses on experiences or symbolic expressions that individuals or groups interpret as *mediating* the presence of God or the sacred, or as reminding them of a transcendent or ultimate dimension of life. Sociological research cannot go beyond these mediated experiences. At one extreme such experiences of a religious presence may come in the mute but symbolic reminders of a spiritual or transcendent dimension of life through architectural or other artistic media, through the visible organizational expressions of religious communities, or through the quiet presence of those who represent a particular religious experience or community. At the other extreme, religious presence may be experienced in the explicit and direct efforts of those who are acting as representatives of a religious

15

experience or community to influence the attitudes and behaviors of individuals or groups. Although the working definition of religious presence used here is rather simple and straightforward, some examples may be helpful.

The buildings of religion—the mosque with its minaret, the medieval Gothic cathedral, the white church on the New England town green, or the contemporary architecture of a church building constructed as part of an urban skyscraper—are efforts of particular communities of faith to express their relationship with God and the relation of their faith to their particular time and place. Whether these efforts always succeed in communicating what their builders intended, and whether social and cultural changes do not sometimes render particular symbolic expressions anachronistic, religious architecture nevertheless is often a powerful reminder of the transcendent, frequently as much to individuals who have no formal relationship to any religious community as to devout believers. In *The Dynamics of Religion* social psychologist Bruce Reed describes individuals who do not belong to any church, but for whom it is important that church buildings remain standing, that church bells ring, and that they see people going to church. In one situation townspeople expressed considerable concern to keep the church tower clock going, not because they wanted to know the time, but because "they were reassuring themselves that the church was still there and the clock still going."[25]

Similarly, a piece of music, a painting, or a play, with or without any ostensible religious content or intent, may be the vehicle through which the religious or transcendent is present to an individual or group. And clergy, especially those who wear distinctive dress, are well aware that their presence is often symbolic, pointing beyond themselves. Many clergy can identify with the experience of the minister who is greeted at the door by a young child who calls to her or his parents that "God is at the door!"

But religious presence, as the term is used here, also has its active, intentional expressions, whether in the efforts to convert individuals through preaching or other forms of religious witness, through the provision of services to those in need, or in the efforts of a religious group to influence decision making in a city or national government. Contemporary American society has no dearth of such visible expressions of presence, including television and radio preachers, religion-sponsored hospitals and homes, and demonstrations on behalf of right-to-life issues or nuclear disarmament. Indeed, electronic media have made it possible for religion to be present in these overt ways on a scale that was impossible in previous generations.

Now how does this use of the term religious presence square with its use in other contexts? As indicated earlier, this concept has not been invented for this study. A brief and somewhat oversimplified excursus into history not only provides background for this use of the term, but also helps one to understand the diverse forms of religious presence described in subsequent chapters.

A sense of the "presence" of that which is at the core of religion has deep roots in human history. It has been thought of in terms of the experience of *mana,* or power, in various primal religions; as the epiphany, or manifestation, of the sacred, as in Yahweh's *shekinah,* or presence, among the ancient Hebrews; and as God's glory (*cabod* in Hebrew; *doxa* in Greek) for both Jews and Christians. In various cultures God or the sacred has also been thought of as being "present" in different ways: in *things,* such as water or a rock; in *processes,* such as fertility or the recurring seasons, especially the rebirth that spring brings; in *events,* such as the exodus or the birth of Jesus; in *special times or places,* such as sacred ceremonies or in shrines or temples; in *special persons,* such as a shaman or priest or saint; or in a *special community,* such as the Jewish understanding of being a Chosen People or the Christian understanding of the church as the Body of Christ. The more primitive a society (in the nonpejorative sense of being relatively simply organized or socially undifferentiated), the more likely it is that the sacred will be viewed as present in most aspects of life. As a society becomes more complex, as social organizations become differentiated, there will be a "withdrawal" of the presence of the sacred from some aspects of life and a tendency to identify that presence with special places, times, organizations, or events. The sacred may in fact come to be viewed as totally transcendent, wholly other, dwelling in a realm above the mundane and profane aspects of earthly existence and in no way identified with this world. And there may be times in the experience of a people when the sacred is not just believed to be wholly other but is even absent. This was the case for the Jewish people when the temple was destroyed and they were carried away into exile in Babylon: "How shall we sing the Lord's song in a foreign land [Ps. 137:4]?" The assumption was that God had withdrawn from the people, that God was not present with them in exile. This feeling of abandonment was also expressed by some contemporary Jews after the Holocaust.

In the later writings of the Old Testament and in the New Testament the glory, or presence, of God was viewed eschatologically, as something that would be revealed in the last days. At the same time, for Christians, there was the belief that in the person of Jesus the glory of God that is to be revealed in the last days was present proleptically; and in the Gospel of John, especially chapter 17, there is the emphasis that the crucifixion of Jesus is the manifestation of God's glory; that is, the presence of the sacred is manifest in the suffering of the cross. Finally, Paul's description of Christians as reflecting "as in a mirror, the splendor [glory] of the Lord" indicates a belief that God's presence is reflected in the life of the believing community.[26]

As Christianity developed from a small, marginal sect to a dominant position within society, religious presence in the West became identified with the presence of the Catholic Church: its hierarchy of popes, bishops, and priests; its various shrines where relics of the saints resided and to which people made pilgrimages to experience the presence of the sacred; and its great cathedrals and church buildings that stood in the center of villages, towns, and cities. In the Europe of the Middle Ages—although the church was a distinct institution, unlike religion in more primitive or undifferentiated societies—religious presence through the presence of the Catholic Church was pervasive in what was essentially a *societas christiana*.[27] This close identification of religious presence with the institutional church "de-eschatologized" the presence of the Holy. Rather than looking for the revelation of God's presence in the "last days," one experienced it immanently in and through the church.

After the Protestant Reformation not only did alternative and competing forms of religious presence develop (Jews had always been present within the *societas christiana* but typically were isolated in ghettos as minority communities), but also the Reformers stressed the transcendence of God and opposed the identification of shrines, relics, or any human institutions—including the churches—with God's presence. God in Christ was graciously present to the church "in, with, and under" the Word and Sacraments, in Luther's words, and was available to faith. But God was not captured, cribbed, or confined in any of these expressions. For Calvin, the world was viewed as the arena or theater in which God was to be glorified as men and women were faithful in pursuing their individual callings, but again, God was not to be identified with any worldly structures or institutions.[28]

Max Weber, in his classic work, *The Protestant Ethic and the Spirit of Capitalism*, saw the Reformers, especially Calvin, as completing what he called the "de-magicalization," or "disenchantment," of the world that had its roots in ancient Judaism, especially the Old Testament prophets. Indeed, in Weber's pessimistic view, this process (aided by economic and other developments) was leading to a future devoid of spiritual or cultural values, a situation that he described as an "iron cage."[29]

Although it involves a considerable historical leap and an ignoring of important developments in other religious traditions, let us skip to the twentieth century and the "rediscovery" of the language of "presence," especially by French Catholics.[30] The historical process that Weber delineated came to a head in France, in the disestablishment of the Catholic Church in 1905, with the juridical separation of church and state. There followed what might be termed a "combative" effort at Christian presence to reassert France as "Catholic and French forever." Conflicts were numerous as Catholic leaders tried to reestablish the church. By the end of the 1920s, however, a different understanding of Christian presence was beginning to emerge in the essentially lay Catholic action movement, both in France and Belgium. There was a beginning recognition that now large sectors of society—especially the French working class—were no longer Christian. A shift was made from a combative presence to one of witness by Christian workers. In the words of Pope Pius XI in *Quadragesimo Anno:*

> *In order to bring these diverse classes of men back to the Christ whom they have denied, we must above all recruit and train auxiliaries in their midst, auxiliaries of the church who will understand their make-up and their aspirations, and who can speak to their innermost hearts in a spirit of brotherly love.*

The worker-priest movement in France, comprising priests with no special privileges who labored in industry alongside the workers, was a direct outgrowth of this new sense of the urgency and meaning of Christian presence. There was a realization that the workers' world had become de-Christianized (or secularized) and later the acknowledgment by an assembly of French bishops that this was true for much of what had once been a Christian culture:

> *It is evident that all around us, and already for a great number of souls, even those who have been baptized, the church is as if absent. There is no longer any geographical or social sector where evangelization is not called for. Contact has either been lost or is yet to be made. . . . The whole church must become a missionary church.*[31]

A later communique of the Bishops' Assembly described the church as "unfortunately partially or totally *absent* when it comes to numerous social groups, especially in the labouring man's world, and also when it comes to much of the modern mentality."[32]

In this acknowledgment of de-Christianization and the call for Christian presence, a common thread was the understanding of presence to be the presence of Christians in the secular world. But different understandings existed as to what that presence was to mean. There was the early emphasis on combative presence, attempting to reestablish the church to its previous favored position, and there was also the early Catholic action movement's understanding of presence to mean active evangelization and witness to the de-Christianized sectors of society by those who were alongside people in those sectors. The concern in this instance was to either convert or reconvert them to the faith.

As the Catholic action and worker-priest movements developed, yet another meaning of "presence" emerged. This meaning was expressed in the term milieu transformation, and it grew out of the insight that the structures of society were unjust and the belief that changing the unjust structures—the milieu—through Christian service and social action would be the means of bringing the masses back to the faith. Later, both among French Catholics and in the Catholic and Protestant missionary movements in non-Western societies who adopted the language of "Christian presence," there developed the understanding that milieu transformation involved Christians in "*being* witnesses" to the gospel in the midst of society (whether a de-Christianized, humanistic Western society or, for example, a Muslim or Hindu society). But this understanding was different from the earlier view of "witnessing *to*" non-Christians in an effort to convert them. The difference could be expressed thus: Rather than trying to "catch more fish," the aim was to "change the water in the pond." Milieu transformation involved not only working to change unjust social structures and practices, but also being present with peoples of other religions and cultures, trying "to sit where they sit, to enter sympathetically into the pains and griefs and joys of their history and see how those pains and griefs and joys have determined the premises of their argument."[33] The aim was not to convert Muslims, for example, but rather to be in spiritual solidarity with them to the end that the Muslim society would be transformed from within, not into a copy of a Westernized Christian society (which had often been the case in the missionary movement), but into one that reflected the highest of both Christian and Muslim truth. In now-secular Western societies the aim of Christian presence as milieu transformation was not to return to a *societas christiana*, but to "nourish the secularization process," as Harvey Cox put it, "to prevent it from hardening into a rigid world view, and to clarify as often as necessary its roots in the Bible."[34] Likewise (to tie the current discussion into the previous rehearsal of the 1960s critics of the churches), Gibson Winter gave expression to the milieu transformation theme in his book *The New Creation as Metropolis,* in which he argues that metropolis, a "unified, reconciled, interdependent society," is the meaning of God's "new creation" toward which human society is moving. The church's task is not to try to escape or to adapt to the present conflicts and problems of urban society, "but to serve God in the world—to point the world toward its fulfillment, to empower it in its realization."[35] This is a call not to a reestablishment of Christendom, but to a transformation of the milieu through a ministry of servanthood within public life.

In an explicit use of the language of Christian presence during the 1960s, the World Student Christian Federation expressed the goals of both evangelization and milieu transformation in a statement entitled "The Christian Community in the Academic World":

> [Presence] does not mean that we are simply there; it tries to describe the adventure of being there in the name of Christ, often anonymously, listening before we speak, hoping that men will recognize Jesus for what he is and stay where they are, involved in the fierce fight against all that dehumanizes, ready to act against demonic powers, to identify with the outcast, merciless in ridiculing modern idols and new myths. . . . "Presence" for us means "engagement," involvement in the concrete structures of our society. . . . In one sense of the word, presence precedes witness. In another sense, the very presence is witness. For us, to be present in the name of Christ spells death to the status quo, both in society and in the Christian community: we will not tire of pleading and working for the restoration of normal manhood as we see it in Jesus.[36]

The statement contains one other note that has been part of the language of Christian presence since the worker-priest movement. Sometimes it is impossible to change unjust structures or even to alleviate suffering in service to those in need. Under such circumstances Christian presence means simply being with those who are suffering. It is, as Peter Berger has expressed it, the "simple presence of those testifying to the fact that Christ continues to walk through the lives of all men, however hopeless or degraded or wicked their condition may be." This understanding of presence is essentially passive, different from service or social action, but nevertheless one way in which Christians may engage the world. It too is a form of milieu transformation in that it involves, to use Berger's words again, "the erection of Christian signs in the world."[37]

Thus the idea of Christian presence has taken on different meanings in its usage by Christians in the twentieth century: from combative presence, to witnessing to non-Christians for the purpose of converting (or reconverting) them, to milieu transformation, to the kind of passive solidarity with human suffering of which Berger speaks. The language of religious presence has not been used much since the late 1960s, perhaps partly because of the overly passive connotation it seemed to convey; however, its various themes have found expression in such recent movements as the Moral Majority (combative); evangelicalism (converting); in various liberation and political theologies concerned with realizing justice in social, economic, and political institutions through structural change (milieu transformation); and in various continuing expressions by religiously motivated individuals or groups in solidarity with the poor and dispossessed, even when change is likely to be minimal. These themes of religious presence are also manifest in the diverse religious expressions—Christian and Jewish—in Hartford and its surrounding suburbs.

In conclusion, two observations can be made. First, although the meaning of religious presence has been broadened here to some extent from earlier uses made of the concept, especially in Christian missionary efforts, there is considerable continuity. As with others who have used the term, we are concerned with ways in which God is present in the world, albeit our focus is on mediated presence, especially in religious institutions. Second, as both the earlier examples of religious presence and the history of the term suggest, religious presence can take on a variety of meanings and expression. This makes the term particularly helpful in trying to make sense of the diverse forms of presence that exist in a religiously pluralistic society.

CHAPTER 2

RELIGIOUS PRESENCE: A CONGREGATIONAL PERSPECTIVE

Chapter 1 provided an overview of issues facing U.S. metropolitan areas in the 1980s, traced in general terms the religious community's response to these issues, and introduced the concept of religious presence. This chapter looks at congregations as institutional expressions of religious presence, outlines a perspective on the study of congregations, and introduces four contrasting understandings of religious presence, or "mission orientations."

CONGREGATIONS AS EXPRESSIONS OF RELIGIOUS PRESENCE

Local churches and synagogues received considerable attention in the "renewal" literature of the 1950s and early 1960s. Commentators differed in assessments of the potential of such churches and synagogues as responsible agents of God's intentions for the world and in estimates of their long-term viability, but placing the congregation at the center of a discussion of the church's role in the world made sense. It seemed natural, for example, for Sidney Ahlstrom, writing of theological trends in *The Annals'* review of religion in 1960, to reflect on theological movements in relation to church and synagogue life.[1] The congregation was, after all, the most visible institutional expression of religious energy and commitment.

Ten years later, writing in the same journal, Ahlstrom looked back and saw a revolution in religious doctrine, morals, and institutions.

23

> *Contemporaneous with this development [the emergence of a radical movement in theology], and closely related to it, was a veritable tidal wave of questioning of all the traditional structures of Christendom, above all, the so-called "parish" church. After Peter Berger's sounding of an early tocsin with his* The Noise of Solemn Assemblies *(1961), "morphological fundamentalism" became the key word of the new critics. In the meantime, the ministry and laity alike have shown an increasingly widespread tendency to regard local church structures as irrelevant, or as extremely unadaptable to the most urgent needs of the time, or even as an impediment to social action.*[2]

Undoubtedly, organized religion and its institutions, including congregations, were affected by the theological, ideological, and value challenges of the 1960s. The effects were especially pronounced on the older, more "established" mainline churches. At the same time these same traditions have exhibited unforeseen capacities for change. Sometimes the change has been quiet and undramatic, but it has taken place nevertheless. In the suggestive words of one "new" Catholic, "I left the church when I was twelve. At forty-two I woke up and discovered that I was Catholic again. I didn't change, but they modified the boundaries without telling me."

The decision to focus on congregations in this study of religious presence was not made lightly. As social scientists, we recognize that understandings of the transcendent find expression in the beliefs, values, and behavior of individuals; in the life of social groups; in the culture and structures of societies; and in a range of institutions. As sociologists of religion, we are aware of the limitations of "parochial sociology" and the dangers of attending only to that which is visible and quantifiable. As individuals, and as Protestant Christians in the Reformed tradition, we are alert to the heresy of uncritical institutionalism and are wary of raising congregations or other temporal expressions of religiosity to objects of worship.

We focus on congregations for four principal reasons.

First, the congregation remains integral to the self-understanding of the major religious traditions. Speaking from within his own tradition, Rabbi Abraham J. Feldman of Hartford made the point nicely on the occasion of the 150th anniversary of the city's Congregation Beth Israel:

> *I want to share with you the thought that until* congregations *and* synagogues *were established, Jews were not acknowledged parts of the larger community and not until then did they become a* Jewish Community. *Because the Synagogue is the oldest institution in Jewish life with a continuous existence across some 25 centuries and because the Synagogue is still the most democratic institution in Jewish life and has always been such, the Synagogue is the center, the heart, as it*

24

were, of the people, which has had its birth in the concept of a "kingdom of priests," which has continued through the ages as a folk dedicated to the knowledge of the Lord, dedicated to provide for the religious needs of its families, dedicated to provide education for its children, dedicated to provide dignified places of worship and also to provide a final resting place for those who are translated from life to life.[3]

The "rediscovery" of the importance of the congregation crosses theological and ideological lines. As Martin Marty has suggested, it grows out of an awareness of the role of social institutions in religious and public life and, in Christianity, of religion's social character. Marty writes:

While efforts to establish an essential form of communal life for Christians everywhere may be futile and may limit imagination, something like the local assembly will remain fundamental. . . . Congregations will take on varied colorings in different times or cultures, but in every case they serve to perpetuate embodiment, which is essential in the whole church.[4]

The importance of the congregation, for Marty, goes beyond its social functions to the fundamentally social character of the Christian faith itself: creation, communion, the fall, the promise of redemption in response to the fall are social acts.

In the covenant in Christ, which is grafted to the original one, the plan remains one of congregants. The choice by Jesus of The Twelve replicates and affirms the tribes of Israel. A new covenant associates the old promise with the new people. Here imagery and reality of Christ as head of a body is in place. The New Testament knows of no consumerist or clientele religion, but always it is the congregation that seeks to transcend caucuses of male and female, causes of bond and free, or coteries of Jew and Greek.[5]

From a considerably different position, that of liberation theology, German theologian Jürgen Moltmann has called for new attention to the congregation as occupying a central role in the religious life. His position is explicit: "The local congregation is the future of the church. The renewal of the church finally depends on what happens at the grass-roots level." His emphasis on the gathered people follows from a particularly nonhierarchical theological orientation: "Undoubtedly," he writes, "religious power is experienced in the church understood as a hierarchy or as under clerical management, but the image engendered is that of an all-wise, all-powerful divine Lord in heaven." Moltmann goes on:

God as love, however, can only be witnessed to and experienced in a congregation small enough for members to know each other and accept each other as they are accepted by Christ. The gospel of Christ crucified for us puts an end to religion as power and opens up the possibility of experiencing God in the context of genuine community as the God of love."[6]

Whether one views the congregation as a carrier of a people's traditions and values, as an embodiment of religious truth and value, or as an agent of social change, its place in the self-understanding of the major religious traditions is undeniable. It is one reason for focusing on congregations in the study of religious presence.

Second, congregations are significant social and economic institutions. The *Yearbook of American and Canadian Churches* counts 336,000 local churches with almost 135 million members. In an average week more than 65 million adults attend services of worship. Financial contributions to religious organizations, virtually all through local churches and synagogues, accounts for 46 percent of all charitable giving and totaled $25 billion in 1980. In a recent year nearly $1.7 billion was spent on construction of religious buildings and a single denomination—the Southern Baptist Convention—established more new congregations than McDonald's added hamburger restaurants.

Given the size and scope of the religion enterprise viewed organizationally, that it receives so little public attention is nothing short of astonishing. Some of this lack of publicity may stem from the justifiable perception that religious institutions are less strong than they once were, but the continuing significance of religious organizations, especially congregations, is ignored. This "presence" takes concrete form in congregations. Just a few of its expressions are mentioned here.

Most obvious perhaps is the role congregations play in providing sustenance for their members and participants. No other social institution has played a more important role historically in providing people with a sense of meaning for their lives and the opportunity to see their own existence in relation to a source and purpose that transcends everyday life. Through such activities as corporate worship, pastoral care, and programs of education, congregations are visibly present to their members and communities.

Sociologist David Moberg has catalogued a number of additional, less visible ways in which congregations have traditionally been present. They function, for example, as *agents of socialization* as they assist in the social development and identity formation of the young. They are *status-giving agencies,* helping people to "locate" themselves in the class and status hierarchies of the society and the local community. They provide *fellow-*

ship and the opportunity for the development of primary group relationships in a mobile society.

Congregations *promote social solidarity* and provide a sense of integration and community for individuals and groups. As *forces for social stability*, they help conserve values and practices that have proved themselves over time. They are *agents of social control* in the regulation of group and individual behavior. They are *agents of social reform,* judging institutional performance in the light of publicly proclaimed values. They are *welfare institutions,* providing for the personal needs of the poor and the homeless.[7] In addition, churches and synagogues are *symbols of continuity,* providing a link between past, present, and hoped-for future. They are also important *economic institutions,* with professional staffs, buildings, and financial resources.

In itself, the functional importance of congregations merits attention in the study of religious presence. Their significance lies not only in their numbers and in economic and social power, but also in the range of specific ways in which they affect the lives of millions of members and hundreds of thousands of neighborhoods and communities. Third, congregations are among the small number of social institutions that "mediate" between the individual and the larger institutions of public life. Peter Berger and Richard Neuhaus argue that modernization tends to force a wedge between the private and the public spheres of life. The state itself, economic conglomerates, big labor, and centralized bureaucracies have become megastructures, institutions of enormous control and influence largely removed from the day-to-day influence of individuals. As noted in chapter 1, "private life" takes its place alongside the emerging megastructures as a "curious kind of preserve left over by the large institutions and in which individuals carry on a bewildering variety of activities with only fragile institutional support."

Berger and Neuhaus continue:

> *For the individual in modern society, life is an ongoing migration between these two spheres, public and private. The megastructures are typically alienating, that is, they are not helpful in providing meaning and identity for individual existence. Meaning, fulfillment, and personal identity are to be realized in the private sphere. While the two spheres interact in many ways, in private life the individual is left very much to his own devices, and thus is uncertain and anxious.*[8]

Relatively few institutions can "mediate" effectively between society's megastructures and individuals, but congregations are clearly among them. They mediate in the sense that they intersect with both worlds: the "outer" world of structures, institutions, and social movements and the

27

"inner" world of individual meaning and purpose. Mediating structures, Berger and Neuhaus suggest, "have a private face, giving private life a measure of stability, and they have a public face, transferring meaning and value to the megastructures."[9]

The work of Parker J. Palmer on the congregation as a mediating structure or bridge between the private and the public spheres of life has been particularly informative to this study. Palmer has reclaimed an earlier and richer understanding of "public life" in which, among other qualities, "strangers meet on common ground." We live in a time, he suggests, in which the private-public balance has been lost and in which the church has a special bridging role to play. If the church is to mediate between private and public worlds, we must "recognize that the church is often seen by its members as an extension of private life rather than a bridge to the public."

Palmer continues:

> To turn the congregation toward the public life we must resist the lure of another image—the image of the church as "extended family," a closed circle of "our own kind," a community in which the pluralism and abrasions of the public world can be avoided and evaded. We must see that the church has often succumbed to one of the great enemies of public life, the "cult of intimacy."[10]

Finally, we emphasize the congregation in this book because we are committed to it. We recognize the importance of the congregation to the larger religious tradition, respect its power and potential for community service and influence, and value its mediating or bridging role with respect to the larger society and its institutions and structures. Each of us has known congregations to be warm and cold, inspiring and dull, open and closed, involved and withdrawn. We nonetheless resonate with the words of Browne Barr in his testimony to the potential of the local church and synagogue:

> They possess resources fully adequate to rescue persons in our society from the frustrations which are suffocating them and to deliver our civilization from the corruptions which can destroy it. Such creative enterprising neither begins nor ends in the top echelons of either church or state. Its vitality and power is in the quality of life in local communities.[11]

AN APPROACH TO CONGREGATIONAL STUDIES

Paralleling the "rediscovery" of the congregation has been new interest in the *study* of congregations as social organizations. Impetus has come from several quarters, for example, a new interest in organizational development and church planning, concern about membership declines and financial strain on congregational budgets, and awareness of the impact of population transitions on congregational life and program.

Congregational studies have stimulated a growing literature on local churches and synagogues from various academic and practical disciplines. One especially important contribution has come from the work of the Project Team for Congregational Studies, an informal consortium of representatives from several theological seminaries committed to interdisciplinary approaches to the study of congregational life and dynamics. The Project Team's book, *Building Effective Ministry*,[12] brings anthropological, ethnographic, psychological, sociological, theological, and organizational development perspectives to bear on the study of a single local church and suggests new possibilities in the cross-disciplinary approaches to the study of congregations.

Our approach to congregational analysis is indebted to various disciplinary approaches but remains essentially sociological. We view sociology as providing a particularly useful paradigm for seeing churches and synagogues in relation to their larger social environment. Although the approach is illustrated in the case studies, a few words of explanation are appropriate here.

Three components of the sociological paradigm are especially helpful in understanding congregations: (1) its comprehensive character, (2) its grounding theory about social behavior, and (3) its reliance on empirical observation to support interpretations and conclusions.

Congregations as Open Systems

The first element of the sociological approach—the one that makes it comprehensive—is its assumption that the congregation is an open system. The congregation may be thought of as an organization of various elements that are related functionally both to one another in the accomplishment of the common purposes of its members and to the congregation's environment. These relationships have certain implications.

1. We view local churches and synagogues as community institutions that have complex and changing relationships to their environment. In open systems terms, one cannot understand the congregation unless one takes seriously its *openness* as a system to the impact of its environment or social context. H. Paul Douglass and Edmund deS. Brunner, pioneer religious researchers of church life, put it this way:

> *The quality and changes of this environment are almost inevitably communicated to the church. Differences in human fortunes suffered by the church's immediate constituencies and changes in these fortunes due to changes in the environment largely control the institutional destinies of each particular church. Where the environment is*

prosperous and progressive the church can scarcely fail to "succeed."
Where it is miserable and deteriorating the church can scarcely avoid
failure.[13]

Douglass and Brunner are more deterministic than we are in the view
that "as goes the environment, so goes the church." We believe that the
environment both limits and provides possibilities for a congregation.
Any perspective that overlooks the congregation's relationship to its social
context misses a signally important aspect of its life.

2. We consider the members of the congregation an important bridge
between the congregation and its environment. Congregations are voluntary associations. A congregation, to achieve its purposes, must secure the
loyalty and commitment of people who contribute their time, talent, and
treasure. Those members are, first of all, community residents. They
share in the culture and social life not only of the congregation, but also of
the community and the broader society. Members' "social worlds," which
reflect their location in the congregation's community and social context,
are brought into the congregation. These "worlds" shape the members'
expectations of the church and influence their participation in it. Likewise, members carry their religious values into their community participation. Thus our sociological approach also leads us to focus on the social
worlds of congregation and community members and their impact on the
functioning of the congregation as a system.

3. We take seriously the internal aspects of the congregation: its distinctive beliefs and values, its organizational structure, and the processes
through which it functions to accomplish its purposes. How these various
internal elements contribute to the congregation's ministry and mission,
how they function in relation to one another, and how they relate to
member needs and interests and the larger context are all important.

Recently, the internal aspects of congregational life have received considerable attention from those who study or work with congregations from
church renewal and organizational development backgrounds. If one can
help a congregation clarify its theological basis, plan better, improve its
organizational functioning, and manage its conflicts, as these approaches
seem to suggest, the congregation will function effectively as a system.
We do not deny the importance of these internal aspects of congregational
life, but we deny that they can be understood apart from the interface
with the congregation's environment and the social worlds of its members.

How Things Work

A second major element in the sociological approach to the study of
congregations is a set of assumptions or theories about how things work.

These assumptions are already implied in what has been said about open systems, but let us add to this by stating two propositions:

1. A congregation—its theology and ethics, its worship, its programs, its style of operation, and what it does or does not do with reference to mission—is profoundly shaped by its social context (especially the local community context) and the social class of its members.

2. A congregation, by virtue of its relationship to a religious or faith tradition, has the capacity, in a limited way, to transcend the determinative power of its context and the values and interests of its members so that it influences them as well as being influenced by them.

These two propositions reflect an *interactionist* view. The first tells us simply that how a congregation expresses its identity—in beliefs, programs, organizations, and behavior—is shaped in part by its social location—the people, politics, economic life, values, and class interests present in its setting. These are the inevitable corollaries of its character as an "earthen vessel." But the second proposition holds out a crucial freedom from determinism. A church or synagogue participates in a faith tradition that contains ideas and inspiration, beliefs and experiences on the basis of which the status quo may be challenged and at least partially transcended. The more leaders and members are helped to see the power of the context on their congregation's life and their behavior in it, the greater is the possibility that they can bring the congregation to fuller expression of its faith commitments.

This is characteristic of open systems: They have the capacity for self-renewal based on feedback and insight. Congregations can never escape the influence of the social context, but being conscious of its power brings some freedom *from* its power and freedom *for* being an influence and shaping force within it.

Attention to Empirical Data

A third distinctive element of the sociological approach is its attention to empirical data in drawing interpretations and conclusions. To be sure, we are guided by theoretical assumptions about congregations as open systems and about their interaction with the social context and the social worlds of members, but we make a conscious effort to test those assumptions with empirical observations of the congregation and its community. We ask ourselves or them, "On what basis do you say that?" "Is there evidence that supports that assertion?" "Says who?"

Why is this important? It is our judgment and experience that all too often congregational leaders and many who consult with congregations fly more "by the seat of their pants," by intuition or imitation of other congregations, than by careful attention to data that are available to them. We are often amazed and distressed by assumptions that are made about the congregation or the community, by plans that are formulated and carried out, and by money that is spent on programs that don't work because leaders have failed to check out the facts in advance.

Empirical data alone do not answer the questions that churches and synagogues ask of themselves or their communities. When used with the interpretive framework one brings to a problem, however, such data provide correctives to inadequate perceptions and stimulate new insights and possibilities. It is amazing what can happen when congregational leaders combine a lively, faith-informed imagination with empirical data on their congregation and community.

The sociological paradigm we bring to congregational studies begins with the assumption that the congregation is an open system, existing in functional relationship to its community context; that it is shaped by and has the potential to shape that context; that one's assumptions and theories about congregations need to be informed by and tested against empirical data. We believe that the paradigm offers the congregational leader/analyst/consultant the opportunity to see some different things and, more important, to see congregations more comprehensively than do alternative paradigms.

THE VARIETIES OF RELIGIOUS AND CONGREGATIONAL PRESENCE

If, as we maintain, congregations are the most visible form of religious presence in U.S. society, it is nevertheless true that the manifestation of that presence through congregations is hardly uniform. To borrow from William James, there are varieties of religious presence, including that expressed through congregations. To make some sense of this variety and to consider its implications for public life, we found it necessary to develop a means of categorizing congregations and other expressions of religious presence. In our discussion of religious presence in chapter 1, we noted several meanings the term has had in the history of its use. Although these meanings—combative, converting, milieu transformation, passive solidarity—are suggestive of strategies, they are not entirely adequate for our purpose. Thus we turned to the various typological efforts in which social scientists, theologians, and historians have engaged.

The efforts at bringing conceptual order to the diverse forms of religious presence, whether in terms of beliefs, values, or organizational forms, constitute a rich heritage. All are indebted to the pioneering work of Max Weber[14] and Ernst Troeltsch,[15] who identified "churchly" and "sectarian" religious forms. Weber and Troeltsch used these categories to interpret aspects of the situation that developed with the breakup of the *societas christiana* and the diversity that developed religiously after the Protestant Reformation. Troeltsch in particular was concerned with the differing social teachings of the two forms of religious organization: the church generally accepting and engaging in compromises with the existing social order in its efforts to dominate or influence it; the sects radically rejecting the world in light of an ascetic ideal. The work of Weber and Troeltsch was extended by H. Richard Niebuhr, in his work on social factors leading to the rise of various Protestant denominations,[16] and a number of other social scientists, who expanded and refined the typology to account for other religious expressions. Particularly suggestive in relation to our study have been the efforts of British sociologist Bryan Wilson to refine the understanding of sectarian groups by classifying them in terms of the answers given to the question "What must I do to be saved?"[17] In another tradition the empirical studies of H. Paul Douglass and others influenced by the Chicago school of sociology have also been important for us, especially the efforts to understand varying types of congregations and their programmatic complexity in terms of their ecological setting.[18] H. Richard Niebuhr's later attempt to specify the differing understandings of the relationship between "Christ" and "culture" in Christian theology and ethics[19] and Avery Dulles' more recent writings on models of the church[20] may also be cited as important contributions to conceptual clarity regarding the diversity of religious presence that come out of more explicitly theological traditions.

Those who are familiar with the literature on types of religious expression and organization will realize that we have mentioned only a small number of contributions to the enterprise of classification. Our purpose is not to review this considerable body of literature, but rather to mention the studies that have been particularly helpful in leading us to the approach at classification we have chosen. This approach has been to focus on the interplay between the church or synagogue (or other expressions of religious presence)* and its environment. In particular, we attempt to classify congregations in terms of the dominant way each congregation defines its relationship to its community or neighborhood. In this way we aim at specifying the diverse ways congregations seek to be "present" in their community and region and at describing the degree to which the structure and programs of congregations support their self-definition. We also hope to gain greater insight into the meaning of the diverse forms of religious presence for urban society and its citizens.

---

*Although we discuss the categories in terms of congregations, the same categories can also be applied to other expressions of religious presence, which we do in several places in subsequent chapters.

In developing our classificatory categories we have chosen to consider them as understandings of, or orientations to, congregational mission rather than as congregational types. We refer to them, therefore, as *mission orientations*. Furthermore, as we reflected on congregations with which we are familiar, it was clear that many have no single way of understanding their relationship to the broader society, but there may be two or more emphases, reflecting the pluralism that characterizes many religious bodies. Generally, however, even when several mission orientations are operative within a single congregation, one will be dominant. Thus we can categorize most congregations in terms of their dominant mission orientations, while acknowledging that other orientations may be present in them as well. This categorization was done using responses to a questionnaire that was mailed to the pastors of all Hartford-area congregations. Included in the questionnaire were items that reflected varying ways of understanding mission. Four distinct orientations were found.*

The mission orientations divide along this-worldly versus otherworldly lines. As the distinction suggests, the former takes with considerable seriousness this present world as an important arena for religiously motivated service and action. There would be general agreement with Calvin's belief that the world is a theater in which God is to be glorified. In contrast, the otherworldly orientations tend, either explicitly or implicitly, to devalue life in the world and stress salvation for a world to come. There is a relatively sharp distinction made between religious and secular affairs. Although we believe that the this-worldly/otherworldly distinction is applicable to non-Protestants as well as to Protestants, it does reflect aspects of Martin Marty's "public" and "private" Protestant categories. Similarly, the distinction between "postmillennial" and "premillennial" beliefs is frequently (although not always) related to this-worldly versus otherworldly orientations, respectively.

Within each of these two distinctions another can be made. It centers particularly on whether the congregation qua congregation is publicly proactive, taking public stands expressing the congregation's mission orientation, or whether there is resistance to any public action by the congregation.

Given the this-worldly and otherworldly distinction and that regarding the appropriateness of publicly proactive stances on the part of the congregation, we have labeled the four mission orientations *activist, civic, sanctuary,* and *evangelistic.* In the descriptions that follow we draw the differences sharply, more so than is the case in actual congregations. Furthermore, although we believe that the orientations are generally

*A detailed description of the sample, the items used, and the results of the statistical analysis are found in chapter 5, which treats the mission orientations of Hartford-area congregations more fully. Here we restrict ourselves to describing the general contours of the four orientations.

applicable to Judaism and other religions (and have used them as such in the research), our descriptions contain some elements that are more applicable to Christian understandings of mission.[21]

1. The *activist* orientation perceives the here and now of the world as the main arena of God's redemptive activity, and humankind as the primary agent of establishing God's kingdom on earth. For the activist church or synagogue, achievement of a more just and humane society is a high priority, and the posture toward the existing social and economic order tends to be rather critical. Lines between public or community life and private or congregational concerns are somewhat blurred, as community issues are brought into the internal life and program of the congregation as matters of great importance. The congregation is understood as a corporate participant in community life, and the rabbi or pastor is expected to be a public figure, free to express his or her views within the congregation and in the community at large. Social action efforts are endorsed and supported by members with time and funds. Adult education programs, often leading to organized church or synagogue participation in social change efforts, are given a high priority. In extreme cases, congregations holding the activist orientation would consider engaging in civil disobedience in the interest of justice.

2. The *civic* orientation shares the activist orientation's focus on this world and its sense of responsibility for public life. But civic congregations are more comfortable with, even affirming of, dominant social, political, and economic structures; less willing to accept, even opposed to, the use of confrontational techniques in the service of change; and more likely to define their public role in educational and cultural terms than in political terms. There is a concern for public life and issues, and the congregation is seen as an appropriate place in which public concerns are discussed and debated in order to help members clarify their opinions in light of their religious beliefs and values; however, there is little expectation or desire that discussion will lead to a corporate decision or action that represents the congregation's stance. If members choose to involve themselves in public issues, it is as individuals that they do so and not as representatives of the congregation. The same applies to the minister, priest, or rabbi. In general, therefore, individualism, tolerance, and civility play important roles in the civic orientation. The sense of moral order is less a call to prophetic change—as is the case with the activist—and more a set of ground rules permitting civil harmony in the middle of political diversity, religious peace in the middle of ecclesiastical pluralism.[22]

3. Whereas the activist and civic orientations are decidedly this-worldly in emphasis, the *sanctuary* orientation is primarily focused on a world to come, in which the cares of this world will be surmounted. The church or synagogue exists mainly to provide people with opportunities to

withdraw, in varying degrees, from the trials and vicissitudes of daily life into the company of committed fellow believers. Inside the congregation one finds considerable unity among members who adhere to a shared vision of religious truth and practice. The shared vision may find its center in a doctrinal statement; it may instead be in a liturgical experience, such as the Mass; or it may be in a religioethnic identity. Concern over deteriorating moral values and opposition to life-styles that represent challenges to traditional patterns of belief or behavior are high in this orientation. God has ordained certain behaviors as appropriate and others as sinful, and the congregation has a responsibility to interpret and monitor member compliance with these standards. Society is viewed as necessary for human existence and therefore God-given, even in its fallenness and sin. Patriotism is generally encouraged, as is adherence to civil laws; efforts to change society are not encouraged. Human beings can do little to change their condition in life or the shape of the world around them, but they can live upright, moral lives, trusting the promise of the world to come and the fulfillment it will bring to the faithful.

4. The *evangelistic* orientation has much in common with the sanctuary orientation. Its focus is on a future world in which temporal concerns are overcome. There is also concern over the deterioration of traditional standards of personal morality. The major difference is the evangelistic orientation's clear sense of a publicly proactive role. Members are encouraged to participate in public life, not for the purpose of social reform or change, but to share the message of salvation with those outside the fellowship. The spirit of the Great Commission of Matthew 28 is alive and at the center of congregational life. Members are expected to make explicit faith declarations to friends, neighbors, and co-workers. The congregation maintains an active program for sharing its faith and incorporating new people. The power of the religious message is such that it overcomes any hesitancy to see members of other religious traditions as candidates for evangelization and conversion.

These four mission orientations are useful in capturing the varieties of religious presence—especially in its congregational forms—that exist in the Hartford metropolitan area. Although we use the orientations to describe several types of religious presence in Hartford, our major application is to congregations. Thus in chapters 6 through 9 we present case studies of a number of congregations in the Hartford metropolitan area that are representative of these orientations. In examining the characteristics of their members, their beliefs and values, their internal structure and programs, and their relationship to the world about them, we begin to get an in-depth picture of the diversity of their religious presence and the degree to which the four orientations are helpful ways of capturing that diversity. Further, we can gain insight into the implications of this diversity for public life in urban society.

CHAPTER 3

A SOCIAL HISTORY OF RELIGIOUS PRESENCE IN HARTFORD

If we were to transport Lisa Alther's Emily from the tower of Riverside Church in New York to the tower of The Travelers Insurance Companies' headquarters in downtown Hartford, we would provide her with a similarly complex but different view of contemporary urban America. Close by she would see the towers of insurance company headquarters that make Hartford one of the nation's financial centers. She would see the Connecticut River, to whose banks some 350 years ago the city's original settlers came and that would, in the eighteenth and nineteenth centuries, help spur manufacturing industries seeking transportation access to the world's expanding markets. She would see a complex system of interstate highways that connect the area's communities with one another and the region as a whole with Boston to the northeast and New York to the southwest.

From The Travelers tower she would see the state capitol of Connecticut, steeples of hundreds of churches, town greens, shopping centers, college campuses, and not far from the center of the city, farmland and rural communities. In every direction she would look down on the homes of the 665,000 people who live and work in the region.

A tower-level view would give Emily a taste of the complexity of the slice of contemporary American life that is Greater Hartford. Without a map Emily would be unaware of the fact that she is looking out over twenty-seven independent towns and dozens of diverse city neighborhoods. Nor would she have a street-level appreciation for the differing cultures and life-styles that characterize those towns and neighborhoods.

There is, in other words, much that one does not see from atop the city, and this chapter points to some of those less immediately visible features of the region's life that help shape relations among its people and its major institutions. In doing so we draw on a number of sources: historical records, census and other statistical data, interviews with a cross section of secular and religious leaders, and a survey of the area's residents.[1] Our intention is not to present a comprehensive history or socioeconomic analysis of the Greater Hartford region, but to establish the context in which congregations and other religious institutions are present in the life of the region and its people.

PURITAN ORIGINS

The story of Hartford's founding in the mid-1630s is similar to that of dozens of New England towns of the time. The Rev. Thomas Hooker, experiencing doctrinal and personality differences with the ecclesiastical leaders at Boston, sought permission to lead his people to the frontier. After some debate, permission was granted, an advance party was sent out to explore alternative locations, and finally, in 1636, Hooker and about 100 men, women, and children began the journey from Newtown (now Cambridge) to the shores of the Little River (now the Connecticut River), where they would join nascent communities at Windsor and Wethersfield.

The settlers were a unified and homogeneous group who moved quickly to construct modest homes on assigned lots of farmland. A meetinghouse followed soon after to serve as the center of religious and public life. Having been together as a congregation since 1632, the residents knew one another well and were willing to follow the lead of Hooker and the assistant pastor, the Rev. Samuel Stone, after whose English hometown Hartford would take its name in 1637.

Hooker's influence on early Hartford can hardly be overstated. Distrustful of centralizing tendencies in the ecclesiastical and civil polity of Massachusetts, Hooker led the colony in forming a system of governance in which church membership would not be a prerequisite for holding public office; the franchise would be open to all responsible landholding white males. Because there was but one church and all residents were required to participate in services and support it financially, and Hooker would remain a key figure in the whole of community life, the division between the religious and secular spheres was more nominal than real. Hooker's motivation was essentially evangelical, reflecting his concern that the meaning of church membership not be diluted: The church was independent unto itself and subservient to no external authority; its au-

38

thority would rest on the covenanting together of converted believers, first with God and then with one another.

Hooker's conviction that governmental authority rests in the "free consent of the people" found expression in the Fundamental Orders, the 1639 document that carried over into the civil life of Connecticut the emerging polity assumptions of New England Congregationalism and that served as the foundation document for the General Court of Connecticut. Each year the free men would choose a governor, a court of assistants, and four deputies from each town to give oversight to the political life of the colony.

Hartford grew slowly but steadily in the late seventeenth and early eighteenth centuries, retaining its agricultural character but taking on some of the qualities of a small New England city of the era. Communications with the neighboring communities of Wethersfield and Windsor and the churches and communities of Massachusetts were adequate, the river provided a means of shipping grain, tobacco, and meat to other colonial settlements; and the community evolved various public institutions to meet local needs. Each male resident gave two days each year to the upkeep of roads, a volunteer fire department was established, schools were founded for the young, and by 1701 the beginnings of what would become Yale College were in place. With the legislature's adoption of the Saybrook Platform in 1708, Congregationalism was established as the official church of Connecticut.

Religious change came early to Hartford and to all New England. The key issue was doctrinal and centered on the religious status of the second generation of New England settlers: What would be the fate of the children of community residents who, because they were not themselves converted and eligible for church membership, could not present their offspring for baptism? The "solution" that gained considerable acceptance across New England was known as the Half-Way Covenant, which admitted people who had not experienced conversion to a form of "half-way membership" and permitted their children to be baptized.

Like most other congregations across New England, the Hartford congregation was divided on the Half-Way Covenant. It eventually accepted the covenant but in doing so generated a split that led to the withdrawal of the orthodox party, in 1670, to form Second Church. It was two years before issues of land and taxation could be resolved fully, and Hartford, like other New England towns, had no choice but to accept the fact that religious diversity existed within its borders.

The controversy within Hartford Congregationalism in the late 1660s was a harbinger of conflicts to come several decades later, when the first Great Awakening swept across the colonies. By the early eighteenth century, as Robert Handy puts it, "there was a sense of decline, a feeling that something was wrong. Especially in New England, but not only there, religious leaders often insisted that in many quarters material concerns were replacing the spiritual ones that had been so strongly expressed in colonial days." Handy continues:

> The undercurrents of Enlightenment thought were making familiar religious assumptions and vocabularies seem antiquated among certain segments of the population, especially among the educated, so that feelings of devout loyalty to inherited church traditions had diminished somewhat by the second quarter of the eighteenth century. The existence of large numbers of the unchurched posed a sharp challenge both to the churches and to the culture, steeped as it was in the premises of Christendom.[2]

The Great Awakening—a revival of religious interest and fervor among both clergy and laity—brought a new spirit and style to the churches of New England. It ushered in a new emphasis on the religion of the heart, personal conversion, emotional preaching, and populism in religious and political life. Divisions between "Old Lights" and "New Lights" became evident, divisions that lasted for longer than a century.

No figure was more important to the Great Awakening than Jonathan Edwards, a son of Connecticut, graduate of Yale, and pastor of the church at Northampton, Massachusetts. Edwards won a sizable following in Connecticut; his most famous but untypically emotional sermon, "Sinners in the Hands of an Angry God," was preached at Enfield—less than thirty miles from Hartford.

Sidney Ahlstrom has suggested that Congregationalism might not have survived as a significant religious movement in New England had it not been for the new energy generated by the Great Awakening.[3] A modest increase in church membership, the new intellectual ferment generated by Edwards' preaching and writing, and a new vitality exhibited by the established churches of the region were all key factors in Congregationalism's renewal from within.

The Awakening had unforeseen effects as well. One was the continuing conflict between the "Old Lights" and "New Lights," each claiming to be the heir of the orthodox tradition. The conflict removed any hope of restoring doctrinal consensus within the established church. A second effect was the opening that the conflict presented to other religious groups; Unitarians, Baptists, and Episcopalians all took advantage of Congregational disunity.

In retrospect it seems clear that with population growth and social differentiation, Puritanism's religious and public role was bound to change. In a recent biography of Jonathan Edwards that focuses on his pastoral ministry, Patricia Tracy discusses his dismissal by the Northampton congregation.[4] She summarizes his hope and the reason for his failure in terms that might well be applied to Congregationalism in early Hartford:

> *What Edwards wanted, clearly, was a church with the intensity of voluntary commitment like the Separatists' but also one with the community inclusiveness like the Presbyterians'—a "come-outer" spirit in an establishment institution. Edwards' church was still the only one in Northampton, and he wanted a permanent revival of pietism within that church. For whatever the reasons that always make surges of communal piety rather short-lived, Edwards' dream was impossible. There was no way to persuade the community to go back to the "city on a hill," to stake their souls on the approval of their neighbors when the community was so rapidly becoming the arena of honest differences and necessary competition.*

Like Northampton, Hartford in the early eighteenth century was no longer the simple community that followed Thomas Hooker into the wilderness of 1636. Diversity had become real. Congregationalism could no longer be the church of all the people and at the same time embody all the qualities demanded by its founders and the leaders of the Great Awakening.

Other periods of religious decline and awakening occurred in the latter part of the eighteenth century. A Venezuelan visitor stopped at First Church in 1784 and found a rundown facility whose members were "inferior" in singing and attire to those at nearby Wethersfield. By this time Second Church had declined to only twenty-seven members (fewer than at the time of its founding, 100 years earlier). The Second Great Awakening brought new strength to both churches and the establishment of still more Congregational churches in the city's expanding neighborhoods. But Congregationalism, still formally established in Connecticut, no longer occupied its central position in the life of the community. By 1818, when disestablishment came, the "established" church had already been joined by Quaker, Episcopal, Methodist, and Baptist churches.[5]

By the time of disestablishment, Hartford was a different place. Its population had grown to nearly 5,000. The town was now a city; settlements to the north, east, south, and west were growing, and the beginnings of what would become important manufacturing and financial enterprises were on the horizon. An era was coming to an end as another was beginning.

It is difficult to trace precisely the ways in which Hartford's Puritan origins have shaped its history, but a few themes are especially important. First, Puritanism fostered a close relationship between the evolving religious institutions and civic institutions. The early Puritans assumed a close relationship between church life and community life, evidenced in

41

the shaping of political structures based on an ecclesiastical polity and responsibility for the moral fiber of public life. From the first days through the Fundamental Orders of 1639 similar assumptions governed religious life. The public presence of the churches changed with time, but the sense of religion's responsibility for public life remained strong. Second, the considerable autonomy reserved for congregations in Congregationalism carried over into the evolution of the New England town. This tradition of local autonomy in municipal life lives on into the twentieth century, sometimes to the detriment of efficiency in governmental affairs and, arguably, with negative consequences for social justice.

Third, from its earliest days, in wrestling with doctrinal and ecclesiastical differences, Hartford was forced to deal with issues of toleration and pluralism. These were not easy struggles, and disestablishment would not come without a fight. Among those who led the Congregational forces in the effort to maintain the church's established status was Lyman Beecher, patriarch of one of nineteenth-century Protestantism's (and Hartford's) most important families. Not one to mince words, Beecher characterized the pro-disestablishment advocates as "nearly all the minor sects, besides the Sabbath-breakers, rum-selling, tippling folk, infidels and rum-scuff generally." Beecher and his forces lost (in Beecher's words: "They slung us out like a stone from a sling"), but before long most Congregationalists agreed with Beecher's assessment of the result:

> For several days I suffered what no tongue can tell for the best thing that ever happened to the State of Connecticut. It cut the churches loose from the dependence on state support. It threw them wholly on their own resources and on God.
>
> They say that ministers have lost their influence; the fact is, they have gained. By voluntary efforts, societies, missions and revivals they exert a deeper influence than they ever could by queues, and shoe-buckles and cocked hats, and gold-headed canes.[6]

The "voluntary efforts" that followed on the heels of disestablishment and the Second Great Awakening channeled energies out of formerly established churches into a host of activist movements for social reform, among them abolitionism, the crusade for temperance legislation, and women's suffrage. They represent one of the most important institutional developments in American religious history, one whose roots are in the response to the reality of cultural pluralism.

1818–1920: A CENTURY OF DRAMATIC CHANGES

If the sixteenth and seventeenth centuries belonged to Hartford's English settlers, the nineteenth century belonged to the new immigrants who built its infrastructure, labored in its factories, and changed its sociological and cultural character. Hartford in the nineteenth century could be the subject of a major volume in itself, for in its life one sees several of the dominant themes that characterized much of urban America as the nation moved into its first full century of nationhood.

Perhaps the most obvious change to occur in Hartford in the hundred years after 1820 was the growth and geographic expansion of the city and its region. From a population of less than 5,000 persons the city grew to 138,000 by 1920. Growth was not limited to the city; Hartford County, which includes Hartford, the smaller city of New Britain, and their neighboring communities, became home to more than 250,000 persons. Other towns, many of them dating back to the late seventeenth century and some with their own industrial and commercial bases, also grew. West Hartford, by now separately incorporated, numbered 8,854 persons; East Hartford, connected to the city by a network of bridges, 11,648; Windsor, 5,620; Wethersfield, 4,342; and Simsbury, 2,958.

By the early twentieth century the city proper had expanded beyond its original settlement on the banks of the Connecticut River and had given rise to a number of ethnically and culturally diverse neighborhoods. Perhaps the best known of these neighborhoods—certainly to those outside the area—was Nook Farm, in the city's West End. This literary suburb was home to a number of Hartford's civic elite, among them Harriet Beecher Stowe and her sister Isabella, writer and editor Charles Dudley Warner, and Mark Twain. Nook Farm (several of whose large, eccentric Gothic houses still stand) reached its heyday, in the last two decades of the nineteenth century, as a center of cultural life and a hotbed of civic activism. Although not the home of the community's wealthiest citizens, it nonetheless stood out as a center of gracious country living in the city.

Nook Farm and its residents represent one extreme among Hartford's new neighborhoods; others were not so fortunate. In 1905 the U.S. Department of Labor reported that among cities of its size, Hartford had the worst housing conditions in the country. Hundreds of desperately poor immigrants were crowded in tenement housing near the original settlement, living in misery. In the 1890s conditions in the neighborhood adjacent to First Church deteriorated to the point where the ancient burial ground was threatened. An inspired member of First Church led what amounted to a crusade to clean up the area and restore it to a state appropriate to its historic importance.* As would happen again in the twentieth century, urban renewal circa 1899 meant urban demolition. The tenements were torn down and their inhabitants transported to similarly uninviting neighborhoods.

*This was not Hartford's first slum clearance effort. Upset with slum conditions near downtown Hartford in the 1850s, the Rev. Horace Bushnell spearheaded an effort to replace a sizable shantytown with the municipal park that now bears his name. Connecticut's state capitol was constructed within the park in the 1870s.

People came to Hartford to work and they found a city with a need for laborers. The nineteenth century saw the city evolve as a manufacturing, commercial, and financial center and as a significant force in the country's economic life.

Hartford began the century with an economic base in agriculture and manufacturing. The Connecticut Valley was an exporter of tobacco, grains, and manufactured goods, using the river as its principal link to the outside world. To this basic means of transportation were added canals, more adequate roads, and, in the 1820s, the railroad. With transportation came an opening to new markets and a succession of entrepreneurs who made Hartford the base of their manufacturing enterprises; among the better known were the munitions industry, pioneered by Samuel Colt, and the machine tools of Pratt and Whitney. By 1880 the city housed more than 800 factories, each employing anywhere from a handful to several hundred workers. During World War I, Colt's payroll grew to more than 8,000 persons, and the city was among the nation's leading manufacturing centers.

As significant as manufacturing was to nineteenth-century Hartford, the city's growth as a commercial and financial center was even more important. In the 1790s the Hartford Insurance Company appeared on the scene. It was the first of many such companies, earning for Hartford the distinction of being the insurance capital of the United States. The reliability of the city's insurance industry was established by prompt payments to clients after major New York City fires in 1834 and 1845, the great Chicago fire of 1871, and San Francisco's earthquake in 1906. By 1920 the companies whose names remain identified with the nation's casualty and health insurance industry, such as Aetna, Connecticut General, Hartford, Travelers, and Phoenix, were solidly established. Insurance was the preserve of Hartford's "old" population, the descendants of its original Protestant settlers. Indeed, the twentieth century was well underway before Catholics and Jews found acceptance in the industry's highest circles.

Another major nineteenth-century change was in the ethnic background of Hartford's new population. Although people of other than English origin had been present in Hartford from the beginning—including a few black slaves among the earliest settlers and a Jew named David, whose name appears in city records for the year 1659—they were a minority. By the early twentieth century this was no longer true.

Immigrants came to Hartford for a combination of reasons: the push of such conditions as famine and persecution in their homelands and the pull of an expanding economy in need of skilled and unskilled labor. The first to arrive in large numbers—and in some respects the least welcome— were the Irish, in the first two decades of the nineteenth century. The

Irish were ill-prepared to enter the increasingly sophisticated cultural life of the city; lacking education and trade skills they came to build canals and roads and to fill low-level factory jobs. Unwelcome in many factories ("No Irish Need Apply" notices were common), they were brought by the hundreds to build the Hartford and New Haven Railroad in the 1830s. By 1860 three fourths of Hartford's foreign-born residents were people who had come from Ireland.

The Germans were not far behind, but because they came from a more technically advanced country and brought needed craft skills they found more acceptance. Many were suited by background and temperament for work in the new factories being established across the city, especially in the firearms plant founded by Samuel Colt in 1855. The German immigrants were not homogeneous; most were Protestant, but Catholics and Jews were also represented. By 1840, when Connecticut law opened religious freedom to non-Christians, about 200 German Jews were living in Hartford.

The 1850s were difficult years for immigrants in Hartford and throughout Connecticut. The American Party (known as the Know-Nothings) attracted considerable popular support, including that of the *Hartford Courant*, the city's oldest and most important newspaper, and took control of the governorship in 1855. Anti-Catholic feelings were strong; the city's first Catholic church was burned by an arsonist and street fights among the city's working classes were common. The conflicts subsided somewhat with the coming of the Civil War but carried over into the city's political life with the emergence of the Republican Party as a coalition of old-line Yankees and blacks, and the Democratic Party as an assemblage of predominantly Catholic ethnic groups.

In the latter years of the nineteenth century, immigration again accelerated and new groups appeared on the Hartford scene. The need for skilled factory workers brought Scandinavians (mainly Swedes and Danes), and by the turn of the century the city began to attract large numbers of Russians, Poles and other Eastern Europeans, and Italians. Between 1890 and 1920 alone the number of foreign-born residents rose from 14,000 to nearly 40,000, with the Russian-origin population increasing from 492 to 7,864; the Italians, from 350 to 7,101; and the Poles, from 19 to 4,880.

Hartford's black population was growing also and by 1920 numbered 4,199 persons, about 3 percent of the city's total. Most were from the rural South, drawn to Hartford by prospects of employment in agriculture, domestic service, and low-level factory jobs. Blacks were concentrated in the city's North End in some of the most dismal housing the city had to offer.

Connecticut was one of the first states to abolish slavery, with adoption in 1784 of a "gradual emancipation" law, which freed children of slaves on reaching age twenty-five. By 1848, when slavery was fully abolished, there were only six black slaves in the state.

In the early nineteenth century Hartford's free blacks were concentrated in several small neighborhoods around the city, neighborhoods that ranged from moderately prosperous to grim. Class lines within the black community were quite pronounced; several black families, mainly descendants of early slaves, owned small businesses and land, whereas new arrivals tended to occupy the lowest rungs on the city's social and economic ladder. In a formal sense, early black residents were integrated into Hartford life, although in distinctly second-class roles. Segregated schools came into being in the 1830s and lasted until 1858, when the public schools were again integrated.

Throughout the nineteenth century there was considerable interplay between the city's old-line black and white communities. The black community produced a number of significant leaders, especially clergy, who were active in abolitionist efforts, both independently and alongside whites. The Rev. James Pennington, founder of the Talcott Street Congregational Church, was a frequent visitor in the elegant homes of Nook Farm and preached in several city churches; he published an abolitionist newspaper during the 1840s. The black community supported an elaborate social life, centering around the churches and the Masonic Lodge.

The latter years of the century saw important changes in the city's black population as the balance shifted toward recently freed southern slaves. In 1860 only 4 percent of the city's black population were southern born; by 1870 the number grew to 25 percent and by 1900 only a small percentage could trace their roots to the early English settlement days.

Most of Hartford's immigrants brought with them the religious heritage of their homelands, which changed Hartford's religious composition radically.

In 1823, responding to the growth of the Irish population, the Bishop of Boston sent a priest to establish the city's first Catholic parish and school. With support from local Episcopalians, the Catholic Church of the Holy Trinity was consecrated in 1830, followed soon after by a school and burial ground. Propelled by continuing immigration, Catholicism in Hartford prospered; a second church was founded in 1849 and a third, in 1851. With the churches came benevolent societies and a weekly newspaper to serve Catholic parishioners.

Until a German Lutheran parish was founded in 1880, the Episcopal Church provided for the religious needs of German Protestants. This pattern repeated itself again and again as older religious groups established missions to new immigrants until groups attained sufficient strength to establish their own churches. Hartford's first Jewish congregation, Congregation Beth Israel, was founded by German Jewish families in 1843—the year that Jews were granted religious rights by the state legislature. Swedish Lutherans formed a congregation in 1889; French Catholics, in 1889; Italian Catholics, in 1898; Polish Catholics, in 1902. Several new Jewish congregations came into being in the 1880s and 1890s to serve Eastern European immigrants, and the city's first Russian Orthodox church was established in 1914.

The Federal Census of Religious Bodies of 1916 documents the change in the city's religious composition. Returns from 88 of the 92 congregations located in the city showed a membership of 73,257 persons. Of that total, 48,329 were Catholic; followed by Congregationalists (6,070), Jews (4,704), Episcopalians (4,241), Northern Baptists (3,479), Methodists (2,459), and Lutherans (1,777).

The change in the denominational composition of the region in the nineteenth century was accompanied by changes in the public role of religious groups within the city.

The churches of the immigrant groups served a number of important functions. For their members they were links with the homeland, places in which one's native language was spoken, one's traditions were maintained, and one's values were reinforced. They were "sanctuaries" in a strange land in which "foreigners" were not altogether welcome. In addition to their sanctuary function, the churches served as bridges to the dominant culture, as agents in the larger process of assimilation. They provided, in other words, a relationship with a valued past while paving the way for fuller acceptance into Hartford's social and economic life.

Representative of the institutions founded by immigrants was the Ararat Lodge of B'nai B'rith, established by German Jewish men in 1851. The lodge was an early center for Hartford Jews and stimulated a number of social, philanthropic, and cultural endeavors. Membership carried with it a number of benefits: material and spiritual support in the event of illness, the opportunity to be heard on issues of concern to the Jewish community, and prestige and social standing in the community at large. Membership was open to men of good health and high moral character, and sanctions were imposed for unethical behavior. Local historian Rabbi Morris Silverman reports that the lodge was a training ground for participation in a democratic society; it provided members with an awareness of current events in the United States and contact with fellow Jews across the world.[7] A typical meeting included time for airing disputes affecting members of the Hartford Jewish community. The lodge helped to provide internal solidarity for Hartford's small Jewish population while forming bridges to the Christian community; one of the lodge's first votes was to purchase an American flag and march in Hartford's Fourth of July parade in 1852.

Over time the role of the immigrant church as sanctuary gave way to an expanded role and to fuller participation in public life. An example of this shift is found in the dedication of the Catholic Cathedral of St. Joseph in 1892 (on Washington's Birthday). In his sermon consecrating the cathedral the Right Rev. Michael Tierney emphasized that the Irish were just as good and loyal Americans as the city's Yankee forebears. Symbolizing their "new respectability," he announced on the same occasion that Hartford's Irish would no longer celebrate St. Patrick's Day in the traditional pattern of elaborate parades and parties, but would keep the day with more acceptable observances, such as banquets and "intellectual exercises."[8]

Hartford's older churches were changing as well, establishing numerous new parishes as their members moved into expanding city neighborhoods and suburban towns. By 1916 more than half the region's Congregationalists and Episcopalians were members of churches located outside the city. These churches had almost no interest in outreach to the city's new immigrants, with whom they had little in common. For the most part their attention was directed toward larger issues. Several churches were active in the growing abolitionist movement and in the Underground Railroad; a number took strong antislavery stands in the form of congregational pronouncements and provided financial support for the social reform endeavors of national missionary societies.

Congregationalism in Hartford remained a center of doctrinal controversy as old battles refused to die and new ones arose. The Rev. Horace Bushnell was, for most of the nineteenth century, the city's leading theological voice. Bushnell tried, with some success, to move beyond old divisions between the denomination's orthodox and evangelical parties, and, principally through his best known work, *Christian Nurture,* became widely known.

During his pastorate at Hartford's North Church, Bushnell remained a minority voice in "official" denominational circles, although his "liberal" theological stance influenced the younger clergy, who dominated Hartford Congregationalism in the late 1800s. Three of the clergy who were influenced by Bushnell became known as the "triumvirate." The three—Nathaniel Burton, Edwin Pond Parker, and Joseph Twitchell—were close friends, members of the Yale Corporation, and pastors of three of the city's "prestige" churches. The triumvirate symbolized the comfortable position enjoyed by Congregationalism in Hartford. Louise Wade summarizes their position:

> They had no interest in the lower classes of Hartford, for they agreed with Charles Dudley Warner (the well-known editor and resident of Nook Farm, in which two of the three pastors lived) that poverty was "the accompaniment of human weakness and crime." None of the three pastors ever indulged in evangelical appeals to his congregation. They preached to complacent, stolid business and professional

48

people, "politically conservative, honest and cautious, content with a high return on their investments, and satisfied with the conditions that made such returns possible." Twitchell, Burton, and Parker "were of them, not above them."

Their leadership in Hartford's Congregational affairs rested on their personal and social position, not their theological acumen or spiritual fervor. They were pastors par excellence for the Gilded Age.[9]

Although the triumvirate was the dominant voice in the city's leading Protestant denomination, it was not the only voice. In 1880 a young Dutch Reformed pastor, Graham Taylor, accepted a call to Hartford's Fourth Congregational Church. Located in the heart of the city, Fourth Church had been founded as Congregationalism's "free church" in the 1830s and was a center of abolitionist sentiment in the pre-Civil War period. At the time of Taylor's arrival, however, the church's future was considered dim. Surrounded by people of immigrant stock and by the poor, its 1,200-seat sanctuary seldom attracted more than fifty worshipers at one time.

Taylor brought to Fourth Church a determination to "raise a voice in God's name in the densest and most neglected district . . . of the city." In a few years he made the church a center of missionary work among the poor the likes of which had not been seen before in the city; by 1883 Sunday attendance had risen to 400, the congregation drawn from all walks of life. Taylor's ministry brought him—and his church—in contact with gamblers, alcoholics, and the "unchurched masses" of the center city, and the church developed the reputation among more fashionable Congregationalists of being the "church for ex-convicts."

Taylor's blend of evangelical fervor and social activism was not especially appreciated by peers. He wrote to his father about the response to an 1883 address on "The Evangelization of the World," in which he argued for the church's missionary responsibility to "the heathen abroad and at home":

> *I was amazed to hear every man but one openly disavow such obligation. . . . One man wished "all missionaries hauled in for 100 years until the church be united." Another would await the Perfection of ministries, ordinances, gifts, etc. before attempting more. Another deprecated the Church's "going down into the Slums." . . . Burton hedged shamefully—even declaring that our Lord was not of "the build of a 6th ward man"—referring to the mission ward of the city. . . . The trouble was that I stuck him heavily in the essay by the declaration that we wanted ministers "who would make men the chief end of their culture and not culture the chief end of man." Such a discussion I never heard in that club. It was such an earthly subject as to disturb its heavenly-mindedness and arouse old Adam.*[10]

Graham Taylor remained a controversial figure in Hartford through the early 1890s, continuing as pastor of Fourth Church and adding duties at Hartford Theological Seminary. He left Hartford in 1892 for Chicago Theological Seminary, where he became a leading figure in the settlement house and Social Gospel movements. Taylor did not transform Hartford or Congregationalism during his years in the city, but he did challenge Protestantism's comfortable and uncritical relationship to public life by demonstrating an alternative to prevailing institutional forms.

A CITY AND REGION IN TRANSITION

In 1920 the city of Hartford was more than 95 percent white and accounted for more than 56 percent of the region's population. By 1980 half the city's residents were black or Hispanic and the city's share of the region's population declined to about one fifth. These two facts summarize the dramatic change that has taken place in the region in only sixty years.

Virtually every point made in chapter 1 about contemporary urban life in the United States can be applied to Hartford: One can no longer deal with the city apart from its metropolitan context; suburbanization has been widespread and selective; municipal government faces severe financial strains; city and suburbs exist in a state of real—yet unacknowledged—interdependence; enclave politics is a reality; and privatization in both public and religious life is widespread. Many of these features were already evident early in the twentieth century, whereas others are of more recent origin.

Beginning shortly after World War II, Hartford experienced a new wave of immigration—this time of blacks from the southern states and the West Indies. They settled in the city's North End and Windsor Street neighborhoods (until the latter's clearance for commercial uses) and found employment in low-paying, unskilled positions. As was true in other northern cities, the new immigrants did not receive a warm welcome. They were relegated to the city's most miserable housing and largely were excluded from opportunities for economic and political advancement. The new arrivals brought new challenges to Hartford's established black institutions—churches, masonic lodges, and political organizations. Hartford blacks provided important early leadership and support to the national movement for racial justice and enlisted considerable aid from the city's white community. In the 1960s, as the focus of the civil rights movement turned from national to local concerns, such as residential segregation in Hartford itself, lack of economic opportunity in the region's financial institutions, poor housing conditions, and inadequate municipal services, black leaders found less white support. The late 1960s saw several summers of racial disturbances, which called public attention to the plight of the city's growing minority population.

Hartford's black population has continued to grow. In the period from 1950 to 1980 the city's black population increased from 8,000 (4 percent of the city's population) to 46,000 (34 percent). Although concentrated in a small number of city and suburban neighborhoods and still far behind whites in economic terms (the 1979 median income for black families was $12,366 compared with $17,437 for white families), the region's black population has become a well-organized political force. Its political power was symbolized in the election of the city's first black mayor in 1982.

During the 1960s blacks were joined by Hartford's newest immigrants from Puerto Rico, many of whom initially came as temporary agricultural workers and stayed in the region. Between 1970 and 1980 alone the city's Hispanic population more than doubled; the 1980 census recorded 28,000 Spanish-origin persons, representing 21 percent of the city's residents. Being relatively new to the city, the Puerto Rican community lacks the social infrastructure and political influence of blacks and other ethnic groups. The Spanish-origin population is young (48 percent are under age eighteen) and poor (the 1979 median family income was $7,473). The needs of the Hispanic community were made visible to the entire region when, in 1982, a group of Puerto Rican demonstrators camped in the local Hilton hotel to protest inadequate housing conditions.

The shift in the racial composition of the city's population is one important change in the region's modern era; the growth of its suburbs is another. Although the city's rate of population growth equaled or exceeded that of its suburbs through the 1920s, in more recent decades it has fallen far behind. Since 1950, when its population peaked at 177,000, the city has lost 23 percent of its population. In the same thirty-year period its suburban neighbors have grown more than 150 percent: West Hartford grew from 44,000 to 61,000; East Hartford, from 20,000 to 52,500; Wethersfield, from 12,500 to 26,000. Suburban growth was not restricted to communities immediately adjacent to the city. Older communities "west of the mountain" began to attract newcomers; the population of Simsbury, for example, rose from 4,800 in 1950 to more than 21,000 in 1980. What were once sleepy New England villages are now large, highly mobile bedroom communities serving the region as a whole.

Hartford's suburbanization has been highly selective. The residents of the towns in the region tend to be white and middle to upper middle class; more than 40 percent have had at least some college education and nearly 30 percent hold professional or managerial positions. The 1979 median income for the region's suburban families was $25,742.

The 1980 census documented city-suburb social divisions. Although the city accounts for only 21 percent of the region's population, it is home for 75 percent of its black and 83 percent of its Hispanic residents. Within the city are half the region's female-headed households, 61 percent of the poverty-level population, 61 percent of those receiving public assistance, and 67 percent of recent migrants from abroad. Family incomes of city residents are only 55 percent of those of suburbanites. Hartford's residents have the fourth highest rate of urban poverty in the United States, whereas incomes in Hartford's suburbs are among the nation's highest.

The relationship between Hartford and its suburbs, however, remains one of interdependence. The city is the region's commercial, media, and financial center. It contains the major television and radio outlets, the region's principal newspaper, a new and thriving civic center, and most of the region's medical, banking, and financial institutions. By 1981 the region housed the headquarters of thirty-nine insurance companies—most still located in the city proper—with worldwide assets of $46 billion.

The key factor in the interdependence of the towns in the region is economic. The city accounts for 40 percent of the region's jobs. The results of a 1976 study done for the Capitol Region Council of Governments pointed out that suburban residents hold 61 percent of the jobs located in the city and take home 70 percent of the income generated by those jobs. Suburbanites, the study estimates, hold nine out of ten city positions paying more than $15,000 per year. What happens to the city's economy affects the whole region: Every 1,000 jobs that leave the city result in a loss of 610 positions for suburban residents (in addition to secondary losses resulting from decreased suburban purchasing power).[11]

Voting patterns in recent elections suggest that demographic and economic differences within the Hartford region are carrying over into the political sphere. In the 1980 Presidential election, for example, the Carter-Mondale ticket received 70 percent of the votes in the city and carried every voting district. In the same election the Republican ticket of Reagan and Bush carried most of the suburbs by healthy pluralities. Reagan-Bush received 43 percent of the vote in West Hartford (to Carter-Mondale's 38 percent), 45 percent in Wethersfield (to 40 percent), and 55 percent in Simsbury (to 26 percent).

A hotly contested mayoral election in 1981 suggested the arrival of enclave politics within the city. The Democratic primary (usually tantamount to election in Hartford) featured a four-way contest involving the incumbent mayor, the deputy mayor, and a Council member—all white—and a black state legislator from the city's North End. The primary, held twice because of voting irregularities, was won with 47 percent of the vote by State Representative Thirman Milner, who went on to become New England's first popularly elected black mayor. Milner won by carrying more than four out of five votes in the city's predominantly black North End, while his opponents were splitting 80 percent of the vote in white neighborhoods. The city divided along racial and ethnic lines, reflecting the new political composition of the city itself.

Privatization—the sixth feature of contemporary urban society noted earlier—is the most difficult to measure. In our interviews with Hartford-area leaders (discussed at length in chapter 4) it most often arose in connection with the responsibilities of suburban communities for problems of the central city. In Hartford, as elsewhere, the separation between the world of work and the world of residence-family-leisure and church or synagogue is real. Local officials spoke eloquently of the retreat "over the mountain" into communities that offers the promise of an escape from the pressures of the "real world" of Hartford. A black politician noted that the desire to escape from the problems of the city is not restricted to whites, that with upward mobility it has become difficult to involve black professionals in the problems of Hartford's minority community.

Most of the leaders were critical of the religious community for what they see as a retreat from active involvement with social problems into the private realm. Even though they were appreciative of the social service, personal counseling, and spiritual nurture roles of churches and synagogues, they used words like passive, reactive, irrelevant, timid, antiseptic, selfish, weak, and uninvolved to describe religious groups and leaders in the public arena. Although our interviews concentrated on the public roles of religious organizations, we suspect that had we been focusing on other social institutions and professions (business, labor, education, the law, etc.) we would have heard similar criticisms. As do most metropolitan areas, Hartford lacks a sense of public life that enables the varying private interests of individuals and groups to come together around shared understandings of public life and responsibility.

If the triumph of the private over the public is more evident in Hartford than elsewhere, it is by contrast with the integration of the two spheres in the city's early history. Frustration with an apparent absence of a larger sense of public purpose—which we found among secular and religious leaders alike—is silent testimony to the historic role of Hartford churches and synagogues in helping to foster a healthy spirit of public consciousness.

The following chapters deal with the presence of religious institutions, especially churches and synagogues, in Greater Hartford and examine diverse responses to the changing urban context in which they exist. Before closing this overview of religious presence in the area, a few general notes on the region's religious community are needed.

Will Herberg's 1957 classic book, *Protestant-Catholic-Jew*—in which Herberg argues that America's three great religious faiths have become three alternative ways of being an American, of expressing one's commitment to the American Way of Life—is particularly appropriate to the change that occurred in Hartford's religious life in the first half of the twentieth century. For nearly 300 years Hartford's Puritan establishment had yielded grudging acceptance of new religious groups, first to Episcopalians, Methodists, and Baptists, later to Catholics and Jews. By the 1950s religious diversity—and widespread acceptance of that diversity—was an accomplished fact in Greater Hartford. It came in part, as Herberg suggested, because the major religious faiths shared common commitments that transcended individual theological beliefs and ritual practices.

An extraordinary symbol of the new era of religious pluralism in Greater Hartford was the emergence of a new "triumvirate" of religious leaders who played a key role in the civic life of the region. The new "giants" in the religious community were described by a Hartford leader:

> *There were three giants in the religious community. Abe Feldman was the key rabbi in town—a masterful speaker, a delightful guy, a real leader. Then there was (Henry) O'Brien who was Bishop of Hartford and later the Archbishop and Walter Gray who was the Episcopal Bishop. The three of them used to form the religious triumvirate of the City of Hartford. I would be willing to say without fear of anyone contradicting me that those three men exercised as much influence in Greater Hartford as any three men you could put together. They were the confidants of the governors. They were the confidants of mayors and leaders of the legislature. Together they were able to bring moral force into the government. And they used to do it together. They were great friends and I think they were very influential on the caliber of life in the area.*[12]

Feldman's daughter writes of the three leaders: "People who came into contact with Feldman, O'Brien or Gray put their best foot forward and tried to rise to the heights which they sensed these religious giants expected of them." She stresses their personal qualities and friendship and their common message: "They all taught and preached love of God, respect for man and men's differences, tolerance."[13]

The triumvirate of the region's leading Protestant, Catholic, and Jewish leaders is an ideal symbol of Hartford's (and if Herberg's larger thesis is correct, of the nation's) religious climate in the 1950s. Its members shared an understanding of the religious community as a full participant in public life alongside other social institutions in support of broadly accepted moral principles and values.

The 1950s were suited to this essentially civic orientation of the religious community. Subsequent decades would challenge the dominance of this orientation. Led by black churches, denominational groups and congregations found themselves in more activist roles with respect to civil rights, the war in Vietnam, abortion, and growing problems in the central city. The region's "liberal" churches found themselves challenged from within and without by aggressive new evangelical churches and movements. Continuing secularization (and in-migration of new ethnic groups) prompted some religious groups to withdraw into themselves as a defense against perceived corruptions in the larger society and in the interest of group solidarity.

To community leaders and to the religious community itself the emergence of new responses to the increased complexity of urban life has been a cause of considerable confusion. In the 1980s it is not possible to point to a small group of leaders as representative of the interests of the religious community as a whole. While for some groups the notion of the congregation as citizen remains dominant, it is by no means inclusive of the variety of religious presence one finds within the region. It is to that diversity, especially as it finds expression in Greater Hartford's congregations, that we turn in the following chapters.

CHAPTER 4

HARTFORD TODAY

Religious presence, we argued in chapters 1 and 2, is multifaceted. Although this book has congregational expressions of religious presence as its particular focus, it would be a mistake to assume that religion is present in Hartford only through congregations. Indeed, non-congregational forms of religious presence are important elements of the context in which churches and synagogues are themselves "present." Building on the historical overview of chapter 3, we touch briefly here on three key aspects of the region's religious life that help comprise that context. Specifically, we will look at community leaders' perceptions of the region and religion's place in it, at the people of Greater Hartford and their religious and social views, and at religious organizations that are active in Greater Hartford that are not congregations.

HARTFORD'S LEADERS

In late 1980 and early 1981 we identified and interviewed a cross section of forty-four Hartford-area leaders representing nine areas of public life. The interviews covered several topics: general attitudes toward religious participation in public life; perceptions of the present impact of religious leaders and congregations on public policy issues in Greater Hartford; the leaders' sense of the major issues facing the region; evaluations of the religious community's performance on issues of concern to the leaders; identification of congregations, other religious groups, and religious leaders having particular impact on Greater Hartford; the contact leaders

56

have had with religious leaders; and the individuals' own religious beliefs and congregational and religious involvements.*

In our analysis of the community leader interviews we identified a number of themes that contribute to an understanding of religion's role in the life of the region. Four are especially important: the "uniqueness" of the region, the problems it faces in the 1980s, the ways the religious community is perceived as an asset in public life, and assessments of religion's involvements in issues of public policy.

The Setting

"Hartford is Holyoke plus twenty corporations . . . and they [the corporations] run the town." These were the words used by one leader in calling attention to the role played by the business community in the life of Greater Hartford. He was not alone in the suggestion of the dominance in public life of a relatively small number of corporations, mainly insurance companies that have their home offices in the city. People stressed both the nature of the work that is performed in the area (mainly white collar and professional, with an emphasis on finance and technology) and the character of the community's corporate leadership. "We have some pretty moral guys in business," said a black activist. "The Hartford business community has been involved in every progressive social issue in the city."

A second common observation has to do with changes occurring within the region. Several leaders spoke of the increasing diversity within the region. As noted in chapter 3, the area has been home for several waves of immigrants. Many feel that Hartford's institutions have had great difficulty keeping pace with the rapid demographic changes that have occurred throughout the past half-century.

Third, the community leaders sense that the religious composition of the region is important. The area's founding by Congregationalists, its significant Jewish population, the key role played by Baptist churches in the black community, the numerical dominance of the Catholic Church, and the lack of a significant conservative Protestant force were all noted by leaders. One suggested that most people view religion as pretty much an individual matter: "Many people feel that religion is one area that is private unto an individual and their relationship to God, and that the rest of us should not interfere with that."

Finally, leaders view Greater Hartford as relatively liberal and open. An attorney put it this way: "Hartford is not the South." He recalled

---

*A fuller discussion of the community leader interviews can be found in William McKinney, David A. Roozen, and Jackson W. Carroll, *Religion's Public Presence* (Washington, DC: Alban Institute, 1983).

attending a meeting of the American Bar Association and sitting next to a delegation from Alabama:

> *Views about minority solicitation or minority recruitment by law schools which I'm sure you won't get anybody from the Northeast to argue about at all, about certain things with respect to civil rights and homosexuals . . . those were not going to get a very good hearing down in Georgia and Tennessee and some of the other places. Of course in the sophisticated Northeast there's no problem with that. But down there they don't have that viewpoint. They're hardback, hardshell Baptists, a lot of them.*

Area Problems

During the interviews the community leaders were asked what they thought were the major problems facing the Hartford area in the next three to five years. Although responses ranged from teenage pregnancy rates to nuclear waste disposal, there was remarkable consensus among the leaders around the following concerns:

Housing. Nearly all the leaders mentioned housing first as one of the major issues facing the area. The problem is viewed as multifaceted and suggests, for many, deeper problems confronting the city and its suburbs.

Housing is an issue that points beyond itself to other area problems. Frequently mentioned were issues of employment opportunity; housing problems are inevitable, explained a physician, unless people have the skills and opportunity to work in jobs that offer hope of economic advancement. This, in turn, requires educational opportunities and skill development that qualify people for jobs.

Other leaders saw the housing issue as symbolic of the refusal of suburban communities to share responsibility for the problems of the city. Some area communities have refused to accept federal funds rather than allow construction of low- and moderate-income housing, which was cited by several leaders as evidence of a desire on the part of those communities to preserve their economic and racial homogeneity. Suburban officials we talked with were quite candid in suggesting that while those opposing low- and moderate-income housing most often spoke of protecting property values and preserving local autonomy in decision making, the real housing issue is one of race and economic class.

Employment. Business leaders and leaders of minority background were especially likely to mention employment opportunities as a key issue. Again and again we heard leaders bemoan the lack of employment opportunities for people without technical skills. The comment of one black businessman is typical:

There have always been jobs here for people who are highly skilled. The problem is to train people for skills. Many of the unskilled are illiterate or they have a language difficulty, and of course this creates an unusual problem. I don't think we're ever going to see the kind of industry here that requires a substantial amount of unskilled labor. And I think this is one of the problems that underlies the city now. We have people here who are functionally unemployable—not because they don't want to work, not because they're not strong human beings but because there's a substantial reduction in jobs that require un-skilled labor. And I see that becoming more and more pronounced in the future.

Education. Most of the leaders think that the development of a strong educational system is the only hope for people to have a chance for decent housing and jobs. In the words of an educator, "if you do not get an education, your chances of breaking out . . . are practically nil. Even if you get it, you still have a lot of problems but at least you have a chance."

Intergroup conflict. Hartford was often described as a collection of communities with loose ties to one another. In most cases this collection was defined as a central city populated by poor and minority people surrounded by affluent suburbs. Officials spoke of "border wars" between the city and suburbs, of racism and anti-Semitism that exist in the region. An attorney spoke of Hartford as a "splintered community, not to the point, at the moment, of explosion but having a fragile set of bonds holding it together." He continued: "There are a lot of potential confrontations within the community: corporate versus neighborhood, black versus white, black versus Hispanic." An educator asked, "How can we get the message across to kids about brotherhood, prejudice, and so on when our city is a segregated city? North End this, South End that. White this, black that. This is the reality they fully recognize. It is almost hypocritical to say man should love his fellow man no matter what color or creed or religion."

Deterioration of traditional values. "There's so much of today's youth that I find so self-defiant, so lacking in initiative, so much of a sense of sitting back and waiting for things to be done for me. You know, going into the classroom or into the workplace and saying, 'Hey, you are lucky I got here. Pay me my salary. Don't ask me to work a couple of extra minutes!'" These words were used by a leader to express his frustration with a seeming deterioration of traditional values of hard work, individual initiative, and determination to make something of one's life. It was a theme raised in different ways by a wide range of people. More than once the present was contrasted with the spirit and energy of the region's founders.

Lack of adequate political structures. "What are the major issues facing Hartford? You can get all the trite answers—housing and jobs—but the basic problem is that we don't have the structure that can deal with them." This was a rather common view: that governmental structures handed down from the past are inadequate to deal with today's problems. "The historic town structure has become counterproductive," said one. "The New England town meeting, as far as Connecticut is concerned, is dead. It's the myth of the wild. It is gone," said another. "It's the most incredible system of government going; you have three people in the same outfield going after the same ball," said a third.

Although many see structural changes in the character of local and regional government patterns as needed, few see change as likely.

Religion and Public Life

> Churches offer far more to towns than they take away in terms of taxes. You couldn't possibly put into place a social service system for the elderly, take care of the loneliness of those who are isolated in their homes, provide personal outreach to families, and provide community concern [such as that provided by religious groups]. As a matter of fact, the churches' dollars are much more effective than the towns' themselves. The fiber of this community is supported by that presence.

This comment from a suburban public official summarizes well the sentiment of community leaders when they were asked to reflect on the extent to which churches and synagogues are assets to the Greater Hartford area.

Leaders cited dozens of churches that are doing an especially good job in their service to the community and a number of ecumenical, interfaith, and para-parochial agencies whose work is important to the area. The comments tended to focus on general areas: service to people and groups with special needs, meeting the religious or spiritual needs of members, providing encouragement to individuals to live responsible lives, and sponsoring special programs that meet area needs.

The leaders view churches and synagogues as important forces in public life. They respect what happens within congregations and the community services the religious community provides. They make a special contribution; in the words of one public official, "anybody who looks at a New England town has to know that the town was founded by a church."

The same leaders were less affirming of the religious community's performance in addressing root causes of major area problems. Most leaders see the religious community's priorities as being elsewhere. Speaking of the leader of his own faith group, one prominent businessman put it this way: "My impression is that he is more interested in prayer and individual sanctity than in social reform. I don't know that this is true, but that's the impression I get."

A few general comments on the public role of churches and synagogues give a flavor of what we heard. A Hartford politician looked at the religious community in relation to other interest groups. "On a scale of one to ten, compared with business, ethnic groups, and so forth," he suggested, "the churches would rate about a two." A medical doctor was equally negative:

> From my standpoint most religious leaders ignore these issues. Certainly they don't become active advocates or take a leadership role in trying to propose some actions or solutions to problems. . . . From my standpoint, most churches—not religions, but most churches—are basically businesses and they're in the business of survival like all others. Maybe they don't have the freedom. Maybe the fight for survival has taken all their strength. I don't know.

The inability to point to active religious community involvement with the moral dimensions of public issues is a source of disappointment for many leaders. "I'm not conscious of much impact from the churches," stated one social service leader, "and that's what concerns me. It bothers me tremendously." He goes on:

> Active as I am [in public policy areas] I should be impacted and I'm willing to be. I'm looking for that. I need that leadership. A lot of people who put us out here as leaders—maybe some of them won't admit it; but I'm one who admits I need it. The ministers and the institution of the church are not involved directly and overtly enough.

The leaders cited several reasons for what was generally viewed as a decline in the involvement of religious groups with public policy issues.

Few giants left. Several leaders pointed to changes in the area's religious leadership. The passing of the "triumvirate" and a lack of "giants" in the religious community were cited often, and leaders are seen as possessing less authority than in an earlier era. One state legislator, an active Catholic, spoke specifically of the archbishop: "There are times when the archbishop comes out and says something. That used to carry a lot more weight on the Catholic Church in Connecticut than it does now. On some things we will rally behind the archbishop and on other things we will say

61

he is not in touch with reality and he really shouldn't have talked about that."

A newspaper editor spoke at length of the leadership issue: "The whole story is the quality of leadership. That's the problem here. There was once a generation of educational and political and some religious leaders who could make the community do what it should do." Now he believes that that leadership is missing. "In the business community we need stronger, enlightened political leadership; in the political community we need stronger, enlightened economic leadership; and in the religious community we need both."

Parish leaders, he thinks, back off from community leadership roles:

> Right now we don't have politically aware ministers. . . . We have ministers who are caring and warm and who like the parish. They get a list of people who are in the hospital and go and see all of them. . . . We had a minister here who was very nice. He was the strongest person I've ever known and he could have had an enormous impact on the community. He didn't get very much accomplished. [I'd go and see him] and he'd sit in his chair and take a deep breath and say, "If you ever have any problems, please take them to somebody else."

The shifting political atmosphere. Several of the leaders noted that the decline in religious activism has paralleled a more general shift in the nation's political climate. Liberalism appears to many to be on the wane, and this has had an effect on the liberally oriented churches and clergy of the Hartford region.

A political leader spoke of the kind of populism he associates with the Reagan administration in Washington, with which Connecticut seems out of step. "Reagan is not an idealist Republican. He did not come out of New England; he is not a Yalie. He is a cowboy. The hero of the cowboy is John Wayne, not Elliott Richardson."

A suburban officeholder shared her sympathy with the churches and her frustration with the inability to make progress on social problems. Problems that once seemed solvable no longer have easy answers. She is typical in the view that as issues become less clearly defined, activist-minded people in general and in the churches have fewer handles on the goals or methods for effective public policy involvements.

A question of will. Many of the leaders traced the low visibility of churches and synagogues to questions of will or intention on the part of clergy and laity. Some charged that the religious community simply doesn't care about social problems.

A newspaper reporter, an active churchgoer, was particularly vocal. The failure of churches to be involved in community life made her angry.

I can think of one particular church in Hartford; if I lived nearby, I would make it a point every day to throw one rock through the window of that church because they contribute nothing to the neighborhood, nothing to the community. Nothing! It's the most ruthless church I've ever seen. It's a white church—a white church in the midst of a Puerto Rican community with an iron fence around its property.

Suburban leaders were hard on local clergy. One called them "rather timid souls." "I used to see them out there, but not recently. They get more and more away from political decisions. I think this is because their own congregations are so split. There's conflict. You can't get a consensus of the congregation." He goes on: "I think there could be an attempt to shake these people up. Clergy are going to have to be a little tougher and maybe take a little abuse from the members and maybe some of them are going to have to relocate."

A businessman who is active in the Hartford Jewish community was critical of laypeople.

There used to be considerable activity in housing in the religious community. Recently, there's been virtually none that I know of any significance. . . . If there was ever a time to get excited about housing, it's now—there are people who don't have a place to live! You know why there is no movement? Because the vast majority, the bulk of the religious community's constituents, are safely ensconced in the suburbs or wherever they are. They couldn't care less about housing.

Running through the interviews is a sense of discouragement and of anxiety about the role of religious groups in the public arena that balances the appreciation nearly all have for the region's churches and synagogues. Religious groups have communicated a vision of a community in which men and women set goals for themselves and their institutions that go beyond what they think they can do. The community's leaders seem to have heard that message and call the churches to do the same.

HARTFORD'S PEOPLE

In the previous section we looked at views of community leaders on issues facing Greater Hartford and at the role of religious groups in addressing public issues. Here we turn from leaders to the general public, using as our principal resource a telephone survey of 500 area residents. The survey, conducted by the Institute for Social Research of the University of Hartford, probed residents' views on a wide range of religious and social issues. The results give another perspective on the religious climate of the

Hartford region. They also help to establish the context in which religion is present in the region.*

Table 4.1 provides an overview of selected demographic and religiosity items for the total sample and for major religious groups. For the most part, the respondents reflect the composition of the Greater Hartford area, although women, whites, and suburban residents are slightly over-represented.

The sample reflects the religious composition of the area in its relatively high numbers of Catholics (43 percent of the sample) and Jews (8 percent). The mainline (23 percent) and conservative (20 percent) Protestant groups are approximately equal in size, and those with no religious preference account for 6 percent of the sample, roughly paralleling the proportion of religious "nones" in the nation as a whole.†

Significant differences exist in the composition of the major religious groups. Catholics are younger and slightly less educated than the sample as a whole. Mainline Protestants are older, have higher educational and family income levels, and are less likely to come from minority groups. Conservative Protestants are more often members of minority groups and have lower income and educational levels. Jews are high in income and education. People with no religious preference are quite young with above-average educational levels.

Religious Commitment

Table 4.1 also shows scores on several items dealing with religious participation and attitudes. Overall, 70 percent of the sample are members of a church or synagogue. Catholics have the highest membership rate (84 percent of Catholics are church members), followed by mainline Protestants (70 percent), conservative Protestants (62 percent), Jews (51 percent), and those with no preference (21 percent).

To summarize the survey data dealing with individual religiosity, we combined items to form four indexes.[1] The first, "Exposure," measures contact with organized religious bodies through attendance at worship, religious education programs, and viewership of religious television. Fifty-four percent of the sample can be viewed as high in religious expo-

*The survey was conducted using standard public opinion polling methodologies. Trained interviewers used a pretested interview schedule developed by the Project Team and Institute staff. A random digit dialing sampling technique was employed with the universe being all residents with listed and unlisted telephone exchanges. All interviews were with persons age eighteen and older and were conducted evenings and weekends during May 1982.

†For our purposes mainline Protestant refers to the following groups: American Baptist, Episcopal, Lutheran Church in America, Unitarian Universalist, United Church of Christ, United Methodist, and United Presbyterian denominations; conservative refers to all other Protestants.

Table 4.1. An Overview of the Telephone Sample

	TOTAL	CATHOLIC	MAINLINE PROTESTANT	CONSERVATIVE PROTESTANT	JEWISH	NO PREFERENCE
Number	498	212	117	97	41	31
Sex						
Male	43%	39%	42%	53%	46%	48%
Female	57	61	58	47	54	52
Race						
White	94	98	97	82	98	88
Non-white	6	2	3	18	2	12
Age						
18 to 35	43	45	28	49	44	62
36 to 55	37	37	42	35	33	28
Over 55	21	18	30	16	23	10
Education						
Less than high school	8	9	7	11	0	3
High school graduate	29	18	21	30	22	16
Some college	25	26	24	24	22	26
College graduate	38	31	43	34	56	55
Family Income						
Less than $10,000	10	10	9	12	6	11
$10,000 to $19,999	20	34	26	30	12	15
$20,000 to $29,999	31	33	30	24	41	26
$30,000 and over	39	39	40	34	41	48
Location						
Hartford	14	17	8	17	17	6
Suburbs	86	83	91	83	83	93
Church Membership						
Member	70	84	70	62	51	21
Nonmember	30	16	30	38	49	79
Religiosity Indicators						
High exposure	54	68	51	53	15	19
High salience	63	68	61	63	45	52
High God-relatedness	74	83	74	72	42	57
High orthodoxy	36	49	17	44	11	17
Public issues						
High economic liberalism	35	38	33	30	28	45
High social liberalism	43	34	44	43	80	54

65

sure. Catholics are highest on this "participation" dimension, the two Protestant groups are average, and Jews and "nones" are low.

The "Salience" index combines items assessing the importance of religion in one's life and the frequency with which a person "talks to friends and neighbors about religion." Sixty-three percent of the respondents have high scores on this index, with only slight differences across religious groups.

The third religiosity index, "God-relatedness," is based on responses to two items; one deals with frequency of prayer and meditation and the other, with the sense of being in the presence of God. Scores on this index of personal (versus corporate) religiosity are quite high; 74 percent of the sample received high scores. Jews are the only group in which a majority have low scores.

The final religious commitment measure taps orthodoxy of religious belief and is based on three items: belief in God as "divine creator who knows my innermost thoughts," belief in the Bible as the literal word of God, and belief in hell as a place "to which some people will be condemned for eternal torment." Only 36 percent of the sample have high scores on the orthodoxy index and the differences are quite pronounced. Catholics and conservative Protestants are above average in their orthodoxy scores, whereas mainline Protestants, nones, and Jews are quite low.[2]

We cannot say, based on this survey, that Hartford-area residents are more or less "religious" than residents of other areas. Comparing data from our Hartford survey with nationwide opinion polls we can say that area residents are average in their rates of church membership (Hartford, 70 percent; United States, 68 percent). On other items, however, area residents appear to be less "traditionally religious" than are other American adults. A higher percentage of Hartford-area residents "rarely or never" attend religious services (Hartford, 26 percent; United States, 18 percent), fewer pray privately (Hartford, 24 percent; United States, 11 percent), fewer local residents watch religious television (12 percent are frequent viewers compared with 21 percent nationwide). Also, area residents less often adhere to literalistic interpretations of the Bible (Hartford, 13 percent; United States, 37 percent).

Public Issues

The interview schedule also sought individual views on a range of current public issues facing the nation and the region. We have divided these issues into two areas: economic liberalism and social liberalism. The former includes provision of low-income housing in all communities within the region and the view that federal budget cuts result in an unfair burden on the poor. Hartford's religious groups have similar views on

66

Table 4.2 Residents' View of the Congregation's Role in Public Life

CONGREGATIONAL EMPHASIS	VERY IMPORTANT	SOMEWHAT IMPORTANT	NOT IMPORTANT
Organizing social action groups within the congregation	28%	38%	34%
Encouraging the pastor/rabbi to speak out in public on controversial issues	26	35	40
Promoting social change through the use of organized collective action or force	15	36	49
Cooperating with other congregations to achieve community improvements	77	20	3
Providing aid and services to people in need in the local community	88	11	1
Helping people resist the temptation to experiment with new life-styles	34	29	37
Encouraging members to adhere faithfully to civil laws, even if they disagree with them	49	29	21
Encouraging members to make explicit declarations of their personal faith to neighbors and co-workers	19	24	56
Protecting members from the false teachings of other religious groups	26	22	52
Actively reaching out to members of other religious groups with an invitation to find true salvation	32	33	36

these issues, with just under one third of each group taking "liberal positions." Only those with no religious preference are exceptional, with 45 percent taking the liberal position on both housing and budget cuts.

The "social liberalism" index combines views on abortion rights (favoring freedom of choice) and homosexuality (viewing homosexuality as "not always wrong"). Jews and those with no religious preference are the most liberal on these issues, Catholics are the most conservative, and both Protestant groups occupy the middle ground.

Religion and Public Life

A major portion of the interview was devoted to an exploration of individual views of the appropriate public role of religious groups. What, in other words, are the proper goals of congregations and other religious organizations in the "secular" arena?

The interview questionnaire contained ten items that explored congregational goals. Respondents were asked whether they considered it very important, somewhat important, or not important that a church or synagogue be involved in each activity.[3] The items and percentage responses are in Table 4.2 (reordered for discussion purposes).

On some items there is high agreement. Fully 88 percent of the sample view aiding neighbors in need as a high priority and 77 percent see intercongregational cooperation to achieve community improvements as an important goal.

On the remaining items there is less agreement. A near-majority strongly affirm encouraging members to adhere to civil laws (a sizable percentage, however, regard this goal as "not important"). There is sharper disagreement on "helping people resist new life-styles," proselytizing, organizing social action groups, and encouraging clergy to speak out on social issues. Two goals—promoting social change by collective action and encouraging explicit faith declarations—appear to be of relatively low priority to sample members.

We combined the survey responses into four mission orientation scales, each of which suggests a different relationship between the congregation and its world, as described in chapter 2. The orientations reflect understandings of the congregation as activist, civic, sanctuary, and evangelist. Table 4.3 looks at scores on the four mission orientation scales. The scales are intended to have an average score of 0 and a range of approximately −3 to +3. The scales were developed using a statistical technique called factor analysis, which reduces a large number of individual items into a smaller number of scales, or factors.

Looking at Table 4.3 we find few extreme differences among subgroups, although there are some differences of interest. The greatest differences occur on the role of the congregation as evangelist. Scores on this scale are somewhat higher for nonwhites, those with a grade-school education, and people with high orthodoxy scores. They are low for college graduates, Jews, and the unchurched (non-church members and people with no religious preference). The same groups have lower-than-average scores on the congregation-as-sanctuary scale as well. Only Jews have high scores on the activist scale; other groups are close to the sample mean.

The religiosity indexes are weakly associated with the four mission orientation scales. People scoring high on these indicators of religious commitment are above average in their understanding of the congregation as citizen, but with the exception of a moderate relationship between orthodoxy and the evangelistic orientation, the relationships are weak.

Finally, the two public issues measures are related to mission orientations. Economic liberals tend to support civic and activist roles, whereas social liberals are low on the sanctuary and evangelistic scales.

What does the survey tell us about the religious climate of the Hartford area? First, the survey confirms the numerical dominance of the Catholic Church and the relatively high numbers of Jews and mainline Protestants in the area. Second, it reminds us that demographic, religious, and

Table 4.3. Group Scores on Mission Orientation Scales

	ACTIVIST	CIVIC	SANCTUARY	EVANGELIST	NUMBER
Total	−0.03	0.08	−0.11	−0.13	500
Sex					
Male	−0.09	−0.01	−0.19	−0.10	217
Female	0.01	0.15	−0.04	−0.16	283
Race					
White	−0.04	0.06	−0.11	−0.17	451
Nonwhite	0.12	0.27	−0.02	0.36	27
Age					
18 to 35	0.01	0.01	−0.25	−0.16	203
36 to 55	−0.07	0.08	−0.01	−0.11	174
Over 55	−0.02	0.20	0.02	−0.08	98
Education					
Less than high school	−0.05	0.11	0.04	0.25	39
High school graduate	−0.08	0.13	0.06	−0.01	146
Some college	−0.05	0.07	−0.16	−0.06	124
College graduate	0.01	0.04	−0.24	−0.34	190
Community					
Hartford	0.11	0.04	−0.16	0.05	72
Suburbs	−0.06	0.08	−0.10	−0.16	428
Church Membership					
Member	−0.01	0.17	−0.01	−0.06	348
Nonmember	−0.07	−0.14	−0.34	−0.29	151
Religious Preference					
Catholic	−0.04	0.12	−0.06	−0.08	212
Mainline Protestant	−0.10	0.19	−0.07	−0.21	117
Conservative Protestant	−0.09	−0.06	−0.06	0.08	97
Jewish	0.26	−0.08	−0.34	−0.50	41
No religious preference	−0.02	−0.01	−0.43	−0.36	31
Religiosity Indicators					
High exposure	0.01	0.18	0.07	0.03	267
High salience	0.04	0.18	0.01	0.03	311
High God-relatedness	−0.01	0.18	−0.01	−0.02	361
High orthodoxy	0.04	0.16	0.15	0.20	164
Public Issues					
High economic liberalism	0.16	0.21	−0.04	0.02	175
High social liberalism	0.06	0.07	−0.37	−0.34	220

ideological differences remain among the major denominational families. Third, social and religious groups differ in their understanding of the community mission of the church or synagogue. These differences, however, cross group and denominational family lines.

PARA-CONGREGATIONAL EXPRESSIONS OF RELIGIOUS PRESENCE

Hartford includes a host of para-congregational expressions of religion—organizational expressions that are not congregations but that exist alongside congregations. These groups are more varied than congregations, ranging from small, loosely organized, and often short-lived fellowships to large-scale, highly organized bodies, and reflect a wide variety of purposes. Although we have no precise count, at least several hundred such groups are in the region.

Statewide Organizations

Hartford serves as the state or regional headquarters of several denominational and ecumenical organizations, among them the Catholic Archdiocese of Hartford, the Connecticut Conference of the United Church of Christ, the Episcopal Diocese of Connecticut, and the State Conference of the American Baptist Churches. The judicatories vary somewhat in the size of their operations, their staff, and the geographic area for which they are responsible.

The largest statewide ecclesiastical organization is the Archdiocese of Hartford. One of three Catholic dioceses in the state, the archdiocese includes cities and towns both within the Greater Hartford area and outside it; however, in Hartford County alone there are approximately 100 parishes for which the archdiocese provides support services. The archdiocese also operates a minor seminary (now used mostly as a retreat and conference center), numerous parochial schools, an urban ministry program, a radio station and newspaper, a hospital, and various advocacy, service, and welfare organizations. The archdiocese joins with the other Catholic dioceses in the state in supporting the Connecticut Catholic Conference, a registered lobbying organization that attempts to influence state legislation on issues of importance to the Catholic Church—especially pro-life concerns—and is also involved in several ecumenical and interfaith ventures.

Diverse organizational and program involvements likewise characterize the other denominational judicatories with state headquarters in Hartford, most of which have large staffs of ordained and lay professionals.

This presence is exercised not only through the judicatories' organization and program involvements, but also as judicatory leaders speak officially as representatives of their faith tradition or as spokespersons of the religious community. We noted in chapter 3 the significance of the new "triumvirate" that emerged in post-World-War-II Hartford. While part of this "triumvirate's" influence resulted from the distinctive personalities of the men occupying these positions, present-day judicatory leaders often are similarly looked to as spokespersons. Interestingly, however, a former conference minister of the United Church of Christ in Connecticut noted that neither the conference minister nor the conference has the public visibility of the Catholic archbishop or the Episcopal bishop, despite the United Church of Christ's historic importance in the state (it remains Connecticut's largest Protestant denomination). He speculated that the denomination's congregational polity, with its emphasis on the autonomy of individual congregations rather than a central judicatory, may be the primary reason for this.

Denominations and religious groups without offices in Hartford are present principally through their local congregations. United Presbyterian, Lutheran, and many black churches are part of judicatories that include several states. The United Methodist churches in the region belong to two different annual conferences, depending on whether they are east or west of the Connecticut River, which forms Hartford's eastern border. This lack of commensurability of judicatory boundaries sometimes makes coordination of denominational efforts difficult.

In addition to the several statewide denominational judicatory organizations located in Hartford, the city is also home for CHRISCON. Formerly the Connecticut Council of Churches, which was exclusively Protestant, CHRISCON was formed in 1976 to include both Protestants and Catholics and is supported by fifteen denominations. With a director and a small staff, CHRISCON is organized into five program units: social issues, communications, ministries, education, and Christian unity. Its primary purposes are informational/educational and coordinating/providing human services, including sponsorship of Operation Fuel, a statewide emergency fuel bank. CHRISCON is also organizational sponsor for the Connecticut Bible Society, in operation since 1809.

Housed in the CHRISCON office, but organizationally independent, are the Connecticut IMPACT network—a coalition of church leaders concerned with sharing information and advocacy around social issues—and the Connecticut Interfaith Housing and Human Services Corporation. The latter is a coalition of denominations (primarily Catholic, Episcopal, United Church of Christ, and United Methodist) established to work at the state level "in developing, initiating, and planning for the provision of human services and housing in areas where resources are nonexistent or severely limited." This coalition's tax status allows it to operate as a nonprofit organization with lobbying rights, which it exercises in collaboration with other social service agencies.

Regional Organizations

In addition to statewide para-congregational organizations Hartford is also the setting for a number of organizations whose activities are restricted to the region. One example, at the ecumenical level, is the Capitol Region Conference of Churches, which, like CHRISCON, was formerly Protestant but now includes both Protestant and Catholic members. Like CHRISCON, this organization is primarily education and social service oriented. It sponsors informational programs, weekly programs on local radio and television stations, and a ministry to homosexuals. Additionally, it serves as the "holding company" for United Way, state, and federally funded programs, especially in low-income housing and services to the aging. The Capitol Region Conference also oversees a chaplaincy program at various Hartford hospitals that provides pastoral care for patients and clinical training in pastoral care for pastors and seminary students. Funding problems for its own programs (as distinct from those it serves as a "holding company") have been rather severe in recent years, partly because of its lack of visibility at the local church level, whose members often fail to associate the conference with the programs it sponsors or houses.

Two rather different nondenominational para-congregational organizations that serve the Hartford region are the Full Gospel Businessmen's Fellowship and Young Life. Both are local units of national organizations and are evangelical in purpose. The former is also an expression of the charismatic movement and brings together regional business leaders for breakfasts and other events, where they hear speakers witnessing to what Christ has done in their lives. Young Life focuses on high school youth, both unchurched and church members, and provides small-group experiences and fellowship aimed at conversion and growth in the faith. These organizations are somewhat suspect in many local churches, where there is both fear that the groups may become a substitute church for involved members and concern that participants' charismatic and evangelistic leanings will be disruptive to existing members.

Evangelism is often consciously combined with service ministries, as in the case of Youth Challenge, a nondenominational organization whose primary focus is to help Hartford-area youth overcome drug and alcohol addiction. Addicts are placed in a residency program funded by gifts from congregations, private foundations, and individuals (no public funds are sought). In this program, prayer, Bible study, and worship is combined with medical, counseling, and educational assistance to help young addicts overcome their addiction, make a commitment to Christ, and learn new job skills. In the words of the program's director:

> [We] ask of the addicts who come to us only that they must both want to be helped and be open to accepting our method of using the spiri-

tual dimension in their cure. We counsel, heal, and teach, providing a sanctuary from the world where the healing can take place as well as training to reenter the world fully as useful citizens who exemplify their faith in God in their work and lives.

A denominationally based regional organization is the United Church of Christ's Christian Activities Council (CAC), founded as a city missionary society in 1850 by Congregationalists concerned for the welfare of the new immigrants coming to the city. In keeping with its heritage, CAC provides social services primarily in Hartford; however, it is supported by member congregations throughout the metropolitan region and views the promotion of city-suburban interdependence as a major goal. As expressed in its constitution, the CAC aims at "encouraging stronger ties among suburban and urban member churches and . . . establishing instruments and structures for lay involvement" to the end of creating "a practical vision of social witness, social involvement and social reform." Since its founding the organization has been responsible for initiating a number of community institutions that are now mostly independent, such as the Newington Children's Hospital, the Oak Hill School for the Blind, and a number of housing and extended-care facilities for the elderly and for low-income families. Among current projects is cosponsorship with two other local organizations of an "urban farming" project, Hartford Farms, which involves the construction of a greenhouse in the city using hydroponic growing techniques.

Other religiously sponsored social service agencies that function within the Capitol Region (and in some cases beyond it) include Catholic Charities, Catholic Family Services, Jewish Family Service (funded through the Hartford Jewish Federation), and the Salvation Army. Similar in goals but statewide in focus are Episcopal Social Services and Lutheran Social Service (operating in Massachusetts as well as in Connecticut and sponsored by four Lutheran denominations).

Town Organizations

Moving to the level of the individual towns, most of the paracongregational organizations are interdenominational or interfaith. Several area towns, such as Manchester, a suburban community east of Hartford, and Rocky Hill, a southern suburb, have a local council or conference of churches. The Manchester organization, involving representatives from fourteen Catholic and Protestant churches, is almost entirely locally focused and service oriented. Developing policy positions across denominational lines has proved too difficult. "We just take up the things we agree on: Feed the hungry, clothe the naked, visit the sick and imprisoned." When Manchester was confronted with the firebombing of a black resident's home, during the period of our research, the conference of churches' director called a behind-the-scenes meeting of the town manager, the chief of police, the chairperson of the board of education, the school superintendent, the head of the human relations commission, and leaders of the black community. The interchange between town officials and black leaders proved extremely helpful and was a valuable service provided by the organization.

Clergy associations are another common type of para-congregational organization found in most towns in the region. Typically, these groups lack formal organization and most are unincorporated. They meet monthly over lunch for fellowship and discussion of common interests or concerns. Beyond informal fellowship and communication, many groups do get into community service activities, such as the development or support of food pantries and fuel banks. For example, the Bloomfield Clergy Association was instrumental in establishing an interfaith housing coalition (now an independent entity) that eventually developed two federally funded housing projects for the elderly. The West Hartford Cooperative Ministries (that town's clergy association) has also launched two ministries, now independent, that serve the town: the West Hartford Pastoral Counseling Center and the West Hartford Street Ministry. The former provides pastoral counseling services to people from the region. The latter, supported by contributions from fifteen churches in West Hartford, provides a ministry to youth, including runaways, who are experiencing family conflicts, drug or alcohol problems, or other issues calling for counseling and support. In addition to fellowship and service activities, local clergy associations sometimes become involved in educational activities around social issues, such as sponsoring a community forum on the nuclear freeze or a prayer vigil for peace. Or, they may engage in advocacy on community issues, frequently in a behind-the-scenes manner. When a local theater was about to change its programming and show all "adult" films, the town's clergy association quietly but successfully worked with the theater manager and town officials to prevent the change.

Some clergy groups are not organized on a townwide basis but are regional associations with particular interests. For example, one association is made up of pastors of several independent, evangelical congregations in the area. Another regional group is the Hartford Ministerial Alliance, a highly visible organization comprising many of the region's black pastors. Meeting twice monthly, the alliance's primary purpose is fellowship; however, the group sponsors an annual citywide revival and has developed a scholarship fund for black youth. The alliance has also spoken out on issues of racial discrimination, employment, housing, and police-community relations, although not always to the satisfaction of members who wish the organization to be more activist. Additionally, because of the important place that the church and clergy occupy in the black community, the ministerial alliance is often visited by both black and white aspirants to political office who are seeking the clergy's support.

Neighborhood or Local Area Organizations

Within the towns, especially within the city of Hartford, are also paracongregational organizations that serve particular neighborhoods or sections of the city, for example, Asylum Hill Christian Community, Southwest City Churches, and Center City Churches.

Center City Churches is particularly noteworthy because of its work in the downtown and inner city. Founded in 1967 as a coalition of eight (now ten) Protestant and Catholic churches, the organization first focused on unmet needs of older city residents. In 1970 member churches came together formally as Center City Churches, Inc. and employed an executive director. Currently, the organization has approximately eighteen full-time and thirty part-time staff. Over the years Center City Churches has undertaken a number of ministries within the downtown area in which its member congregations are located. These include a tutorial program for both public and parochial schoolchildren; the Friendship Center, serving alcoholic and alienated adults; numerous programs for children in the city, including summer programs and a children's theater; a food pantry; a health and nutrition ministry, providing basic health care and meals to residents of downtown hotels, rooming houses, and apartments; holiday meals for street people at Christmas, Easter, and Thanksgiving; and a rooming house for low-income people—St. Elizabeth's House—where meals and health screening are also available. Additionally, Center City Churches has sponsored a cooperative lenten series and other worship and study opportunities for church members and interested adults. The organization's annual budget of almost two thirds of a million dollars is supported by member churches (who also provide important free contributions of space for programs); federal, state, and city government funds; and gifts from foundations, corporations, local businesses, and individuals. The cutbacks of government funding of social programs that have occurred during the Reagan administration have dramatically increased the pressure on organizations like Center City Churches. Says the director:

> Other city agencies have taken to sending us their clients, without even checking with us first to see if we can provide the needed food, housing, counseling, jobs, or whatever. . . . Even the Salvation Army has cut back and started referring clients to us. Well, often we don't have the resources either. But rather than do nothing, we have hired someone whose job it is to do advocacy for these people who are sent to us—try to find them the agencies that will help and send them

(after we telephone to make sure the agency or group can provide them the help).

Mission Orientations

We organized this brief overview of para-congregational organizations within the Hartford region according to their "turf"—the geographic territory they serve—because that is one helpful way to view them. The four mission orientations introduced earlier offer another way of thinking about para-congregational forms of religious presence. As with congregations, many of the para-congregational organizations exhibit multiple orientations; however, with them as well, it is often possible to indicate a dominant orientation.

The *activist* orientation is perhaps most evident in the work of the Connecticut Catholic Conference, the official lobbying organization of the state's Catholic dioceses. The orientation is also evident (and combined with the provision of services) in the Connecticut Interfaith Housing and Human Services Corporation. This combination of activism with service is a natural one for church organizations. As the director of one organization expressed it: "Advocacy without service is ungrounded, and service without advocacy is ineffective." An activist orientation is also present in more ad hoc and informal para-congregational coalitions—some pursuing issues of peace and justice, others concerned with such issues as abortion, homosexuality, prostitution, and pornography. One such unofficial Catholic group, the Blue Berets, has protested publicly against issues, legislation, and programs viewed as inimical to traditional Catholic theology and practice. A local group of young Jews, L'Chaim, pursues an activist stance from a liberal perspective, combining study and action relating the imperatives of the Jewish heritage to current social and political issues and sometimes antagonizing more conservative Jews in the process.

The *civic* theme is dominant in many of the para-congregational organizations described earlier. Much of the work of the ecumenical and denominational service agencies is aimed not at bringing about social and political change or evangelism (seeking converts), but at alleviating suffering and need. In so doing the organizations themselves play the role of good citizens. Indeed, maintaining the civic orientation by avoiding evangelism or action to bring about social or political change is often necessary if cooperative action in providing human services across denominational or interfaith lines is to take place. Furthermore, the decision to seek government or United Way funding for some service programs necessitates maintaining a civic orientation.

The *evangelistic* theme is also a dominant orientation in several para-congregational organizations, such as the Full Gospel Businessmen's Fellowship, Young Life, and Youth Challenge. Other para-congregational organizations also give expression to the evangelistic theme in some of their activities. For example, evangelism has been a major concern of the Catholic archdiocese's radio and television ministry, with lapsed Catholics being a special target. The Hartford Ministerial Alliance's annual revival meeting is also an evangelistic outreach program, although, as noted, evangelism is not the alliance's major purpose. Because evangelism frequently is interpreted as involving a particularistic concern for conversion to one's own religious group, it is often left to local congregations to pursue, either individually or in coalition with others of their denomination. A major exception in recent years was the sponsorship of a Billy Graham Crusade in Greater Hartford by a broad coalition of denominations and churches.

The *sanctuary* theme is perhaps the most ostensible raison d'être of some Catholic religious orders in the area and of various retreat centers, many of which are operated by religious orders. Holy Family Retreat House, for example, provides weekend retreats for individuals, married couples, members of Alcoholics Anonymous, and occupational groups (doctors, lawyers, police, firefighters, and so forth). The Cursillo movement, which has both Catholic and Episcopal expressions, brings together laypeople for long weekend retreats of prayer, meditation, and faith development. Para-congregational organizations that primarily reflect a sanctuary orientation at a less formal level include a number of neighborhood Bible study groups and the Feminists of Faith, a Hartford-area group of women representing various denominational traditions who meet periodically for fellowship over a meal, shared worship, and discussion of their faith from a feminist perspective.

Several observations may be made concerning the importance of para-congregational organizations for the presence of religion in a city like Hartford. First, because they are statewide, regional, local, or neighborhood in their organizational level, they frequently are positioned to exercise a presence on the level they occupy in ways a local congregation cannot. Whether para-congregational organizations always do so effectively is another question; however, their potential for doing so is especially important in a complex, highly organized, and differentiated society.

Second, as noted in chapters 3 and 4, a majority of white Protestants, Catholics, and Jews in the Hartford region currently live in the suburbs. If they and their congregations (most of which are also suburban) are to play any role in the city or region, they must do so through ecumenical and denominational para-congregational organizations or coalitions that do have a presence in the city or, more broadly, in the region.

Third—and closely related to the first two points—some issues are too large or, on occasion, too controversial to be undertaken by a local congregation or sometimes even by a denominational judicatory acting independently. An existing para-congregational organization or coalition, such as the Connecticut Interfaith Housing and Human Services Corporation, may be able to address the issue with greater effectiveness.

Fourth, para-congregational organizations that are interfaith or inter- or nondenominational enable individuals to experience fellowship or pursue a common goal with those of other faith traditions in ways not generally possible in their local congregations. At the same time, however, the very interdenominational or interfaith character of the organization may preclude addressing some of the more controversial issues that divide religious groups.

Finally, many para-congregational organizations that depend on the support and participation of individuals or the support of individual congregations experience considerable organizational precariousness. Their special-purpose goals must continue to capture the commitment of members and supporting congregations—always a difficult task as circumstances that brought them into being change or as money and volunteer time become scarce.

These observations highlight the importance (as well as the precariousness) of para-congregational organizations in the overall economy of religion's presence in the region's public life.

CHAPTER 5
AN OVERVIEW OF CONGREGATIONAL PRESENCE

Chapters 3 and 4 pointed to some of the key historical and current elements of the context in which congregations carry out their ministries. With this background we turn to the specifics of congregational presence in Greater Hartford, doing so from two perspectives. First, we offer an overview of the region's churches and synagogues based on a survey of congregations. The overview provides a descriptive profile of the area's congregations, including their engagement of public life. It also gives a preliminary look at how various factors affect congregations' engagement of public life. Second, beginning with chapter 6, we present case studies of ten congregations whose lives and ministries reflect the richness and variety of congregational presence that exists in the Hartford area.

THE CONGREGATIONAL SURVEY

The congregational survey was conducted in late 1981 by means of a questionnaire mailed to the pastoral leaders of the 413 Protestant, Catholic, Jewish, and nondenominational congregations in the twenty-seven towns in the Hartford region.* Leaders were asked to respond as repre-

---

*At their request, a small number of Muslim, Christian Science, and Mormon congregations were not included.

sentatives of the congregations. The range of topics covered included the congregation's attitude toward involvement in public life; involvement in various types of programming; social issues addressed within the congregation in the previous year by various means; membership and neighborhood characteristics; and membership, participation, and budget statistics.

After two follow-up mailings, usable questionnaires were returned by leaders of 177 congregations, an overall response rate of 42 percent. The response rate was higher for some groups, most notably mainline Protestant congregations (61 percent), and lower for others, most notably conservative Protestant churches (20 percent). To compensate for this unevenness of return, we weighted the data for purposes of analysis to reflect the known denominational distribution in the region. This commonly used technique has the effect of making the sample more truly representative of the universe of area congregations. Even after this adjustment, some known biases remain in the sample. Specifically, congregations located in the city of Hartford, especially small churches serving minority constituencies (e.g., storefront churches), are slightly underrepresented, whereas large, white, suburban congregations are slightly over-represented.

Hartford's Congregations: A Profile

There are slightly more than 400 local congregations in the Greater Hartford area, one for every 1,600 residents. They represent a wide range of denominational traditions, reflecting both the immigrant waves of the area's historical development and the denominational diversity that is characteristic of the United States in general.

Mainline Protestant groups account for a little more than a third of the area's congregations, conservative Protestant groups for another third, the Catholic Church for 21 percent (in comparison to 43 percent of the area's population), and Jewish groups for 5 percent. The "denominational mosaic" is rounded out with a sprinkling of Christian Orthodox, Muslim, and interfaith congregations.*

A disproportionate share of the congregations are located in the city itself—30 percent compared with 19 percent of the population. Suburban communities account for 50 percent of the congregations, and the remaining 20 percent are in small-town and rural areas to the city's northeast and northwest. In the Hartford region, as in other areas of the country, many suburbanites continue to commute to city churches as they do to work.

*As in the telephone survey, so in the congregational survey, mainline refers to American Baptist, Episcopal, Lutheran Church in America, Unitarian Universalist, United Church of Christ, United Methodist, and United Presbyterian denominations. Most of the remaining Protestant congregations in the area are independent congregations or are affiliated with evangelical bodies that are not members of the National Council of Churches.

The "average church" in the Greater Hartford area has a total active adult membership (defined as people age fifteen and older attending services at least once a year) of just under 600. Weekly worship attendance averages slightly more than 425, with approximately 150 youth and 40 adults participating in religious education activities each week. Extrapolating from these figures, we estimate that the area's congregations include an estimated 238,000 active adult members, with more than 178,000 persons attending services in a typical week. More than 61,000 children and 17,000 adults are involved in religious education each week.

The average budget of Hartford-area congregations for 1980 was almost $110,000; mission/benevolence expenditures accounted for approximately 12 percent of this total ($13,200). Again extrapolating to the region's congregations in total, an estimated $44 million was expended by area churches and synagogues in 1980, with mission/benevolence expenditures of $5.5 million. Forty percent of congregations have endowment funds to help support their budgets; almost 20 percent report endowment funds of $100,000 or more.

The variation in membership, participation, and finances by denominational family is considerable. Catholic parishes have the largest average membership (1,800) and the highest weekly worship attendance (1,500) and religious education attendance (428 youth, 53 adults). In terms of members, mainline Protestant churches are only one fifth the size (365 adult members) of Catholic parishes, and weekly worship attendance (179) is only one tenth that of Catholic parishes. Conservative Protestant congregations are half again smaller than their mainline counterparts in terms of members, but their worship attendance is only slightly lower (average membership 160, average worship attendance 151). Despite their small memberships, conservative churches in the area are equal to mainline congregations in education attendance of youth (74 conservative to 76 mainline), and their average weekly adult education attendance surpasses even that of Catholic parishes (conservative 55, Catholic 53, mainline 27). Conservative Protestant churches are also twice as likely as mainline Protestant congregations and four times as likely as Catholic parishes to have increased in membership by as much as 25 percent in the past five years.*

Total church and mission/benevolence support is highest, on average, for Catholic parishes ($175,000 total, $18,600 mission), followed by mainline ($104,000, $12,800) and conservative churches ($73,000, $12,000). When participation and financial support are looked at on a per-member basis, strikingly different patterns emerge. Weekly worship attendance

---

*The small number of Jewish congregations in our sample (seven) limits our ability to generalize about their characteristics, so we don't in what follows. Jewish congregations are, however, included in all totals.

averages fully 94 percent of adult membership for conservative churches, 81 percent for Catholic parishes, but only 49 percent for the mainline. In 1980 total expenditures averaged $456 per member in conservative churches, $285 in mainline congregations, and $97 in Catholic parishes. Mission support shows a similar pattern, with conservative churches spending $75 per member, mainline groups $35, and Catholic parishes $10. The high per-member expenditures reported by conservative churches take on added significance when it is noted that such churches are, for the most part, without assistance from endowment funds. Only 7 percent of these churches report endowments of more than $100,000 compared with 12 percent of Catholic parishes and 21 percent of mainline Protestant congregations.

Variations in membership, participation, and financial patterns among city, suburban, and rural congregations are not as great as those among denominational families. Suburban congregations are slightly larger (average membership 860) than city (840) or more rural congregations (620). City congregations, however, reported higher expenses in 1980 ($151,000) than their suburban ($125,000) or rural ($75,000) counterparts. The higher expenses of city churches are affordable, in part, because a third of city congregations have endowments of $100,000 or more—a welcome cushion against the reality of older and larger buildings often supported by declining memberships. Not all city churches are declining in membership, although a fourth are; less than 15 percent of suburban congregations report membership declines. At the same time many city congregations *are* growing; most of the growing city churches are either affiliated with conservative Protestant denominations or serve predominantly black or Hispanic memberships.

Overall, the congregations in the Greater Hartford area are predominantly white and middle class and are made up of people who have been members for lengthy periods, not unlike the population as a whole. Compared with the area's total population, however, church and synagogue members are older and more likely to be married, to own their own homes, to live in the suburbs, and to be long-time area residents.

Denominational family differences in membership characteristics are slight but important. Mainline Protestant churches tend to have older, more geographically stable memberships than do other churches and the population in general. Catholic parishes also tend to have relatively stable memberships and sizable numbers of blue-collar families. Members of conservative Protestant churches are more likely to be young, to be single, to be renting their homes, and to be relatively new to their churches.

Membership differences among city, suburban, and rural churches tend to parallel known differences in the demographic makeup of the communities in which they are located. The major exception is the significant number of both white and black mainline Protestant churches located in the city that draw a sizable portion of their membership from the suburbs.

Mission Orientations

In an effort to map the various ways congregations understand their role in public life we use the four mission orientations described in chapter 2 and to which we have also referred in describing other aspects of religious presence in Hartford. As noted in chapter 2, the four orientations were derived from analysis of responses to items included in the congregational survey. The survey questionnaire included twenty-three items constructed from the insights of H. Richard Niebuhr, Avery Dulles, church-sect theorists, and others. Each item looks at a community-based activity in which some churches and synagogues are engaged. Leaders were given a choice of five responses, ranging from "basic to" the congregation's understanding of its ministry to "contradictory to" that understanding. Responses are summarized in Table 5.1.

On some of the questionnaire items there is considerable consensus. More than 70 percent of respondents see acts of charity on behalf of local residents in need, encouraging members to accept—as individuals—a sense of responsibility for civic life, and inviting the unchurched to active religious participation as at least "quite important" to the life of their congregations. Providing financial support to social and political action groups, attempting to promote social change through collective influence or force, trying to "convert" members of other religious groups, and helping people accept their status and condition in life as ordained by God were viewed as "not really important" or "contradictory to" their congregation's self-understanding by 40 percent or more of the sample.

The sharpest divisions in the sample have to do with emphases on "preparing church members for a world to come in which the cares of this world are absent" and "encouraging members to adhere faithfully to civil laws as they are mandated by governmental authorities." Twenty-four percent see the former as "basic to" their understanding of ministry, whereas 21 percent see the same emphasis as "contradictory to" their view. Similarly, 19 percent see encouraging obedience to civil law as "basic to" their self-understanding, whereas 15 percent see it as "contradictory to."

Because dealing with more than twenty individual items is rather awkward, and in an attempt to identify themes in congregational understandings of their public role, we used a statistical technique known as factor analysis to identify underlying patterns among responses to the questionnaire items. This analysis is the source of the four mission orientations

Table 5.1   The Congregation's Public Role

CONGREGATIONAL EMPHASIS	BASIC TO	QUITE IMPORTANT	SOMEWHAT IMPORTANT	NOT REALLY IMPORTANT	CONTRADICTORY TO
		IMPORTANCE OF ITEM TO CONGREGATION'S UNDERSTANDING OF ITS MINISTRY			
1. Providing adult education that brings laity face to face with urban problems, racial discrimination, world poverty and hunger, and other social issues	10%	45%	35%	4%	5%
2. Providing for members an earthly refuge from the trials and tribulations of daily life	22	31	30	11	5
3. Cooperating with other denominations and faith groups to achieve community improvements	17	39	29	10	5
4. Helping people accept that their condition and status in life is determined and controlled by God, and that therefore one has only to accept it and live the best life possible	7	15	9	13	56
5. Promoting social change through the use of organized, collective influence or force	4	20	31	20	25
6. Helping people resist the temptation to experiment with the new "pleasures" and "life-styles" so prominent in our secular society and media	24	30	21	17	8
7. Providing aid and services to those in need within the local community	33	40	22	3	1
8. Maintaining an active, organized evangelism program; inviting the unchurched to participate in the life of the congregation	40	33	19	6	2

Table 5.1   The Congregation's Public Role—Continued

	IMPORTANCE OF ITEM TO CONGREGATION'S UNDERSTANDING OF ITS MINISTRY				
CONGREGATIONAL EMPHASIS	BASIC TO	QUITE IMPORTANT	SOMEWHAT IMPORTANT	NOT REALLY IMPORTANT	CONTRADICTORY TO
9. Actively reaching out to members of other religious groups with an invitation to participate in the life of the congregation	7%	13%	5%	21%	53%
10. Encouraging the pastor to speak out in public and from the pulpit on controversial social, political, and economic matters	6	22	29	27	15
11. Preparing church members for a world to come in which the cares of this world are absent	24	16	15	24	21
12. Encouraging members to make specific declarations of their personal faith to friends, neighbors, and strangers	31	23	24	17	5
13. Providing financial support to political or social action groups and organizations	2	11	24	27	37
14. Maintaining a proper distance between the congregation and governmental affairs	7	16	28	32	17
15. Helping people to understand that they are "agents" of God's hope, responsible for actualizing the good and humane as they share in the development of history and society	41	34	15	9	1
16. Fostering a sense of patriotism among the congregation's members	10	22	31	32	5
17. Encouraging members to reach their own decisions on issues of faith and morals	43	36	12	2	7
18. Involving the congregation corporately in social and political activities	5	20	32	24	19

85

Table 5.1   The Congregation's Public Role—Continued

	BASIC TO	QUITE IMPORTANT	SOMEWHAT IMPORTANT	NOT REALLY IMPORTANT	CONTRADICTORY TO
		IMPORTANCE OF ITEM TO CONGREGATION'S UNDERSTANDING OF ITS MINISTRY			
CONGREGATIONAL EMPHASIS					
19. Organizing social action groups within the congregation to directly accomplish some social or political end	4%	22%	31%	27%	17%
20. Protecting members from the false teachings of other churches and religious groups	15	24	23	24	14
21. Listening to what the "world" is saying in order to understand what the congregation's ministry should be about	19	39	28	8	5
22. Encouraging and inspiring members, as individuals, to become involved in social and political issues	15	51	22	10	2
23. Encouraging members to adhere faithfully to civil laws as they are mandated by governmental authorities	19	28	17	21	15

Some items modified in questionnaire to Jewish congregations.

introduced in Chapter 2.* Rather than repeating the description of the four orientations, we have attempted to show them schematically in Figure 5.1. In it we see both the this-worldly versus otherworldly division and that between those who see a public role for the congregation as opposed to those who restrict activity to within the congregation. Cross-cutting these two dimensions yields the four orientations—*activist, civic, sanctuary,* and *evangelistic.*

*Factor analysis is a technique for data reduction whose product is a table of correlations between individual items and a smaller number of factors, or dimensions. By examining this table, one is able to "name" the factor. In naming the themes discussed below we have tried to be faithful to the patterns in the data while at the same time communicating their meaning to a nonstatistical audience.

Figure 5.1. Mission Orientations

	MEMBERSHIP-CENTERED	PUBLICLY PROACTIVE
This-worldly • Stress the establishment of the kingdom of God in society • Concern for the welfare of all people • Ecumenical cooperation • Membership involvement in public life • Educate members on social issues	**Civic Orientation** • Stress civil harmony and avoidance of confrontation and conflict • Individual members making their own decisions on moral and social issues • Affirmation of existing social structures	**Activist Orientation** • Stress justice and a critical posture toward existing social structures • Affirmation of member and congregational involvement in social action, including the expectation that pastor/rabbi will be leader in this regard • Openness to confrontation, conflict, and civil disobedience
Otherworldly • Stress salvation in a world to come • A sharp distinction between the religious and the secular • Acceptance of existing social structures • Opposition to "sinful" life-styles	**Sanctuary Orientation** • Acceptance of one's status in life • The congregation as a refuge from this world • Tradition and doctrine • Opposition to congregational involvement in social change • Patriotism and adherence to civil law	**Evangelistic Orientation** • Stress personal witnessing to and sharing one's faith with others • Strong openness to the Holy Spirit • Conversion of everyone to the "one true faith"

Congregational Characteristics and Mission Orientations

Strong support for each of our mission orientations can be found in the Judeo-Christian biblical and theological tradition. Perhaps reflecting this diversity of inherited imperatives, few congregations in the Hartford area limit their understanding of their public role to a single orientation. Rather, most congregations give evidence of each orientation to varying degrees, with one or two orientations being dominant. It is also the case that few congregations give extreme expression to any one of the four orientations. For example, only 4 percent of the congregations in our survey affirm all four of the strongest indicators of the activist orientation (items 5, 10, 13, and 19 in Table 5.1) as basic to their understanding of mission. The comparable figure is 5 percent of the evangelistic orientation (items 8, 9, 12, and 20), 17 percent for the sanctuary orientation (items 4, 6, 16, and 23), and 22 percent for the civic orientation (items 3, 7, 15, and 22). This last figure, along with the general affirmation of civic items evidenced in Table 5.1 across all congregations, supports other data from our study in suggesting the dominance of the civic orientation in the Hartford area.

For examining the relationships between mission orientations and other characteristics of congregations we have classified a church or synagogue scoring in the top third of all congregations on an orientation as "strong" on that orientation. That is, those congregations which scored in the top third on the civic orientation scale *relative* to all other congregations in the Hartford area are considered to have a "strong" civic orientation; those scoring in the top third on the activist orientation scale *relative* to all other congregations in our sample are considered to have a "strong" activist orientation; etc.* Given what was noted above in regard to the percentage of congregations affirming all four of the key indicators of any orientation as basic to their understanding of mission, this relative ranking approach probably overestimates the number of congregations that would be classified, particularly, as strongly activist or evangelistic if more absolute criteria had been available to us. Nevertheless, until such time as more normative criteria can reasonably be derived, the relative ranking approach does permit a conservative starting point for exploring the extent to which different understandings of a congregation's public role reflect differences in location, denomination, and organizational or membership characteristics, and/or get translated into programmatic differences.

Using our top third criterion for classifying a congregation as strong on each orientation, we found that a little more than a third of the congrega-

---

*The orientation scales were computed using the factor weights and individual congregational responses across all twenty-three items.

tions give major emphasis to a single orientation; four out of ten give strong emphasis to two or more orientations; and slightly more than 20 percent of congregations do not score high on any of the four. Activist-civic and sanctuary-evangelistic combinations are twice as common as any others.

All three major denominational groupings contain some "strong" congregations of each orientation. At the same time there are clear denominational differences. Two thirds of the conservative Protestant churches are strongly evangelistic, compared with less than two out of ten Catholic parishes and mainline Protestant congregations. Catholic and conservative Protestant churches are more than twice as likely to have a strong sanctuary orientation as are mainline Protestant congregations (40 percent and 20 percent, respectively). Nearly half the area's Catholic parishes embody a strong activist orientation, compared with just less than a third of mainline and a fourth of conservative Protestant congregations. The three denominational families are about equally represented in the "strong civic" category, although if there is a group with an edge-up in this category, it is the mainline Protestant congregations.

Mainline Protestant congregations are most likely to have no strong orientation, a finding that may support the thesis of James Smylie, among others, who argues that mainline Protestantism in the late twentieth century is suffering from either a crisis of identity or a failure of conviction.[1] In comparison, conservative Protestant congregations are the most likely to score high on the sanctuary and evangelistic orientations, exhibiting qualities of "social strength" and "strictness," cited by Dean M. Kelley and others as contributing to membership growth in recent decades.[2] And Catholic parishes are most likely to have both multiple strong orientations and strong activist orientations. The former may be due to both their sheer size and their historical tendency to embody considerable diversity under one "authority." The latter is perhaps attributable to the relative freedom or insulation Catholic priests have from the direct control or dictates of local parish members.

Congregations located in the city are more likely to have strong activist orientations than are their suburban or rural counterparts, which is perhaps understandable given their more immediate proximity to the groups and conditions around which activist causes tend to rally. Similarly, the proximity of city churches to the "disestablished" may explain the reason city churches are also decidedly more likely to have strong evangelistic orientations than are congregations in other locales.

Suburban churches are about equally divided among the four strong orientation groups and are the most likely to have no strong public orientation. Churches and synagogues in the region's outlying towns also tend to have less strong orientations than do city churches, especially with respect to activism.

Within denominational families, having a single strong orientation appears unrelated to congregational size, participation, or budget. Among Catholic parishes, however, those with strong evangelistic orientations appear to be more marginal than do parishes with other orientations. Finally, of conservative Protestant churches, those with strong otherworldly orientations—sanctuary and evangelistic—have exceptionally high rates of participation and per capita financial support.

Among both mainline and conservative Protestant churches the expected relationship between a strong evangelistic orientation and exceptional rates of membership growth does appear. But without being able to control, in particular, social contextual factors in our survey analysis, we urge caution in overinterpreting any possible causal relationship. Similarly, we note as an apparent anomaly that deserves further scrutiny the fact that in our study Catholic parishes with strong evangelistic orientations have lower membership growth rates than parishes with any other strong orientation. Perhaps this is due to the fact that, as some have suggested, they have adopted an evangelistic orientation as a means of confronting imminent survival issues.

Congregations and the Engagement of Public Life

Congregations engage public life in at least two ways. One way is to bring public issues into the life of the congregation, placing them before the membership in the congregation's liturgical and educational programs. A second way is to provide services for those outside the congregation's membership. We will look at each in turn.

To examine the public issues addressed by Hartford-area congregations we listed twenty-one representative issues in the congregational survey. We asked whether, in the past year, each issue had been dealt with by the congregation as the topic of a sermon, in a liturgical prayer, in an adult study group, in a social action program, or as the recipient of financial support from the church or synagogue budget. The issues that were included and the overall responses are shown in Table 5.2.

The issues most commonly addressed within Greater Hartford congregations included world hunger and poverty, concerns of the elderly, and the Iranian hostage situation (the survey was conducted shortly after the hostages' release). More than 90 percent of the congregations indicated that they had addressed these concerns. World hunger and poverty, for example, were dealt with in prayer and preaching by just under 70 percent of congregations and in adult study or action groups by nearly a third. Concern about the hostages in Iran was more often the subject of pastoral prayers than was world hunger and less frequently the topic of sermons or the focus of study or action groups.

Other issues receiving widespread attention include alcoholism, the 1980 Presidential election, drug abuse, women's rights, energy conserva-

90

Table 5.2. Congregations Addressing Particular Public Issues

ISSUE	LITURGICAL PRAYER	SERMON TOPIC	ADULT STUDY	ACTION GROUP	GIVEN FUNDS	NOT DEALT WITH
World hunger and poverty	68%	68%	32%	30%	53%	8%
Iranian hostage situation	82	45	11	4	1	11
Concerns of the elderly	63	42	20	40	43	11
Racism	50	60	23	10	15	18
Alcoholism	28	40	21	13	14	30
Presidential election	52	31	8	5	1	31
Women's rights	21	40	23	7	5	36
Energy conservation	27	33	19	16	7	38
Drug abuse	33	39	24	12	12	31
Abortion	27	36	25	14	7	38
Environmental pollution	36	35	12	3	4	44
Anti-Semitism	34	32	16	4	6	44
Crime in the streets	29	30	11	5	4	50
Open housing	19	26	11	13	11	55
Public education	18	25	14	10	3	55
Homosexuality	15	26	20	6	1	56
Child advocacy/children's rights	20	18	14	9	7	60
Equal opportunity employment	18	22	10	5	3	64
Pornography or prostitution	16	24	10	3	3	65
Communism	20	14	7	1	0	71
Tax reform	4	3	5	3	1	88

tion, pollution, abortion, Christian/Jewish relations, and crime—all receiving at least some attention in more than 70 percent of congregations. Housing, children's rights, and public education were dealt with less frequently (by 40 percent to 50 percent of congregations), followed by homosexuality, equal opportunity employment, and pornography or prostitution. The issues least often addressed were communism and tax reform.

The most common means of dealing with an issue were liturgical prayers and preaching. Adult study and organized congregational action groups were less frequently used, and with the exception of world hunger and concerns of the elderly, few issues received congregational funding.

Statistical correlations indicate that the four mission orientations have a moderate relationship to the kinds of issues and concerns brought before church and synagogue members. Strong activist congregations are far more likely to have addressed most of the issues included in the survey than are congregations with either high scores on other orientations or no strong orientation. The only issues for which this is not true are homosexuality, crime, pornography or prostitution, children's rights, and communism.

The two sex-oriented issues—homosexuality and pornography/prostitution—appear to be of special concern to evangelistic congregations. Such congregations, however, are no more likely than are others to have dealt with other "personal morality" concerns, such as drug abuse, abortion, and alcoholism. Strongly evangelistic congregations were less likely to have dealt with the issues of environmental pollution, energy conservation, racism, and open housing than were congregations with high scores on other orientations.

Churches and synagogues with a strong sanctuary orientation appeared especially concerned with communism, crime, children's rights, drug abuse, and tax reform.

The most consistent pattern in the analysis appeared for congregations with a strong civic orientation. A strong civic orientation was *not* significantly related to addressing *any* of the twenty-one issues. Civic churches and synagogues appear to have staked out the middle ground; they are no more—and no less—likely to have dealt with specific community or world concerns than has the "average" Greater Hartford congregation.

The survey asked only if the church or synagogue had addressed issues in the past year; it did not ask what position, if any, the congregation had taken on the issue. Other evidence from the study, including the case studies, supports past research indicating that activist congregations lean toward liberal positions on most issues, whereas sanctuary and evangelistic congregations tend toward conservative positions on most issues.

Orientation toward public life is not the only factor that influences which issues are addressed by congregations. We looked at the possible effect of three other such factors: membership size, denominational family, and location (city versus non-city). Denominational family had the greatest overall impact of the three, followed by location. To summarize: Mainline Protestant churches were most likely to have dealt with environmental and energy issues and less often with abortion; conservative Protestant churches were especially concerned with pornography/prostitution and homosexuality; Catholic parishes were especially likely to have dealt with abortion; city churches were most likely to have dealt with equal opportunity employment, tax reform, and housing issues.

To discover whether the differences we found by mission orientation in addressing public issues within a congregation were merely surrogates for the factors just noted, we submitted the survey data to one further analysis. We again looked at the relationship between strong orientation congregations and the list of twenty-one issues, this time controlling for size, denominational family, and location. We found that, for the most part, the original relationships that had mission orientation retained their strength.

Table 5.3. Congregational Involvement in Outreach Programs

PROGRAM	INVOLVED IN THE PAST YEAR			NOT INVOLVED	
	WITH ANOTHER CONGREGATION (A)	ALONE (B)	BOTH (A) AND (B) (C)	APPROPRIATE (D)	INAPPROPRIATE (E)
Building use by community	5%	64%	3%	13%	14%
Emergency need programs	17	38	9	29	7
Membership recruitment program	1	55	1	34	9
Neighborhood Bible/prayer groups	4	47	2	41	5
Scouting	3	47	4	40	6
Summer vacation Bible school	18	30	0	45	6
Senior citizen programs	14	30	3	49	4
Adult study groups: social issues	1	38	4	46	10
Music, art, dance, drama programs	4	35	2	43	15
Programs for the handicapped	7	22	2	63	6
Public policy: personal morality	8	19	4	56	13
Public policy: social justice	9	17	4	58	12
Day-care or nursery center	2	24	0	57	16
Radio or television advertising	1	21	0	55	22
Elderly housing	14	6	1	66	14
Adult sports	1	19	2	57	22
Low-income housing	10	4	0	66	19
Parochial school	2	12	0	45	40

The only major exception is that the heightened attention that evangelistic congregations give to the issue of pornography/prostitution seems to result more from their close affinity with conservative Protestantism than from the evangelistic orientation per se.

To gain further perspective on how congregations in the Greater Hartford area are reaching beyond themselves, a major portion of the survey was devoted to a list of eighteen community-oriented programs in which churches and synagogues could be engaged. Congregations were asked whether they had been engaged in each type of program in the past year. If involved, they were asked whether they acted on their own, with another congregation, or both. Those not involved were asked to indicate whether participating in this activity would or would not be appropriate for the congregation. The list of programs and overall responses appears in Table 5.3.

The most often-noted community-oriented activities were permitting community groups to use the congregation's building, implementing programs to meet the emergency needs of local residents and the needs of the elderly, sponsoring scouting groups, and initiating member recruitment programs, all of which were mentioned by more than half the congregations.

Community-oriented activities least often cited (by a fifth or less of the congregations) were parochial schools, housing for the poor and the elderly, radio and television advertising, day-care centers, and sports programs for adults. Thirty percent of the churches and synagogues said they had undertaken "organized attempts to influence public policy" on a "social justice issue or issues"; 31 percent indicated that they had done so on a "personal morality issue or issues."

Programs dealing with summer vacation church schools, sponsorship of elderly and low-income housing, emergency assistance, elderly assistance, and public policy efforts were most often undertaken cooperatively, with neighboring congregations, although only housing programs were more likely to be cooperative than "single-congregation" ventures. Adult study groups on social issues and day-care centers are, somewhat surprisingly, almost never done as cooperative ventures. Membership recruitment programs, advertising, and adult sports activities are also most often done unilaterally.

The effect of mission orientation on community-oriented programming is stronger, overall, than was the case for addressing public issues within the congregation. Strongly activist congregations are somewhat more likely to be involved in social service programs and much more likely to be involved in advocacy programs than are churches and synagogues with other strong orientations or no strong orientation. Civic congregations are especially likely to be involved in sponsoring programs for senior citizens and scout groups.

Congregations with strong sanctuary orientations are more likely to maintain parochial schools and programs for the handicapped than are others. They also give above-average attention to public policy efforts regarding issues of personal morality, although not nearly the attention as do activist congregations, nor do sanctuary congregations' public policy efforts in the area of personal morality carry over to social justice issues. In addition, sanctuary congregations are less likely to involve themselves with programs in the arts and day care than are others. Congregations with strong evangelistic orientations are unusually active in membership recruitment, neighborhood Bible study groups, and vacation church school, but less active than average in programs for the elderly and adult study groups on social issues.

Membership size, denominational family, and location are also more strongly related to community-oriented programming than was the case for addressing public issues within the congregation. Large congregations

94

in particular are more likely to be involved in senior citizen programs, emergency assistance, and low-income and elderly housing. Mainline Protestant congregations seem to have a special affinity for permitting other community groups to use their buildings; conservative Protestant churches, for sponsoring neighborhood Bible groups and vacation church schools and for using radio and television advertising; Catholic parishes, for maintaining parochial schools. City congregations are more likely to be involved in public policy concerns of all kinds.

Controlling for the effect of size, denominational family, and location on community-oriented program weakens congregations' relationship to the mission orientations somewhat, but the basic patterns remain. There are two major exceptions:

1. The extensive involvement of evangelistic congregations with vacation church schools and their lower-than-average involvement with elderly housing seems to be due more to their affiliation with conservative Protestantism than to their affiliation with the evangelistic orientation per se.

2. The propensity of sanctuary congregations toward programs for the handicapped seems to be due more to their large memberships and location in the city than to the sanctuary orientation itself.

In summary, what does the survey data tell us about congregations in the Hartford area and their engagement of public life? First, the survey calls to the attention the fact that although Catholicism dominates the region in terms of numbers of people, there are actually fewer Catholic parishes than there are either mainline or conservative Protestant churches. Related to this is the fact that the membership of Catholic parishes is, on average, five times larger than the membership of mainline Protestant congregations and nearly ten times larger than the membership of conservative Protestant congregations.

Second, the survey points to significant differences among denominational groups in terms of member participation and financial support and membership characteristics. Conservative Protestant churches have by far the highest levels of member involvement and per capita financial support. Their memberships are more likely to be young, single, and growing.

Third, the survey confirms that many, particularly mainline Protestant congregations in the area, have sizable endowments; that area congregations are disproportionately located in the city; and that many city churches draw a majority of their members from the suburbs.

Fourth, the survey clearly indicates that the dominant mission orientation in the Greater Hartford area is civic. This dominance is evident not only in the number of congregations giving it primacy, but also in the extent its varying dimensions find expression in congregations giving primacy to other orientations. The sanctuary orientation is also prevalent in the ethos of Hartford-area congregations, whereas pure expressions of either of the two publicly proactive orientations—activist and evangelistic—are quite limited in number.

Fifth, the survey suggests that although congregations giving strong expression to each of the mission orientations can be found within all denominational families and locations, there are clear denominational and city-suburban differences. City churches are decidedly more likely to have strong identities than are congregations in other locales. This is especially true, again, for the publicly proactive orientations. Catholic parishes show an affinity for both the activist and sanctuary orientations; conservative Protestant churches, for the evangelistic and sanctuary orientations; and mainline Protestant congregations are most likely not to have any strong orientation and those that do, tend toward the civic orientation.

Finally, the survey data suggest that, overall, mission orientation has a slightly greater and independent effect on both dealing with social issues within a congregation and outwardly oriented programming than do denomination, size, and location.

THE CONGREGATIONAL CASES

The open systems approach to the study of congregations, which was discussed in chapter 2, is an especially useful paradigm for viewing churches and synagogues in relation to their larger social environment. It has informed the congregational case studies presented in chapters 6 through 9.

The concept of "system" as applied to a congregation assumes multiple parts working together more or less interdependently toward the definition and accomplishment of a central purpose. This overall sense of purpose is a congregation's understanding of what it is called to be and do. It reflects the attempt of leaders and members to understand the meaning of their professed religious tradition (its identity) in a particular time and place (the context).

Major components of the "congregational system" include the congregation's members and the social worlds they bring to congregational participation, and its leadership, organizational structure, programs, and community context. That these parts are interdependent implies that they all interact with and therefore affect one another. Within a free church polity, to cite just one example, members have a determinative voice in choosing their pastoral leaders, who in turn through their person and impact on program have a determinative effect on members choosing to affiliate with the congregation.

"Open system" implies that a congregation's existence in a particular time and place both affects and is affected by its history and environment.

Although the impact of churches and synagogues on their social context is the central concern of this book, it does not denigrate the importance of a congregation's history or its social context in shaping the congregation's current mission. Nor does it ignore the importance of the internal dynamics of congregational life and the unique gifts and limitations of a congregation's members in mediating the exchange between church or synagogue and society. On the contrary, we take these features with great seriousness, as the cases will show.

The ten churches and synagogues presented in the cases were chosen, on the basis of the congregational survey, to represent the four mission orientations. Although each congregation has obvious strengths and weaknesses, the cases were not chosen because these were the most effective or the "best" in the metropolitan area; rather, they were felt to illustrate, in a particularly instructive way, an aspect of congregations' relationship to their community and world. In making the choices, attention was given to denominational, ethnic, and city-suburban diversity of area congregations.

The case studies were conducted through what may perhaps best be described as "directed participant observation."[3] Backed by the data supplied by the pastor as part of the general congregational survey, by community data obtained from the 1970 and 1980 censuses, and by a seventy-five page research guide, a researcher spent at least six days in the congregation and its immediate geographic neighborhood.[4] The time was spent interviewing (staff, laity, community residents), observing (worship services, committee meetings, outreach programs), and reading relevant documents (annual reports, newsletters, congregation histories, educational curriculum).

The case researchers set out to answer three general questions that combine the concern with religious presence and the open systems approach to the study of congregations:

1. *What is the congregation's understanding of the ways it should be active in relationship to the world beyond the doors of its building?*
2. *In what ways is the congregation, in fact, present to its neighborhood, community, and world?*
3. *What is it about the congregation, its membership, and the community in which it is located that influences (1) and (2) and the congruence or incongruence between them?*

In answering these questions the case researchers were instructed to emphasize description over interpretation. At several points along the way each consulted with the authors to check progress, explore gaps in the data they had gathered thus far, and plan strategy for obtaining specific additional information needed. A preliminary report of about thirty pages was prepared by the case researchers and submitted to the authors and the pastoral leaders of the congregations for their review. Where necessary, revisions and additions of factual material were made. The revised report and field notes were then used to prepare the case accounts that appear in this book. In these accounts the names of people, congregations, and locations (except for Hartford) have been altered, as per the agreement with the participating churches and synagogues.

Building on the systems framework, the following questions should assist the reader's consideration in approaching the case materials:

1. Purpose and mission orientation. To what extent do leaders and members share a clear and concrete sense of purpose? What is their understanding of that purpose and the place of the mission orientation in it? How is this sense of purpose informed by the congregation's history and heritage; by the mix of beliefs, needs, and resources embodied in its membership; and by the geographic turf it occupies or serves?

2. Social context. To what extent does the congregation have a sense of parish? What are the characteristics of the community or neighborhood in which the congregation is located? Who lives there, works there, and otherwise shares an interest in its future? Do the congregation's members live there? Work there? To what social, economic, political, and other religious institutions does the church or synagogue relate? What expectations and perceptions do its neighbors have of the congregation? Does the congregation have an accurate understanding of the community's needs, resources, expectations, and perceptions?

3. Members. Who are the congregation's members? What are their beliefs, values, and life-styles? Their ethnic, class, vocational, educational, and religious backgrounds? How do they describe their social worlds? Are members representative of the neighborhood or community? To what extent do they interact with one another outside congregational activities? Is there evidence of members feeling cross-pressured by multiple commitments, and what priority is given to religion? What is the nature of and motivation for their participation in congregational life?

Underlying all these questions on membership is the recognition of a congregation's members as its primary link with public life. Members not only bring into the congregation needs and resources, expectations and commitments, all shaped to a greater or lesser extent by their social location and involvements outside the congregation; they are also the principal carriers of the congregation into public life, bringing whatever transformations of values, life-style, and commitment the congregation has engendered in them.

4. Pastoral leadership. What role does professional leadership play in the life of the congregation? Specifically, with respect to a congregation's sense of purpose and mission orientation, is its current definition primarily owing to the pastor's influence? Or, is the pastor's involvement more that of managing or facilitating a preexisting lay consensus? What is the pastor's role in shaping program decisions? In carrying out programmatic activities? How is the pastor's time divided among different congregational tasks and the different congregational constituencies to which he or she must attend? What cross-pressures does the pastor feel in this regard? How sensitive is the pastor to the needs and resources of members? To the congregation's social context? To what extent are the pastor's personal beliefs and activities consistent with the mission orientation and activities of the congregation? In multistaff congregations, how are leadership responsibilities divided and what does this division imply about the congregation's sense of pastoral priorities? How qualified or effective is the pastor, both overall and in regard to specific tasks? In addressing each of these questions about pastoral leadership one needs to consider not only the specifics of role and effectiveness, but also the extent to which these specifics are affected by what the pastor brings to them in his or her own person and how they are shaped by, for example, the congregation's polity and members' expectations, perceptions, and support.

5. *Congregational program and organization.* How does the congregation's dominant mission orientation get expressed programmatically? In what other kinds of outreach-oriented programming is the congregation engaged? What priority of resources and attention do these programs receive? Is this consistent with the priority given to outreach concerns within the congregation's general sense of purpose? What effect does the congregation's prior experience with mission concerns have on its current program? What is the congregation's perception of the needs that exist in the community, and how does it decide which of these it will address? How and to what extent are mission concerns and social issues incorporated into the congregation's worship life and educational programming? What is the level and quality of lay involvement in and awareness of the design, sanctioning, and implementation of mission-oriented programming? Is it any greater or less than for other kinds of programming? To what extent are outwardly reaching programs seen to be mutually supportive of other tasks of the congregation? Detrimental to or in competition with other tasks? To what extent are such other tasks seen to be supportive of mission programs? Detrimental to mission?

The thrust of these programmatic and organizational questions is not only toward the specifics of how the congregation attempts to relate to public life, but also toward the relationship of these attempts to other aspects of a congregation's program and organization, and how these linkages facilitate or hinder the congregation's public ministry. Questions of program and organization inevitably involve a consideration of purpose, social context, membership, and pastoral leadership.

99

CHAPTER 6

THE CONGREGATION
AS CITIZEN

Civic congregations focus on the here and now as the main arena of God's redemptive activity. They express their concern for public life primarily through the education of their members and secondarily through funding or sponsoring social service activities. They are comfortable with, even affirming of, dominant social, political, and economic structures; indeed, many of their members are well placed in those structures. The congregations are pluralistic, tolerant of diversity, and embrace ecumenical involvements. They put a premium on civil harmony and religious peace.

The survey analysis shows that the civic orientation is the dominant cultural expression of religious presence in Hartford. To the extent that it is coupled with a strong secondary orientation, there is some tendency toward the activist. But activist involvements are the exception, not the rule; they seem too threatening to the preservation of unity within the congregation itself.

The survey findings also suggest that although congregations of a strong civic orientation are evenly distributed between city and suburbs and across denominational lines, there is some affinity with a suburban and a mainline Protestant environment. Reflecting this, two of the three cases that follow are of suburban congregations and two are of mainline Protestant denominations. Yet each congregation has a distinctive flavor, thus enriching the possibilities for comparison and contrast.

Two of the congregations are located in the suburban community of East Town, and in some ways their recent histories have been intertwined. Although First Church, East Town is nearly as old as the town itself and River Plains Jewish Congregation is fairly new, each has assisted the other at moments of difficulty. The congregations' members share one of the region's most affluent and beautiful communities and in significant ways both reflect and help shape its values.

The physical location of Carmel Baptist could hardly be more different. Its building is located in the heart of one of Hartford's poorest neighborhoods. Nearly all of Carmel's members commute to their church from suburban communities not unlike East Town. In some respects Carmel Baptist is the most complex case in this book. One finds evidence of all four mission orientations in its life and program, although priority is clearly given to the congregation's role as citizen.

FIRST CHURCH OF CHRIST, EAST TOWN

THE UNITED CHURCH of Christ has eighty-nine "First Churches" in Connecticut, fifteen in Greater Hartford alone. Most are of white frame construction, most are located on or near the town green, and virtually all refer to their sanctuary as the meetinghouse. The meetinghouse image is a legacy from the period of Congregationalism's religious establishment in New England. As one historian notes, meetinghouse names "a building which should be associated with, and stand for the social, political and religious life of a community." Appropriately, most early New England meetinghouses were located at the center of the community, and the Congregational minister functioned quite broadly as custodian of the civic culture, being an official of the town as well as minister of a congregation.

The meetinghouse image remains an important rallying point for many of Hartford's "First Churches." First Church in East Town is no exception. Thus, at a recent planning retreat, the following goal, listed under "Christian Concern," was particularly telling:

> *Increase [establish?] the role of the church as a forum for discussion of community issues.* Return the church to its position "At the Center of the Community" [*emphasis added*].

Historical Aspects

First Church's current meetinghouse, a white, frame Georgian structure built in 1830 and several times renovated, stands on the town's main thoroughfare, visible to all who drive north into the town's center. First Church has had three buildings—the first constructed in 1683 on a nearby site and the second in 1739 at the present location. Until officially gathered and organized in 1697, the parish was an outpost of Congregationalists in a neighboring town.

The physical site of the first meetinghouse had been the source of bitter controversy. It took twelve years to make the choice, and twenty-nine years later, when the building proved too small, another controversy arose over whether to enlarge the existing structure or to relocate. That dispute lasted for twenty-seven years, until a new meetinghouse was built on the present site. A local historian states that the controversy over the site reflected the difficulty encountered in serving the large, somewhat irregular geographic area of East Town, which is divided by a river over which there was no bridge in the eighteenth century. More important, he continues,

> the disputants were shrewd, farseeing. . . . They knew that the meetinghouse was a magnet which would attract to its vicinity homes, schools, stores, businesses; that every mile which separated them from it meant a discount on valuation of their property.

During the 1950s and especially in the 1960s, East Town grew rapidly from a one-industry mill town sufficient unto itself into a "bedroom" suburb for the middle- and upper-management families of Hartford's commercial establishment. The town's population was approximately 4,800 in 1950, 10,100 in 1960, and 17,500 in 1970. The 1980 population was 21,000, indicating a slowdown in the rate of growth.

The post-World War II baby boom, coupled with suburbanization, lay behind East Town's growth, with profound effects on both community and church. At the end of the war, in 1945, active church membership at First Church was 504. It increased to 776 by 1955 and was 1,069 in 1960 and 1,398 by 1970. Such rapid growth created tensions between old-timers and newcomers. As the pastor recalls it, "new members were taken into the church twice a year, with an average of one hundred fifty each year. That meant about seventy-five newcomers standing before the old-timers twice a year." The newcomers brought church experiences and expectations often at variance with existing First Church practices. The resulting conflicts are now mostly in the past. Most current members have joined within the past twenty years; few "natives" remain.

The rapid membership increase had a dramatic effect on the church school. Enrollment was 185 in 1945, 334 in 1955, and 843 in 1965, a 355 percent increase in twenty years! The school was so large that double sessions were necessary on Sunday mornings; some 100 adults taught in the programs. The church school was a source of great pride to the members and a major attraction in the community. One member recalled that "having one's kids in our Sunday school was the 'thing to do' in those days. That all changed about the same time the town built its recreational complex and began an extensive sports program for all ages."

To accommodate the burgeoning church school in the mid-1950s, First Church bought a large sandstone house across the street that had been the home of the town's major industrialist. A chapel and other meeting rooms were added in the late 1960s. These facilities now serve as a parish hall and are also available to various community groups. An independent nursery school and a branch office of the YMCA rent space.

The postwar period also brought a proliferation of other Christian congregations to East Town. Methodist, Episcopal, and Catholic churches had arrived earlier, but Presbyterian, Lutheran, and Baptist churches were postwar additions and attracted some First Church members who had previously belonged to one of these denominations.

Also influential in the church's life was a 1965 fire that damaged the meetinghouse extensively and destroyed an adjacent parish hall. The restoration of the sanctuary was possible, and the additions to the house across the street were made to replace space lost with the parish hall. Members refer to the fire as a traumatic experience that provided a significant challenge to First Church. Several members believe that a comparable current challenge—although not a fire—is needed to get the congregation "moving again."

Two social issues had special impact on First Church during the 1960s and early 1970s. These were the civil rights movement—particularly its implications for East Town—and the Vietnam war. "East Town was a very racist community," said one long-time community resident, "and there were certain pockets of the town where racist feelings were especially high and where people threatened to 'shoot any niggers who tried to move in.'" Although most of the members preferred not to deal with the issues of integration and open housing, a group within the church believed that a stand should be taken against racism. A proposed antiracism program, including a series of six sermons, was overwhelmingly approved by congregational vote, but considerable negativism was expressed privately and in comments to the church staff. Several members gave public support to efforts aimed at breaking racial barriers in the larger community.

The war in Vietnam became an issue in response to a letter in which the pastor offered draft counseling about conscientious objection to all seventeen-year-old men in the church. The letter generated considerable controversy and several families reportedly left First Church because of it. One member, who strongly objected to the letter, asked, "Is convincing one student to take alternative service worth losing six families?" Despite the furor, the counseling took place.

Current Situation

First Church's membership stood at 1,133 active and 670 inactive persons* in 1980, a slight decline since 1970 despite East Town's growth.

*"Inactives," as defined by First Church's bylaws, are those "whose addresses have been long unknown or who for a period of two years have not communicated with the church or contributed to its support."

Church school membership was 175 in 1980, a decrease of 668, or 79 percent, from the peak year of 1965. Average attendance at Sunday worship during the fall and winter months (1980) was 292; average summer attendance was 119.

All members are white and most are upper middle class. The average family income is approximately $40,000 annually. Several individuals, transported by members, come from a local home for the retarded. The membership is aging, and available figures suggest that the First Church membership is significantly older than the town's population. Taking only town residents age nineteen and older, 38 percent are forty-five and older, whereas 60 percent of First Church's members are over age fifty.

The minister of First Church is in his nineteenth year of service. A minister of education, who also functions as assistant minister, joined the staff in early 1981. Other staff include a minister of visitation (a part-time retired pastor), a choir director, a junior choir director, an organist, two secretaries (one full and one half time), and a sexton.

The 1981 budget was $225,800, of which $175,000 was pledged by members. An additional $27,000 was projected from endowment sources, and the remainder was expected from various sources, including a $13,800 balance from the previous year. The stewardship committee estimated that the 1981 average pledge of $407 was 1 percent of family income. Budget allocations to major expense categories included Christian concern, $51,750; Christian education, $6,300; worship, $4,000; per capita assessments (United Church of Christ), $2,300; administration, $9,000; personnel, $45,000; buildings and grounds, $48,750.

A majority ($43,600) of the Christian concern budget was designated to the United Church of Christ's Our Christian World Mission. Most of the remainder goes to local and regional outreach, including ecumenical programs and United Church urban ministries.

As renovated after the fire of 1965, First Church's meetinghouse is an attractive Greek revival structure with a plain, well-appointed interior that can seat approximately 400 worshipers on the main floor and in a balcony around three sides. Choir and organ are in the rear balcony. The recessed chancel has a free-standing communion table in the rear center. A wooden cross hangs overhead. The pulpit is on the chancel right, facing the congregation.

Church offices, meeting rooms, and a library are downstairs. Plans are underway to provide access to meeting rooms for handicapped people. First Church has a large parking lot behind the meetinghouse and some space for automobiles on the north side.

The parish house, situated on a three-acre tract across the street, consists of church school rooms and offices, a living room, a large fellowship hall with kitchen, and the chapel. This building is well kept, although it needs a new roof, costing $60,000 if the original slate is replaced and

$30,000 if asphalt is used. The physical separation of the parish building from the meetinghouse creates a problem for First Church. For some members, the division is a psychological barrier, a split between elements of church life. For others, the concern is for the safety of those who must cross a busy thoroughfare. Some officials believe that this problem "turns off" certain potential members.

A plan to consolidate all church buildings on the meetinghouse side of the street was developed in 1975 but has not yet been implemented. The plan was recently revived and is high on the agenda being discussed by a long-range planning committee. Proposed changes in town streets may add incentive to the consolidation of facilities.

The perceptions First Church members have of their community are generally positive. They take considerable pride in the quality of life in East Town. At the same time some indicated an uneasiness—perhaps even guilt—about the high quality of public service and standard of living.

Most community residents share First Church's pride in the community. It is described as a good, even "ideal," place to live. The physical setting—semirural, rolling hills, woods and meadows, attractive houses on large lots—is highly appealing. East Town has little blight. Schools, both public and private, are considered to be excellent, as are several public and private recreational facilities. Most residents are into sports, one community resident noted, "and there are strong pressures for everybody to be active, if not in sports, then in something else."

The predominance of affluent, well-educated white people makes East Town a comfortable home for many of the residents, largely members of managerial or professional families accustomed to employment mobility. The constellation of pluses attracting people to East Town makes it hard for some to recognize any local problems or needs. "Needs tend to be invisible," one resident said. For example, the minister of First Church met considerable resistance in his attempt to set up a town social service (welfare) department because opponents saw "no need" for such an agency. "East Town is a community trapped by its own mystique and affluence," said a resident.

When problems and needs are discussed the two most commonly mentioned are (1) isolation—East Town's isolation from the region or the real world and residents' isolation from one another—and (2) the high degree of stress that seems characteristic of life in the town.

Isolation from the concerns of the surrounding region, particularly those of the city, troubles some residents. East Town, in fact, is perceived to be a haven from urban problems. "The city is a symbol of decay, and people fear it," said one person. "They fear that people from the city want to come out here and take what we have." Some East Towners wonder if they are too protected. One woman said that her mother constantly asks,

105

"Are your kids going to be ready to face life when they grow up? They don't know any blacks; they haven't experienced a ghetto."

But even people who criticize the isolation are reluctant to change it. One person endorsed the idea of low- and moderate-income housing in East Town but added, "I would strongly object to having it in my neighborhood where there is one-acre zoning; no, I wouldn't like that at all."

Isolation characterized the town government for many years. This has begun to change as new leadership has become involved in regional affairs and may signal a shift toward greater participation by residents in the real world, although many are doubtful.

The personal isolation found in East Town is partly attributed to the town's large geographic area and the zoning-enforced, dispersed nature of housing. "People don't really know each other," said a town resident, "and there's no real sense of community."

Much of the stress is tied to work-related pressures. People feel "owned" by the corporations for which they work. This generates a widespread sense of powerlessness. East Town also imposes pressure to achieve, a factor related to the cost of living and maintaining the "expected" life-style. Such pressure takes its toll on marriages and family life and carries over into schools, where parental anxiety is translated into pressure on children to prove themselves scholastically or in sports. Alcoholism is a problem for both adults and teenagers in East Town and several residents view it as stress induced. As one person said, "if a teenager can't achieve scholastic or athletic status, he can try to prove himself as the best beer drinker or the heaviest pot smoker."

Conception of Membership

The bylaws of First Church contain the following paragraph regarding membership:

> The Church welcomes to its membership all who desire to unite with it, as followers of Jesus Christ in worship of God and in service to men. Applications for membership should be made to one of the Ministers or a member of the Board of Elders. Those recommended should be publicly propounded at least one week before the admission of the applicants. If in this time no objection is made to their admission, they shall become members by entering into covenant with the Church.

There are apparently no criteria for membership other than those stated in the bylaws, and the statement carries no explicit expectations (and none could be ascertained, in the church's practice, by this study). New members usually have at least one meeting with the minister before joining, but this practice is not always followed. The minister's failure to insist on this meeting has been criticized at more than one meeting of the elders. The reasons for rendering a person "inactive" (being out of touch for two years or failure to contribute) perhaps imply certain expectations, but in general, First Church has few announced standards for membership and those it has are not applied rigorously.

Confirmation training is required of youths joining the church for the first time (but not of adults). The minister of education recently introduced clear requirements for completing the training, including a written statement of faith. Students must have completed this assignment to be confirmed, an apparently new element of rigor in the preparation for membership. Also, students are now given the opportunity to decide whether or not to proceed with confirmation after completing the class. When two young people recently decided not to join, elders expressed surprise and concern. An elder asked the minister of education if the students were ready for membership. "Yes," he replied, "if confirmation is understood as a stage along the way and not as an expression of closure on what one believes."

When asked what belonging to the church means to them, most members mention two things: (1) an opportunity to be exposed to Christian values (especially the love of God and neighbor) and (2) fellowship. Many members recognize that the values and the fellowship inherent in First Church are socially and politically conservative, although not monolithically so. One member's description of the church as "the Republican Party at prayer" was disputed by others; both the Democratic and Republican town chairpersons belong. However, the general conservatism is not seen as a hindrance to the discussion of controversial social issues as long as "all sides are presented fairly."

First Church members are active in both town and regional affairs and are described as being "highly civic minded." The minister estimates that more First Church members are active on town committees and in town affairs than is true for all other town churches taken together. But neither he nor others were sure of the degree to which these people saw their civic involvement as a matter of Christian vocation. As one person put it, much of the participation in civic and regional affairs results from the expectations imposed by employers. Corporate executives belonging to First Church sit on the boards of directors of various Hartford civic and cultural institutions, but there is little evidence of a connection between these affiliations and Christian service.

Several persons noted that First Church members, probably reflecting the East Town ethos, were overcommitted to organizations and activities and that this has a negative effect on church involvement. The consensus was that the church is relatively low on a long list of priorities. Underscoring this, one church leader speculated that his involvement would likely be curtailed: "I've just bought a piece of vacation property in Maine that I want to develop, and my job also is requiring more and more time. You know, there just isn't enough time to respond to all these commitments." Another leader voiced frustration over the lack of commitment of some church school teachers: "They'll call on Friday and say that they won't be there on Sunday; they're playing tennis, going skiing or to a dog show. They don't say, 'I'm sorry.' Rather they imply, 'Of course, I won't be there, because you know that these other things are more important than the church.'" A sermon on commitment by the minister of education used a text from Jeremiah about Israel's straying to false gods; however, there was little application to East Town and the connection was probably missed by most hearers.

Theological Self-understanding

The lack of explicitly religious references in board and committee meetings and the difficulties many members have in describing the congregation's theological identity suggest that First Church has no common theological self-understanding. There is a formal statement of faith, to be sure, one adopted by the United Church of Christ in 1959, and there is a formal statement of purpose. Members appear to be in general agreement with these statements, although most do not seem to be familiar with their specifics. They are not required to give assent to them.

A pluralism of beliefs is not only acceptable at First Church, but also a reality of life. Despite the general social and political conservatism, the minister noted, most congregants share a strong belief in the right of individuals to their own private beliefs. "After all, they are part of the UCC [United Church of Christ], and the United Church is a left-of-center liberal denomination." Some of the more religiously conservative members find meaningful participation in a local charismatic Presbyterian congregation but nevertheless retain their membership in First Church. As for typical theological knowledge, one person termed it on a "Sunday school level, that is, about junior high."

Implicit and occasionally explicit theological themes can be discerned in First Church programs, notably Christian education. The minister of education described the approach as "classical theological liberalism, in which the historical-critical study of the Bible is accepted and various personal and social issues are considered in relation to Christian values." To that might be added an emphasis on the "fatherhood" of God and the brotherhood and sisterhood of humanity, also a classic liberal emphasis. A document prepared by the Christian education board expressed this in terms of "vertical" and "horizontal" Christianity. Other documents and programs bear out the essential liberal stance in operational theology. Programs serve as a center where individuals clarify values and the meaning of life in relation to God and find avenues to serve those who are in need. Much of the service is carried out through institutionalized means supported financially through the church, especially denominational mission programs. The relatively strong support of mission, both in giving and in programs, reflects in large part the minister's personal interests.

Structure and Decision Making

In keeping with its congregational polity, First Church vests final authority in the congregation, which has an annual meeting and special meetings on call. Twenty-five members constitute a quorum.

The bylaws authorize a Church Council to act on behalf of the congregation between meetings. The Council consists of designated officers, board chairpersons, various committee representatives, and three members elected at large. Although the Council has formal authority to act, an executive committee made up of designated officers, board chairpersons, and the senior minister exercises de facto power. The Council meets quarterly; the Executive Committee, monthly. The fact that the smaller Executive Committee is the real decision-making unit was mentioned negatively by several members who would prefer a larger, more representative body. Presiding over the annual meeting, the Church Council, and the Executive Committee is the president of the congregation, who may serve up to five consecutive annual terms. The position of president is an influential one, described by some members as similar in function to the chairperson of a corporate board.

First Church has six administrative boards: Christian concern, responsible for outreach; Christian education; finance; elders, responsible for "the spiritual life of the church, its members, and *its community* [italics added]"; and trustees, responsible for endowed funds and real property. A deacon's committee administers the Deacon's Funds and is responsible to the Board of Christian Concern.

These boards meet monthly and operate with considerable autonomy. Each has constitutionally designated tasks and a portion of the church budget to administer. Except in matters that involve a major change in emphasis (for example, when a new church school curriculum was being selected) or a venture into new territory that requires a church policy decision, boards conduct their own affairs. Indeed, there seems to be considerable concern over turf; each board is loath to take action or propose changes in matters that may pertain to another's area. Thus some things "fall between the cracks." This concern for turf was also said to "hinder cross-fertilization among the boards. Each does its own thing." When turf disputes arise the Executive Committee or the congregation is called on to settle them. Communication between the boards takes place through the Executive Committee and the Church Council. Also, some boards report on activities in the church newsletter.

Several persons commented that the church was organized and run like a corporation, and some complained about it. In the latter's view, the president and the Executive Committee served as "board chairman" and "board of directors," respectively, with the ministers as managers, employees of the "board of directors" (the Executive Committee), who in turn represent the "stockholders" (members). What is more, according to those who resist such a business mentality in the church, in the conduct of the "corporation," too much emphasis falls on planning and efficiency, "holding the fort," minimizing losses but also minimizing risk—"damage control," in the new jargon of beleaguered businesses. They cite, for example, three scenarios for the church's future projected by the Board of Elders: one optimistic (calling for venturesome programs with some risks to the church), one pessimistic (projecting declines), and the other middle of the road (essentially maintaining the status quo). The latter was the one recommended by the elders, calling for "a 'moderately paced' program of physical and spiritual improvements."

Administrative responsibility for First Church's presence in the East Town community and beyond is lodged formally in two boards. The Board of Elders, as previously noted, is given some responsibility for the spiritual life of the community. Specifically, it is to "interpret the role of the church in the life of the community." How this task is, or is to be, carried out is less than evident, and little reference to this role of the elders is made by members of the church.

The major responsibility for relating the church to the town and the world falls to the Board of Christian Concern and the Deacon's Committee. In addition to recommending priorities for mission giving, the board has several other duties as described in the bylaws:

> *The Board shall be responsible for the development and implementation of a program of interpreting the mission of the Church.*
>
> *The Board shall be responsible for identifying social and moral issues or practices with which Christians should be concerned. It shall make recommendation to the Church Council on any issue on which it feels the Church should speak or act.* While the Board may express its mind on any issue, it shall not of itself take a stand on any issue in the name of the Church [*emphasis added*]. . . .
>
> *The Board shall be responsible for relating the life of our Church to its community.*
>
> *The Board shall be responsible, through its Committee of Deacons, for disbursing the Deacon's Funds in accordance with the terms of the bequest.*

The Deacon's Funds are endowments of some magnitude left to the church over its long history and designated for use in meeting the needs of East Town residents or those who are "of East Town," that is, those who are natives but may now reside elsewhere. At times the deacons have had difficulty spending the benefactions, and a surplus of $30,000 accumulated at one point. Current practice entails close cooperation with the town's Social Service Department in disbursing the money, with the department doing initial screening of needs and making recommendations for grants. There is a policy against making unrestricted gifts to organizations; however, allocations have been made to help organizations initiate specific programs, such as home care for the sick or elderly.

Its bylaw charge notwithstanding, the Board of Christian Concern functions in two principal areas: first, in supervising the allocation and disbursement of mission funds—most of which (85 percent) are given to the United Church of Christ's Our Christian World Mission; and second, in informing itself and the congregation on issues. Individual board members relate to specific programs funded by First Church or monitor specific types of issues. For example, one person monitors world mission, another national affairs, and another regional and local concerns. These individuals report at board meetings. Recent reports have included world population growth, El Salvador, the Nestlé boycott, CIA pressures on missionaries to be informants, changes in the food stamp program, the Connecticut Prison Association, a local program to aid battered teenagers and runaways, and the local Interfaith Refugee Resettlement program. Some of these programs were candidates for receiving funds; others were discussed as matters of information. In the past the board has presented some issues to the congregation with recommendations for action by individual members, if they were so inclined. The Nestlé boycott is an example. Also, at least one Christian concern issue is highlighted in the church newsletter each month.

Although effective in its recommendation to the congregation of priorities for mission giving and in broadening the perspectives of its members, the board is less successful, according to its chairman, in keeping issues before the congregation. In part this is because so many issues come before it. But also involved is the fact that there is no, even implicit, agreement at First Church about what issues are appropriate for the church to address, much less agreement on appropriate types of action. One leader, for example, spoke strongly against any activist role for the church or minister, except for relatively safe forms of service and attention to noncontroversial issues. He was especially negative toward either the congregation or the clergy doing anything to challenge the "law of the land." "If it's the law, then we have an obligation to support, not challenge it." He is not alone in these sentiments.

The senior minister's role in support of the outreach efforts of First Church deserves special mention, as does his involvement in community affairs. Despite some complaints about aspects of his leadership, especially the activist bent of his preaching, he commands considerable overall support, respect, and appreciation. He is described as a strong individual who frequently makes his influence felt quietly, although he is not reluctant to speak out forcefully when he believes that this is needed. He sometimes influences decisions by "planting seeds with various lay leaders that later emerge as recommended actions." He also regularly uses the pulpit to deal with issues about which he feels strongly. Said one member, "It's hard to get by a Sunday when he doesn't have something to say on a social issue either in his sermon or prayer." Although this has generated conflict, most believe that the elders support his right to express his conscience from the pulpit. Also, as one person said, "he's been doing better in recent years in owning his perspective, saying, 'I as an individual believe this.' People react more positively to this than in cases when he seemed to be speaking or acting for the church. There's less conflict now than ten years or so ago." Still, the minister is not just an individual, but one of the most visible representatives of the congregation and its professional leader. This means that, even when the minister speaks as an individual, some identify his speaking with First Church. Although this gives his position greater authority, it also angers those who disagree with particular positions. His endorsement of amnesty for Vietnam draft resisters, for example, created enough conflict to prompt attempts to limit his involvement with the issue.

When asked what loss there would be to East Town if First Church should cease to exist, the minister answered in terms of the loss to the community of the role that he, as minister, plays. His comment was not made in a bragging fashion. Instead, it reflected the actual importance attached to the pastor's role in the community, perhaps an expression of the legacy from early New England. Others confirmed that First Church's minister has, indeed, played a significant part in town affairs for the last two decades—prodding the town government to establish a social service department, helping to establish a coalition of human service professionals, speaking out against racism, providing leadership in the Nestlé boycott, and so on. Perhaps indicative of his stature in the community is the fact that the local clergy association chose him to be their spokesperson in advocating a resolution supporting the nuclear freeze. Also of note in this regard is the fact that as he rose to speak in favor of the resolution at the town meeting, he introduced himself only by name, with no mention of his church or of the fact that he is a minister.

Church Program and Activities

The 10:00 A.M. Sunday worship service is the primary gathering of the First Church congregation. The order of service, led by the minister or assistant minister, includes considerable congregational participation—responsive sentences of adoration, a unison prayer, a responsive assurance of pardon and versicles before the pastoral prayer, and hymns. An exceptional choir leads the singing and offers one or more anthems.

The Sunday service on a Memorial Day weekend gives the flavor of a typical service. The opening prayers and hymn were appropriate to the weekend. There was a service of Christian baptism, with a brief comment on the importance of children to Jesus and on the need to be concerned for the kind of world in which the young grow up. The pastoral prayer by the senior minister centered on the theme of Memorial Day. He prayed that Americans might honor the memory of the dead by a commitment to freedom, justice, right relations among people and nations, and peace. He thanked God that American Christians are not prisoners in their own nation, grown harsh and callous, but that in Christ they can reach across separating boundaries and through mission programs they can teach intelligent nutrition, adequate health care, and just labor relations. He mentioned the needs of developing nations and of the hurt and poor at home.

The minister of education read the lessons and preached, focusing on the subject of commitment. He developed the theme of the Israelites' adaptation of their religion to a pagan culture, leading to the worship of false gods. The preacher reminded the congregation of Jesus' call to unconditional discipleship and the example of Jesus' own commitment unto death. He made little application to East Town, although in private conversation he said that the low church commitment and multiple loyalties of many members were motivations in his selection of the sermon topic.

At a lenten service the sermon—one of a series on discipleship—focused on the responsibility of Christians in the world. The imperative to serve all people in society, including the least lovable, was stressed. In particular, the minister cited the example of a local corporate executive who entered into a contract with Jesse Jackson's Operation PUSH to provide jobs to minorities. This action by an active church member (not First Church) was termed an instance of Christian service, and the example was commended to other members with corporate connections. The impact of the sermon is debatable. As one observer noted, "the church expresses more genuine concern for victims of racism in the South than it does for victims within the shadow of its spire."

Worship is followed by a fellowship period downstairs or, once a month, by a "Second Hour" program. At the social gathering, members seem unconcerned about greeting newcomers or strangers; instead, they cluster in small groups of acquaintances for conversation.

Church school is the major program of Christian education and includes children and youth from age three through eighth grade. It meets during the morning worship hour, except on fourth Sundays, when children attend worship with their parents, those above the fourth grade remaining for the whole service and those younger returning to their classroom after a children's sermon. On the wall of one classroom is a collage of pictures showing world hunger and other forms of human need. A caption asked, "What would God like to change in the world? What does God like?" The answer, in large letters, was "JUSTICE."

Young people "graduate" from church school into the confirmation class. There is also a junior high fellowship and a Pilgrim Fellowship for senior highs. Both youth organizations are more oriented to fellowship than to education, and the senior group is not notably strong. A Bible study for youth was tried but discontinued because of low participation. The Pilgrim Fellowship sponsors a breakfast for the entire church each Sunday before worship, except during the summer. One adult said that he and a friend, whose jobs are quite different, frequently sit together at these breakfasts to discuss ethical matters they face on the job. He described this contact as an important form of Christian support.

There are a variety of adult education programs. The best attended are the "Second Hours," held once a month after Sunday worship. In the past Second Hour programs had tended to avoid controversial topics and, frequently, to be organized on intergenerational lines. However, the Board of Christian Concern was asked to suggest or present programs on social issues. This request resulted in programs on hunger in the metropolitan area and on cults and their appeal. Second Hours are mentioned with appreciation by members; if there is criticism, it is of the infrequency with which they are held.

Other adult education includes a Bible study led by the ministers each Wednesday night, excluding the summer months. A women's fellowship is organized into six circles that meet monthly to study a book. And an annual lenten series features adult study, usually on a currently topical ethical issue. Issues addressed in recent years include genetic engineering, medical ethics, ethics in the workplace, and the concept of a "no risk" society. Average attendance is about thirty persons.

In response to adult fellowship needs, First Church has the women's organization (also for study and service) and a couples' club that meets monthly on a Friday evening for a meal, a program, and fellowship. The club has been in existence for twenty years, having been started by single women to provide social life for themselves and their dates. It evolved into a couples' group whose members are now mostly middle aged. Hope was expressed that a new group for younger couples might be launched. There is a fellowship organization for older women, and the church sponsors a New England Holiday Fair, held every other year.

A nursery school in the parish building is independent of the congregation, but First Church supports regional outreach programs and facilities affiliated with the United Church of Christ. This involvement, according to the pastor, gives First Church regional ties lacking in other Protestant congregations in East Town.

In general, the programs just described are congruent with the identified and inferred theological orientation of the church. They provide fellowship and opportunities to reflect on life from a Christian perspective. Issue-related programs are chiefly informational rather than action oriented. Although the senior minister issues challenges to social action, the week-to-week activities are definitely low risk.

Is First Church "at the Center of Community Life"?

The Board of Christian Concern's goal to return First Church to "its position 'at the center of the community'" certainly implies that now, at least for those at the leadership retreat, it is not. What is more, there is little common agreement among members when asked what that might mean. Three general types of responses are given: (1) that it's a geographic reference; (2) that it's a reference to the perception by newcomers that this is *the* church to belong to in East Town if one wants to associate with the influential people; and (3) that it's a reference to the influence of the church in the community, once considerable but now reduced.

Which is right and what *really* is meant? The retreat planners clearly seem to have meant the latter, intending through education to stimulate the congregation's concern for the community. And they are bothered that the church is not presently central in the community. How central is it? Are they correct?

A number of programs and other factors, some mentioned previously, suggest that First Church is already a strong presence in East Town, regardless of whether it is actually at the center of things. In recent years First Church has participated in or helped to initiate most of the new social institutions or programs in East Town and the region. These include refugee resettlement, assistance for youth from homes with conflict, outside aid for prison inmates, and support for people with alcohol-related conflicts with the law. The church also took part in the Nestlé boycott and a program to bring inner-city youth into the community to be part of the local schools and community. There is also the Deacon's Funds and the various educational programs that have addressed ethical issues.

Additionally, First Church has a minister who has a significant role in congregational education for mission and in community affairs.

Finally, there are those laity who, individually, are involved in civic affairs locally and regionally. The number of such persons is not insignificant, even if it remains a question whether people who enjoy—or whose employers expect—such involvement are attracted to First Church or whether there is an ethos in the church that fosters the involvement.

As one observer concluded after a study of First Church's outreach efforts:

> First Church is definitely present in East Town and, to a lesser degree, in the region. But its presence, constructive as it often is, ap-

pears to be relatively safe and nonthreatening. The church involves itself in local and regional problems primarily through the pastor's presence and by giving money to others to act in the church's behalf. It engages in service to needy persons in East Town while generally accepting and supporting the status quo of the town's life-style and ethos, which may create or contribute to the problems. Thus, while First Church is present in the community, it is also very much of the community.

RIVER PLAIN JEWISH

ARCHITECTURAL DESIGN, at its best, is attentive not only to function, but also to the symbolic embodiment of the meaning of place. River Plain Jewish Congregation's striking contemporary building tucked away on a wooded, secluded lot in East Town bespeaks as loudly as words and deeds the fundamental tensions that inform its unique identity. On the one hand, it is composed of well-educated members, concerned about, established in, and comfortable with the best of the modern world. On the other hand, as a minority in a Christian culture, the members are in need of and search for a "place of their own," a place to affirm and maintain their Jewish existence.

River Plain Jewish Congregation is situated off one of the major thoroughfares of the suburban community of East Town.* Although near a well-traveled road, its building is hardly noticeable to passersby because a virtual forest hides it from view. Indeed, the synagogue is difficult to find for anyone who is unfamiliar with it. A driveway marked by an ordinary street lamp and an inconspicuous sign are the only indications of its sheltered location.

The building is rustic, modern, and distinctive in design. It has multiple levels, integrated with the rolling landscape of the wooded lot, and its vertically grained wood siding is finished in natural hues. Compared with many city synagogues, the structure is diminutive. Facilities include the original sanctuary and a more recent addition housing a school, a social hall, and administrative offices. A new parking lot is also relatively small. The total effect is of a tasteful yet eloquent blend of cosmopolitan and country. The synagogue's interior is harmonious with the message conveyed externally. Newly redecorated, it is in no way ornate; rather, it blends a feeling of intimacy with an emphasis on function (religious and social). Like many synagogues, River Plain leaves its worship space small until the high holy days, when a movable partition allows for the greater seating required. Classrooms, meeting rooms, the library, and even the

*For an extended discussion of East Town, see the First Church, East Town case.

rabbi's study are similarly functional. Signs of a lively educational program decorate the hallways in the basement.

Historical Aspects

River Plain Jewish is a relative newcomer to the East Town area. Until the early 1960s the town and nearby communities had virtually no Jewish population. One of the earliest Jewish residents of East Town recalls that when he set out to found a synagogue twenty years ago, "there were no more than seventeen Jewish families in the vicinity." These people were aware of one another, felt a sense of closeness, and shared a sense of alienation from their gentile neighbors. They felt different in part, according to the synagogue founder quoted above, because "we were flaming liberals. We were Jews, not Yankees."

The beginnings of the synagogue were informal. Perhaps a dozen families met in a space provided by the area's largest corporation. This corporation would later donate the land on which the synagogue building stands, as well as land for a cemetery. Area churches also had a part in helping to establish the Jewish congregation. Space for worship was provided and one local Christian minister is credited with offering strong encouragement toward establishing a formal synagogue.

From its inception, River Plain Jewish Congregation grew with a sense of self-definition. Founders envisioned a complete center—a "temple" in contemporary Reform language—including a sanctuary housing an ark and Torah scrolls, an education facility, and a social program. The founders' need to identify as Jews and to share their Jewishness with one another expressed itself in the kind of congregation that was built. They also wanted to maintain a sense of intimacy, a sense of a mutually supportive local "family." They had no rabbi, so they used their own liturgical expertise in services, found their children's teachers within their own number and organized their own social activities.

As the congregation grew, changes occurred, but the initial vision remained intact, according to founders. A major step was taken in 1964, when a rabbinical student was hired to lead services—"in a manner not to dull the sense of congregational participation." A member became the cantor (or liturgist). This person has since left East Town but returns each year for the high holy days and is still considered part of the community.

River Plain Jewish was a functioning congregation long before the services of a rabbi were sought. After the first rabbi came in, the community tried to retain its homegrown flavor. Whether it has succeeded is a matter of divided opinion within the congregation.

Perhaps the most profound change in the tenor of the congregation took place in 1971, when its house of worship was officially dedicated. This event brought greetings from the President of the United States, the governor of the state, and local politicians. Consistent with the spirit of community cooperation that helped to establish the synagogue, the rabbinical student was joined at the dedication by clergy from several Christian denominations.

Current Situation

Today the congregation's leadership is still concerned with maintaining a sense of group identity. With approximately 400 member families, River Plain Jewish finds it a challenge to provide the services required by a group that large and yet retain a sense of family. Growth has made it difficult for people to assume responsibility for one another and for the synagogue's corporate welfare; perhaps the founders' need to identify as Jews has diminished as the area's population, including the Jewish population, has increased. Leaders bemoan the transiency of corporate executives and professionals, who now make up a large percentage of the membership. At the same time to be part of the area's Jewish community is equivalent to joining the synagogue, just as it was twenty years ago.

Other aspects of the congregation's life are also undergoing change in the early 1980s. River Plain Jewish is in the process of replacing its first full-time rabbi. And the Hebrew school has expanded to the space provided in the recently added wing to the ten-year-old sanctuary. Approximately 230 students currently are enrolled, a far cry from the original educational system.

River Plain Jewish is officially a synagogue of Reform Judaism, although the congregation—like other "liberal" Jewish groups—makes modifications in ritual and practice. Its members are scattered across a large area, but virtually none of them work in the town in which they reside. Jews continue to be a small minority in the vicinity; however, the proportion of Jews to Christians now moving into the area is roughly the same as the existing ratio among residents.

Synagogue leaders believe that the community at large is aware of the synagogue's existence, with church people and groups being the most aware. No hostility seems to hamper relations between the Jewish congregation and Christian churches. Christians are invited to the synagogue for various events and there has been a sharing of programs for Jewish and Christian young people. The rabbi is an active member of the East Town Clergy Association.

The membership is relatively young, mostly falling between thirty and early forties. Most of the families include a father who works for a corporation in Hartford or an adjoining town; almost all are upper middle class, although not necessarily wealthy. The congregation does not expect much change in the composition of its religious community in the near future, partly because the region is not experiencing major social changes. However, there is concern that young adults and senior citizens in the congregation are finding it increasingly difficult to secure affordable housing.

Conception of Membership

According to River Plain bylaws, accepted in the late 1970s, the purpose of the congregation is "to provide for the religious needs of all its members and to do any and all other acts or things to carry out the above purpose." Thus the program is left flexible and responsive to expressed needs.

Unlike churches in East Town, and unlike synagogues in areas of heavy Jewish concentration, the synagogue has little competition (although a few Jewish families prefer to commute to West Hartford). When a Jewish family moves into the vicinity and wants to join a synagogue, River Plain is the most likely choice. It is *the* local temple. But the need to absorb new people who may bring set expectations with them means that the synagogue must be religiously broad enough not to alienate any segment within the local Jewish community. Members, in turn, must at times be willing to make compromises to accommodate Jewish diversity.

The synagogue does not actively solicit new members in any formal manner. It is assumed that Jews moving into the area who are interested in religion will learn of the congregation by word of mouth. Inquiries are usually handled by personal visits by leaders who explain the benefits and requirements of membership. In keeping with the family ethos, every member is on the Membership Committee; all are expected to extend themselves to new Jewish residents. However, given the fairly rapid growth, all members do not necessarily know one another. A statement on "Temple Etiquette" drafted by the Religious Committee says, "Extend a WELCOME to strangers, no formal introduction is needed, they may be your fellow members you have not met as yet, make them feel at home."

Membership is primarily a matter of paying dues, at least in an objective sense. A written application submitted for approval by the Board of Directors is more for the record than for purposes of exclusivity. Any Jewish person who is willing to pay the dues seems acceptable. In cases of financial hardship, reduced rates or a time-payment schedule are possible. In theory, no one is denied membership because of a money shortage. Pragmatically, given the affluence of the community, reduced dues are seldom necessary.

The dues are annual contributions that vary according to category of membership: full (family), single, "head of household under twenty-eight years of age, and having no children of religious school age," or senior (over age sixty). Full membership in 1981 was over $700 per year. In addition, a building fund pledge is expected from each full member. The

Hebrew school has registration fees and tuition, and the temple sisterhood has annual dues.

Apart from financial commitment, the synagogue places no explicit demands on members. Personal conduct is considered the business of the individual; criteria for seeking a resignation from membership do not exist. The chief objective inducements for membership are the social programs and the school. (The sense of being Jewish and of giving allegiance to God do not depend entirely on formal religious affiliation.) Many young Jewish couples typically begin to consider membership in a synagogue when their children reach the appropriate age for Hebrew school. Synagogues often reinforce this tendency because in most cases a family may not send children to the school of a congregation to which it does not belong. This is the case at River Plain Jewish.

Another, more subjective factor must be considered with regard to membership in the River Plain congregation. Joining the synagogue, as already noted, is tantamount to a statement of solidarity with the area Jewish community. To this extent the fact of belonging is both self-definitional ("I am a Jew") and supportive ("I want to do my share to see that a synagogue in this area can exist"). This factor is notable when it is observed that, as one friend of River Plain puts it,

> the Jews who move to East Town and environs are not traditionally observant Jews, certainly not Orthodox, which would require walking to the synagogue. The Jews who move in are not identifiable as such by any external criteria; they are not people thinking first and foremost about their proximity to an active Jewish center when they buy homes. They are relatively assimilated Jews for whom joining the synagogue is all the more a statement of religious and cultural identity—a matter of appreciable substance.

Nonetheless, it is clear that membership in River Plain Jewish Congregation has subtle implications. Joining is at least tacit acknowledgment that being Jewish is different. Although Jews may live comfortably in homogenized American culture, the community bears witness to an underlying stratum of perceived difference. Whether impelled to join by an inner sense of Jewish identity, by external factors confronting them with the "difference," by projections of future events, or by the fact of wanting their children to be knowledgeable Jews, membership in the synagogue says something. As part of a minority group, openly identifying themselves as such, the members of the congregation are acting and representing themselves in a specific way. Membership, then, includes a great deal more than the explicit criterion of paying dues.

Religious Self-understanding

Early in its history the synagogue faced a decision about its denominational affiliation. With which major branch of American Judaism would it identify—Orthodox, Conservative, Reform? A Committee on Judaism (precursor to the Religious Committee) presented a report on "The Differences Between the Various Divisions." After much consideration the committee proposed affiliation with the Reform movement through the Union of American Hebrew Congregations (UAHC); it would generally tailor its programs to Reform specifications. That was the logical choice, especially in light of the assimilation factor mentioned earlier. But to accommodate those who were more concerned with keeping the tradition, several concessions have been made.

With regard to *kashruth* (dietary regulations), there is a range of possible options—some strict, others lenient. Thus food brought into the synagogue kitchen may not be prepared in any member's home, since this would violate *hashgakhah* (ritual supervision by the rabbi). To overcome this problem a list of kosher caterers who were allowed into the synagogue was drawn up. Yet all wines are permitted. Certain dishes are requested but not required; platters containing fresh fruit and vegetables from non-kosher homes may be brought into the building but not the kitchen.

A similar blend of tradition and reform remains in the sanctuary. For example, the document on "Temple Etiquette" states that "yarmulkes [skull caps] and tallithim [prayer shawls] may or may not be worn at the discretion of the worshipper." Yet the synagogue stipulated that any individual called to the pulpit as a participant in the service "will wear these garments without fail." Women are counted in the *minyon* (minimum of ten worshipers needed for a complete service) and may read from the Torah, practices almost universal in Reform Judaism and increasingly acceptable in the Conservative branch.

The pattern of accommodation and compromise seems to work well in the congregation of religious diversity. "A good solution is one that makes everyone a little unhappy," said one member of the synagogue Board of Directors. Individuals, however, do not always capitulate. They continue to hold their own beliefs and make peace with the fact that they cannot have everything their way. A past president of the congregation said that discussions of ritual observance and religious tenor bring out the differences that divide the group, but she added that such discussions, although lively, are not mean or bitter.

Judaism expects a synagogue to provide its members with a number of services. By definition, a synagogue is a place of worship, of study, and of gathering, and all these are considered part of each Jew's religious life. It is not unusual, therefore, to find members who are dedicated to one or another of the synagogue's functions but not to all three (although a sabbath service combines all three, containing study of Torah and being a gathering). Religious commitments and theological beliefs can be extremely diverse, and River Plain congregation is typical in this regard. No system of belief is imposed. One member who was interviewed imagined it possible for an atheist to belong, if he or she were Jewish.

A few men have questioned the participation of women in the service, but dissent is not a real problem and the congregation seems relatively content with things as they are, including the affiliation with the UAHC. The only rumblings about UAHC have to do with the amount of dues paid to the Reform organization in relation to the perceived few services provided.

That the synagogue is content with its modified Reform character seems clearly implied in the fact that it is seeking a new rabbi through the Union's placement apparatus. The interview questions prepared for the selection process provide a good picture of the congregation's religious self-understanding. The following are from "Interview Questions for Rabbinical Candidates":

- How does a rabbi effectively deal with a congregation which must meet the needs of a religiously diverse population because it is the only Temple in a five-town area?
- Is it the rabbi's responsibility to build attendance at weekly services? How have you or would you do this?
- What is the purpose of a sermon in a Jewish service?
- Tell us how you choose a subject for a sermon?
- Should worship be creative?
- To what degree do you observe ritual in your conduct of the service, and to what extent do you expect your congregation to do so?
- Please describe your interpretation of Halacha (law).
- Is there anything about your style of delivery that keeps people awake during sermons?

On an interview form that each member of a selection committee was expected to complete after talking with each candidate, religious philosophy was a major category. The form asked, "How compatible are his/her religious attitudes with those of the congregation?" (The presence of the male/female pronouns is worth noting, because it seems to suggest the acceptability of a female rabbi; however, one source said "her" appeared only because it was required by the UAHC, not because a woman rabbi was a real option.)

Structure and Organization

River Plain Jewish Congregation follows the typical organizational structure for Reform synagogues, a plan not unlike that of free-church-policy Protestant congregations. The form is essentially democratic, but one question at the time of this study concerned the number of votes allotted each family.

Congregational offices include president, first and second vice-presidents, secretary and assistant secretary, and treasurer. These are elected (except for the assistant secretary) at an annual meeting of the membership. This meeting also considers and adopts a budget for the year ahead. The Board of Directors, on which the officers and the rabbi automatically sit, is chosen by the members for three-year terms, up to two terms each. The board meets monthly and members chair the various committees.

The Board of Directors, according to common perception, is an open body that is receptive to divergent views and is interested in all opinions. A good example of its openness is the "Directors Are Listening" program, which was initiated in 1980. This program, not fully implemented when this study was conducted, has two prongs. It was designed to solicit views of the congregation from active members and from those who decide to terminate affiliation. One directive resolves that any terminating member will be visited within a week to ascertain the reasons for withdrawal ("expectations; likes and dislikes; specific problems"). A schedule of visitation of active members sets a goal of interviewing one fourth of the member families each year.

A few persons in the congregation complain that the Board of Directors is a clique of old-timers who want to dominate the decision-making process. Actually, the synagogue has trouble getting its members to take leadership positions and must rely on those who are willing. Almost any member who shows an interest is taken into the leadership ranks.

Program and Activities

In the historic Jewish pattern, the program at River Plain Jewish Congregation has three components: worship and ritual (including rites of passage), education, and social interaction. Of these, education seems to get the most attention.

The educational program, a source of great pride, is designed for children, youth, and adults. Especially appealing to the young families is the Hebrew school, which is directed by a long-time member. An enrollment of 230 students (out of a congregation of 400 families) shows the relative youthfulness of the members. The rabbi, elected leaders, and members devote considerable time and effort to the school and seek constantly to improve it. The 1979 report of the rabbi to trustees focused on education. He wrote:

> Since my arrival we have made several changes in our religious school program. First, we have restructured the Hebrew curriculum.

123

> We feel this change will stimulate more interest in Hebrew and give
> the students a better background for prayer. . . . Parents should
> instill in children the feeling that religious education is just as impor-
> tant or more important than their secular education. . . . Second, we
> have introduced the concept of family education. Teachers have been
> asked to invite parents into their classes on one or more occa-
> sions. . . . Parents and children learning together is an important
> element of Jewish education.

In the same report the rabbi made suggestions for the long-term future
of the educational program. He proposed (1) strengthening the education
committee, (2) strengthening the curriculum in history and Jewish values,
(3) increasing the responsibility and accountability of teachers, and
(4) considering a midweek Hebrew class for fourth graders.

Education for teenagers is less formal, but the youth groups for junior
and senior highs are active and well attended. These organizations sponsor religious services and social activities and interact with other Reform
youth groups in the Hartford area. They also participate in programs
sponsored by the Greater Hartford Jewish Federation and the Jewish
Community Center.

Adult education is provided primarily through a lecture series that goes
beyond the confines of the synagogue in terms of both topics and speakers. All in all, according to one who is knowledgeable about Hartford-area
synagogues, "River Plain Jewish has what is probably one of the most
successful ventures in Jewish education in the region."

Religious services are largely the responsibility of the rabbi, with the
advice of the Religious Committee. The services are similar to those of
other Reform synagogues, although an emphasis on congregational participation and a sense of family have been maintained. Sometimes various
grades in the Hebrew school are in charge of the Friday evening services.

Typical worship at River Plain synagogue combines the spiritual, the
educational, and the communal. For Jews to gather in worship always
entails prayer, praise, and humility. It includes affirmation of the people
as a group (the rationale for the *minyon*), and there is an expectation that
something will be learned.

Some members criticized the educational component of the services
led by the current rabbi. They thought the sermons "were not stimulating
enough" or mentioned a low-key delivery. Others complained that the
rabbi failed to take stands on issues confronting the congregation, the
community, or the world, but an inconsistency lurks in this complaint.
Pressed on the point, congregational leaders admitted that strong stands
on issues by the rabbi would cause divisions within the membership.
What the congregation apparently wants is a rabbi who will be more
forcefully ideological but who will support the mutually exclusive posi-

tions found within the body. During the interviews ambiguity over the ideal rabbi's style of leadership also surfaced. Some members said the former rabbi passed back to the congregation too many questions of observance and philosophy, yet they admitted that had he made unilateral decisions, he would have created antagonisms.

The social activities are organized primarily around the Jewish holidays and festivals and the rites of passage. There is an active temple sisterhood and a men's organization. A book club is fairly active.

The building of the addition onto the original structure has consumed considerable time and energy in recent years. Now that the project is complete the leaders seem happy with their programs, their physical plant, and the outlook for the future. No financial problems loom on the horizon. Someday the congregation will be faced with the problem of an aging membership—but not now.

Presence in the World

The River Plain Jewish Congregation knows that beyond its door—and the woods surrounding the temple—is a world of which it is part, and a sense of presence in that world is basic to its self-definition and mission in at least four respects.

First, the synagogue is part of the family of Jewish congregations in the metropolitan area. It participates in the activities of the Jewish Community Center and the Jewish Federation. Members take part in the Israel Walk-a-thon, a fund-raising event for the State of Israel. They support and promote the United Jewish Appeal. These involvements identify the congregation with the larger Jewish community; indeed, the establishment of both internal and external ties to that larger community was a founding and continuing motivation for the congregation. A testimony is made to all who will hear and see: "We are here; we are Jews, too. We are one."

Second, the congregation identifies itself as part of the inclusive religious community in East Town and the surrounding area. It remembers with appreciation the assistance provided by Christians in its formative years. For five years it met in space made available by the First Church of Christ, East Town, and when the First Church meetinghouse was heavily damaged by fire, in 1967, members of River Plain Jewish contributed to its restoration. The synagogue donated a new pulpit Bible used in the rededication of the Protestant sanctuary in 1967. Christians are welcome at services and the synagogue takes part in reciprocal educational programs with churches. The rabbi is visible and active in area religious and public life.

Third, River Plain Jewish understands that it is part of the social fabric of the area as a whole. Its leaders sense the congregation's opportunity and obligation to educate the broader community on the history and meaning of Judaism. If joining and supporting the synagogue are acts of consciousness, it follows that informing the population as a whole on the values of Judaism is part of the congregation's goal.

Fourth, the synagogue evidences a type of presence that is difficult to define because it is seldom articulated. This pertains to the congregation as a buffer between Jews and the non-Jewish community and as an advocate on behalf of Jews. Although relationships between the synagogue and local Christian churches have been quite good, Western history and culture reeks with Christian hostility and brutality against Jews. A sense of uneasiness based on centuries of persecution is hard to eradicate. Like minority religious and ethnic communities elsewhere in the United States, the River Plain congregation bespeaks an urge for a solid religious organization headed by a strong leader. This seems to lend security in a largely Christian environment.

A drive toward security can be detected in the members' concern to educate themselves, their children, and the community at large in the meaning of Judaism. Education, in short, emerges as a defensive and offensive tool against anti-Semitism: The better educated a Jew is, the better able he or she is to counter anti-Jewish sentiment; the better educated Christians are about Judaism, the less likely they are to be anti-Semitic.

No one who is affiliated with the synagogue spoke of overt anti-Semitism in East Town. However, members do cite incidents that make them wonder about subtle, beneath-the-surface resentment, if only because people have not made conscious attempts to free their minds of religious bigotry. To overcome vestiges of prejudice that could flare into open anti-Semitism is part of the synagogue's mission. "You run into individuals who are not aware," said a member of the Board of Directors.

Synagogue leaders are not sure whether problems encountered by Jews in community affairs are the result of anti-Semitism or of ignorance; for example, conflicts over the public school calendar and Jewish holidays, and the decision of a public camp to become a "Bible school" in order to circumvent insurance problems. Jews had been active in starting the camp and the change of emphasis stung, was seen as perhaps anti-Semitic. The synagogue—by its very existence—offers protection against present or future discrimination. As one member said, "an important reason for the existence of the synagogue, and the reason I am active, is to advocate for the Jewish community in cases of overt and covert anti-Semitism."

Anti-Semitism is not, however, a major topic of conversation within the life of the congregation. The term itself seems to be avoided, at least in talking with non-Jews, almost as though to speak it would invoke the reality. Synagogue leaders were not pleased with a local newspaper article on the temple that dealt at length with anti-Semitism. The topic raises discomforting questions of "difference." Anti-Semitism, or the fear of it, is an issue with the people of the River Plain temple, but they would like to deal with it quietly.

In addition to the four types of presence just discussed, the synagogue is also active in response to human need and emergencies. Typical is the aid provided to tornado victims when devastating winds struck a nearby town. The synagogue organized a team from East Town to take direct aid and worked with the Red Cross in other relief measures. River Plain has been in the forefront of local efforts to resettle refugees from Southeast Asia and takes an especially active part in efforts to counteract racism. A cross burning at the home of a black family was decried by the synagogue, which, in the wake of the incident, launched a letter-writing campaign against such atrocities and stepped up its antiracism program in the Hebrew School.

Generally, the synagogue does not—as an organization—become directly involved in political issues. Reasons cited or implied are twofold: (1) political stands, especially when controversial, might make the congregation vulnerable; and (2) to identify with a particular side in a political debate would divide the congregation. Members of the synagogue who function politically do so as individuals.

The amount of attention public issues should command within the internal life of the congregation is a matter of disagreement. Some members would like a greater emphasis on social questions in the educational program. As stated earlier, the rabbi was sometimes criticized for not saying more in sermons about social concerns. But when the rabbi did identify a group of issues he wanted the synagogue to address, he found himself in relative isolation (issues he proposed included human values, drugs in the schools, and alcohol abuse). Congregational leaders tend to think such issues should be handled by other organizations or addressed through interreligious channels (such as the ministerial association). The congregation, according to the rabbi, was more interested in taxes, land development, schools, and recreational facilities, matters that he thought were not within the religious scope.

An attempt to organize a social action committee failed. The committee was to identify those broader social issues that might merit the attention or efforts of the congregation. The task of determining the issues became divisive and the committee disbanded.

The lack of a social platform is somewhat out of step with the tenets of Reform Judaism, which historically has stressed social justice as a prophetic aspect of the faith. However, the Reform movement in America has grown to considerable affluence and has encountered difficulties in translating its identification with the downtrodden into practice. River Plain Jewish Congregation has the same problem.

In summary, the congregation is conscious of the importance of its presence in the community. It serves members as a locus of Jewish identity in a largely Christian environment; as a source of education in Judaism for members and the community; as a source of comfort—a buffer—for a minority; as a forum for the discussion of social concerns; and as a locus of action in cases of human need. The synagogue participates in the larger religious community but is hesitant as an organized entity to become actively and publicly involved in political and social issues.

The overriding concern for presence is probably that of Jewish existence—there; definitely there, but like its temple in the woods, peacefully protected.

CARMEL BAPTIST CHURCH

TWO LONG-TIME MEMBERS of Carmel Baptist Church reflected on their church's involvement in the civil rights movement of the 1960s:

> Even then [the 1960s] there was not too much church involvement in it [the civil rights movement]. It was not that the congregation wasn't interested. It was hard for us to get involved too closely, though, because a lot of us were seen as outsiders from the suburbs even though our church was here on the main street. We were never told outright that we weren't needed, but people in the neighborhood made it clear that they didn't want us to tell them what to do with their lives. So most of our activities were church-related, and building on that, whatever personal persuasion we could have on those with whom we worked and knew.

> I tried to find ways on a more intellectual level to work with it, and therefore was never very successful with many of the organizations that were formed at that time. I just could not think the way they thought, and since I couldn't think the way they thought, as far as they were concerned, I was not of too much value. But I think in my own way I did just as much or more. Many of us, each in our own way, had a great deal of, and an important, influence on those whites with which we were associated. But you didn't find us out parading about.

Historical Factors

Carmel Baptist Church is the oldest black church in Hartford. Its beginnings can be traced to migrants from Essex County, Virginia, who, according to the church's history, "finding themselves in a new place, sought comfort and divine guidance in meeting together for the worship of God." Initially, they met in members' homes. In 1871 they began meeting in a boxcar in downtown Hartford. Even then several members lived in the suburbs. The historian continues: "Swinging their lanterns in the night, many of the members of this little church walked miles from their homes as far away as Wethersfield."

Despite a controversy just before the turn of the century that resulted in half the members splitting off to found their own church, Carmel Baptist's continuing growth led to a succession of relocations to ever larger facilities. The present building on the North End's major thoroughfare was purchased from an Episcopal congregation in the mid-1920s.

Carmel Baptist has always sought and been blessed with "pastors of stature." The pastorate of the Rev. Dr. Marvin C. Dixon is pointed to by members with particular pride. He was president of the New England Baptist Convention before coming to Carmel in January 1922, where he served until his death in 1953, at age eighty-six. The mark he left on both church and community is summarized in the tribute that was published at the time of Carmel's 100th anniversary:

> During his tenure in the pulpit the "old Patriarch," as Reverend Dixon came to be known, made his influence felt in the greater community in civic as well as in religious circles. He gave twenty-seven years of eminent leadership to the New England Baptist Convention. He worked unceasingly for the employment of Negro teachers in the Hartford School System and for Negro case-workers in the City Welfare Department. In 1943, while traveling on a train through Alabama, Dr. Dixon was set upon and cruelly beaten by two white men when he passed through a coach reserved for whites to join some friends. The assault left effects upon his health from which he never fully recovered. While the incident was widely reported in the press, he was unable to get a trial from the Department of Justice. Popular indignation at home and the resulting concern over the treatment of Negroes in Connecticut bore fruit in the passage of a law by the Connecticut General Assembly, effective June 29, 1943, creating an Inter-Racial Commission to compile facts concerning discrimination in employment, violations of civil liberties, and other related matters, and to make recommendations to the Government for the removal of injustices. One of the original members of the commission was the man whose experiences had inspired its creation—Reverend Dr. Dixon. In 1947 the Commission was charged with enforcement of the Fair Employment Practices Act which forbids discrimination by employers, labor organizations or employment agencies against any person because of his race, color, religious creed, national origin, or ancestry. Presently known as the Commission on Human Rights and Opportunities, this agency is a fitting memorial to a life spent in service to his God and his fellow men. As a leader in the civil rights movement Reverend Dixon was a driving force behind the local branch of the National Association For the Advancement of Colored People and, during his tenure, Carmel purchased a life membership in this organization. . . .

*Reverend Dr. Dixon's death, which was widely mourned, sym-
bolized the end of an era for, due to the length of his pastorate—31
years—he was the only pastor whom many members of Carmel had
known.*

After the Reverend Dr. Dixon's death, Carmel called "a minister of
youth, intelligence, ambition and vision." He was a graduate of Yale
University and Yale Divinity School and had served three years as an
education specialist and assistant chaplain in the armed forces. He is
remembered as a "scholarly and dynamic preacher." He maintained Carmel's strong ties to the community through service on the boards of
numerous civic organizations. He professionalized Carmel's music program. He began "the custom" of honoring black high school and college
graduates of the Greater Hartford area with a banquet. As recalled in the
church history, "at the first banquet, held in the Parish House, ninety
graduates were honored and presented with a silver dollar as a con-
gratulatory token. In subsequent years, a great increase in the number of
graduates necessitated limiting the number being honored to those who
were members of the church." This young man of intelligence and vision
served Carmel Baptist until 1959.

After two extended interims and one short pastorate, a period that was,
in the recollection of a member, "especially trying and during which the
continued existence of the church itself sometimes seemed at issue," the
current pastor was installed on June 26, 1966. As remembered on the fifth
anniversary of a pastorate that is now reaching into its eighteenth year:

*With the coming of the Reverend Mr. Henry, Carmel acquired a
minister with a rich educational and religious background. He is a
warm, friendly man who loves people and is loved in return by them.
He is particularly diligent in his ministry to the congregation—
visiting the sick, comforting the bereaved, and counseling those in
need of guidance. He is a man of courage willing to take an unpopular
position if he believes it to be the right one. He is a scholar, a lover of
good books both religious and secular. He is equally knowledgeable in
the ancient religious philosophical writings and the current fads in
sports, dress and customs. By his personal warmth and kindness he
was able to unite a church of diverse elements behind his leadership.
His ministry has truly been one of healing.*

The above statement, which also marked Carmel's 100th anniversary,
goes on to list almost a dozen civic and religious organizations with which
the Reverend Mr. Henry has been involved since coming to Hartford, as
well as several church improvements initiated under his leadership. It
then concludes with the following look to the future:

130

With God's help Carmel Baptist Church has gone from a box car to its present glorious structure. With God's help Carmel has grown from a handful of souls to a congregation of over five hundred. With God's help Carmel has weathered physical and emotional storms which threatened to destroy it. As it enters upon its second century of existence, it is the hope and prayer of all that, with God's continued help, Carmel will continue to progress both in its witness to the Christian Faith and in its service to mankind.

The Local Community

The membership with which Carmel engages its "second century" of ministry is almost entirely middle class, with most living in the suburbs. The community within which it ministers is decidedly different. In Hartford's North End signs of poverty and despair are everywhere.

The immediate vicinity around Carmel church has experienced four ethnic changes in the past sixty years. The first residents were mostly white Protestants, with a relatively large Catholic minority; only a few black families then lived in the area. Jews next came into the area, moving out as blacks from both the South and the West Indies began arriving in large numbers during and immediately after World War II. In the late 1960s, Hispanics began to replace the blacks.

Puerto Ricans now outnumber blacks, at least in the mile or so that separates Carmel from downtown Hartford. A nearby street mural, once bright but now chipped and faded, bears witness to the black pride that created it a decade or more ago. Today signs are as apt to be in Spanish as in English. The area is filled with abandoned buildings and substandard housing. Its aging public housing developments bear witness to unemployment and general neighborhood neglect. Hope that an influx of federal money would lead to a restoration of area housing has faded as those funds have dwindled, and the "gentrification" found in other sections of the city is nowhere in evidence.

The designation of Carmel's neighborhood as a federal "Enterprise Zone" offers, at best, a glimmer of economic hope for the future. But at least it is an appropriately directed hope; according to a local Salvation Army worker,

> *as bad as the area looks, housing is not the major problem. People in the North End say their major concern is jobs, not housing. People say, "The reason I don't have a house is I don't have a job; I don't have any money to pay for housing." Or, "The reason I don't want to go to school is because I can't afford clean clothes."*

"No one *wants* to move into the area," a long-time resident comments, "though many are forced to do it. And few willingly visit, except to ride or

131

drive through on the way to somewhere else." The main thoroughfare on which Carmel Baptist happens to be located is only a conduit, primarily carrying traffic into and out of downtown.

A search turns up a few pockets of physical improvement. Near Carmel Baptist two brick duplexes are being restored; a nearby side street has a row of well-tended single-family homes. But few stores or small businesses remain; there are no supermarkets, clothing stores, restaurants, or banks. For blocks around the church building there are no commercial establishments except a single corner grocery store. Looking out from the church, the view includes a graffiti-smeared housing project, a cemetery, a huge vacant lot, and boarded-up buildings. The city occasionally plants new trees and lays new sidewalks, tokens of improvement, as one community leader put it, "that do not change the fact that the area is one of Hartford's 'ghettos' and will be for a long time to come."

If anything offsets the bleakness it is the churches. Within two blocks of Carmel Baptist are eight more churches: three Baptist, two African Methodist Episcopal, one African Methodist Episcopal Zion, one United Church of Christ, and one Episcopal. Not far away are several storefront missions and a Catholic church.

Rather than seeing the concentration of churches as a cause of religious competition, Carmel's pastor applauds it. "This is a real advantage. Each church has resources for aiding our people." But he regretfully admits that many neighborhood people know little about any of the churches unless they happen to attend one of them.

On Sunday mornings the "high steeple" churches in the area are not patronized, in the main, by neighborhood residents. Ushers dressed in formal black suits and bow ties wait near curbs to welcome parishioners arriving by automobile. By 11:00 A.M. cars are triple-parked for blocks on both sides of the main street that Carmel shares with several other churches.

Except for a Salvation Army station that resembles a 1950s-style gymnasium, the church buildings in the two-block area around Carmel Baptist are all old and traditional, most built by congregations that have since moved elsewhere. The church buildings remain, however, the most attractive properties around. Carmel's building, in particular, stands out in its gray, stone Gothic.

Constructed by an Episcopal church, which now has a newer building around the corner, Carmel Baptist's sanctuary sits well back from the street, almost obscured to approaching traffic by a three-story tenement on one side and the old rectory—currently housing Carmel's offices—on the other. The sense of the sanctuary's distance from the main street is reinforced by the fact that the front of the building has no doors; entrance is through doors off the side driveway and the rear parking lot. The building is quite impressive. The high arches of the sanctuary are freshly painted; the red carpet along the center aisle shows little sign of wear. Muted light through stained-glass windows falls on late-nineteenth-century mosaics. This is where the congregation worships together—from the physical evidence alone, clearly its highest priority.

Yet evidence of lost grandeur can be seen even here. Painters complain that a leaking roof makes it difficult to keep the fresh paint from flaking off. Broken sections of stained glass have been replaced with clear panes. Some of the stonework needs repair. And the restorers' touch seen in the sanctuary is not at all evident in the Sunday school wing extending into the rear parking lot: walls need paint, furniture is old, and carpeting is patchwork. As one worship attender commented, "for the suburban children who come here on Sundays with their parents, the Sunday school rooms stand in stark contrast with their bright, new public schools." Carmel Baptist is well aware of this and is currently in the middle of a fund-raising campaign to remodel its educational and office facilities.

Church offices and the pastor's study are located on the first floor of the old rectory (a new parsonage was purchased in the suburbs) standing next to the sanctuary; Sunday school and nursery rooms occupy the rest of the building. On entering through the front door, one comes first to the pastor's study; there is no buffer and little privacy. A secretary's office, work rooms, and a lounge are to the rear. The arrangement underscores the fact that at Carmel Baptist the pastor is very much at the center of all that goes on.

Membership

Carmel Baptist has slightly more than 500 members. All are black. About half are elderly, but a significant number are young adults and children. Most are middle class. Many families have two incomes. There is a sense of pride in upward mobility and educational achievement, although the congregation encompasses a broad range of educational backgrounds, including many who are "not very well educated at all." The membership includes a strong complement of professionals and "leaders in the community." There are several lawyers, a few doctors, many teachers, and a scattering of nurses and government workers. There are a few domestics and a few skilled craftsmen. But while discussing needed repairs on the church parking lot, one member bemoaned the fact that not one man in the congregation had carpentry or masonry skills.

The congregation's image in the community is clear: Carmel Baptist is a "higher class" church than most of the other area churches. And that, many members concede, is not entirely a blessing. "We're a status church; that's obvious," one noted with mixed feelings. Another adds, "At the same time that you are improving yourself, you are also alienating yourself from your roots and from your neighbors. And face it, they [the nonstatus people] are about the only kind of people Christ related to."

Even the pastor reluctantly acknowledges that "there are those who look on us as a cold, aloof church, where there is a certain pride in achievement." Several members also acknowledge that many in the community perceive Carmel as a cold and aloof church, but most of these members attribute this more to the lack of "vocalization" in worship than to any pervasive sense of pride.

Few residents of the immediate neighborhood are members of Carmel, a fact the pastor sees as an indictment against the church. "Sad to say," he states, "there is a cleavage between 'them' and 'us' along class lines." But he likes to think of neighborhood people as part of the church. "I think a church does have some obligations, yes, even geographically." Most members share the pastor's concern about Carmel's inability to involve more people from the local community and the class distinctions implicit in the situation. They also share the pastor's puzzlement over how to do anything about it and remain resigned to things as they are. As one member puts it, "we try to appeal to everyone, although it's up to them whether or not they come." Another notes: "We are a quiet, dignified congregation, while most of the people living in the church's area are drawn to the more emotional, vocal churches."

Of the 369 active families who are members of Carmel Baptist, more than 60 percent are commuters, many of whom have moved "up and out" of the core city; a few have lived in the suburbs all their lives. The commuter families are scattered throughout Hartford's suburbs, but there is some concentration to the north, where the pastor also lives.

Being a congregation of commuters presents a variety of problems. One member commented that as a result, "we really do not know one another very well. We go through the procedures of small talk with one another on Sunday morning, but the fact is that we're transient people, a lot of us." Several other members noted the negative effect of commuting on Sunday school attendance and involvement in the church's youth programs. And more than a few remarked about the obstacles it presents to dealing with the concrete social issues of Hartford—or of any specific community.

What keeps the commuters coming back into the city? "Their parents attended before them, and sometimes their grandparents," the pastor explains. "In times like these, people need roots; they come back to the place of their origin for strength." The members themselves, many of whom have looked and traveled about, are more singular in their assessment: "Carmel Baptist is unique. There is no other church like it in the area." In particular, they cite the scholarly and dignified nature of its worship, the quality of its music program, its emphasis on educational achievement, and its outstanding programs in the arts. These same qualities also appear to be the primary attraction of Carmel to new members. Membership has been growing recently, the pastor notes—"nothing

134

really outstanding, but we are holding our own." The new members are, by and large, young black professionals moving into the Hartford area.

Membership in Carmel Baptist Church is open to all Christian believers who have been baptized by immersion. Some come by transfer from other churches, some by a profession of Christian experience, and still others by restoration of faith. All who join, however, are expected to respond to the "invitation" given at the close of the Sunday sermon. By coming to the front, prospective members make their intentions public before God and the congregation.

All new members are expected to attend classes, and special instruction is required for those who have never been baptized. The sessions cover the history and mission of the congregation, as well as Baptist beliefs and history. The text on the Baptist tradition is *The New Life: A Baptist Perspective,* published by the American Baptist Churches. Illustrations in the edition used at Carmel show only white people enjoying "the new life." The pastor regrets that he has never had time to prepare his own study materials on Baptist beliefs and history. "After all," he notes, "the budget allows for only one minister."

Expectations for membership are explained to new members, who receive a "check-up chart" on which they are asked to keep a daily record of prayer and Bible reading, attendance at both Sunday school and worship, tithing, and occasions of having "witnessed for Christ."

Members new and old review the expectations of membership by repeating in unison a "church covenant" during most communion services. The lengthy covenant, read with considerable conviction by the congregation, includes promises to attend worship, to provide financial support, to practice private and family devotions, to abstain from alcoholic beverages, and to join another church if they should move away from Carmel. The covenant, according to the pastor, is "pretty standard for our Baptist churches" and calls members "to witness in all areas of life" and "to become part of an area of service in the church."

The extent to which members live up to the promises is difficult to ascertain, although the pastor admits "that commitment, involvement, and discipline are not as strong or deep as they might be or perhaps once were." Yet membership is not taken lightly. New members who miss worship are telephoned by the church secretary. Members who do not attend or contact the church for two years are placed on an inactive list and then dropped from membership if they do not respond to the invitation of a deacon to resume active participation.

Most new members, said the secretary, "are good members and we keep up with them. They are usually here to stay." New members also fill out forms that help the church know what each can and wants to do within the life of the congregation.

135

Membership cards are given only to "certified supporting members," and financial support is stressed in the church newsletter and bulletin and in persuasive appeals before the offerings. People who tithe are singled out regularly for special recognition; they bring forth the tithe before the offering is collected, making them visible models for others.

Members apparently give generously. A recent year's annual budget of $106,082 was 23 percent higher than that of the previous year, and this does not include the many special offerings given to visiting speakers. As one member put it, "most of our members are busy people, so they are not so able to give of their time. But when they see a need, they dig down into their pockets to help, and it's really surprising, sometimes, how much they give."

Theology and Beliefs

According to its pastor, Carmel Baptist Church exists for two reasons:

> First, we exist to have Christ become Lord in the life of everyone, for them to be an exemplification of his teachings—especially the Sermon on the Mount—throughout the home, the school, the business, the community, and the world. The black church must also exist, second-arily, to be an institution, an arena of life that deals with the totality of black concerns in America.

In his 1981 annual report the pastor stated more succinctly that the church is "in the business of leading people to Jesus Christ. He alone can save."

There is a creative tension implicit in the pastor's theology that he believes is endemic to the black church experience. It is the wedding of an evangelical and otherworldly fervor with a strong social concern. "No matter how conservative the theology," he comments,

> there has always been that social thrust. It's part of its history. You have got to remember that when the black church came into being during slavery and shortly after slavery, it came as a protest move-ment; and it has continued as the arena of almost complete living for its members. Even today black churches are the one institution that blacks feel they hold free and unencumbered from white domination. And for that reason, it perhaps means considerably more to the people than appears on the surface.

Pastor Henry's theology is hardly fundamentalistic, however. He is as apt to quote from Tillich or Augustine as he is to quote from the Bible, and he is constant in seeing ministry in holistic terms. "We must be a part of all that has to do with making life more abundant—better and more whole, particularly for our people. I think a complete ministry has a personal aspect and certainly a social outlook. If it begins with the individual, it begins. If it ends with the individual, it ends."

That the pastor may be overstating the uniqueness of the black church experience for at least some members of Carmel Baptist is suggested in the following comments from two laity:

> While it is certainly true historically, and even for many blacks today, that the church is the single most important institution in their lives, this is no longer the case for most Carmel Baptist people. Our mobility, both geographic and socioeconomic, means that even timewise, much less from the perspective of white domination, the church is just not the dominant social institution it once may have been.
>
> Members in the church are often in management and supervisory positions where they are dominant over whites. Therefore, the sense of the church as a place to be free from white domination is just not the same in our personal experience.

That the divergence of experiences encompassed in Carmel's membership may also have theological implications is suggested in the following comments, the first from a deacon, the second from an educator who has traveled around the world:

> If you ask fifteen different people what the church believes, you are likely to get fifteen very different answers.
>
> I used to be a science teacher and sometimes have had real problems bringing some of these things together with religion. I think I have been able to make some sort of sense out of it. But I wrestle with it a lot and am still working on it. I have sort of formulated some principles that I just try to live by, but as I formulated them I didn't think, well, in the second chapter of Genesis, verse so and so, it says such and such. In fact, my whole philosophy goes back to one statement: Do unto others as you would have them do unto you. I don't even know for sure where you would find it in the Bible.

And so it would seem that the theological tension between Carmel's evangelical and activist theological heritage is confounded by the tendency, particularly among its more educated members, to construct and articulate their own personal set of beliefs.

Organization and Program

Authority in Carmel Baptist is vested theoretically in the congregation. As its primer on church polity states, "each Baptist church controls its own business and ministry as the members decide." Yet, according to the pastor, "in practice we become presbyterial. Joint boards are the primary decision-making bodies of the church." Deacons and trustees "wrestle with business and spiritual decisions" and their recommendations are "almost ninety percent affirmed."

Disagreements do arise and are often settled by votes in quarterly meetings of the congregation. For example, divergent points of view arose over a proposed lottery for raising money. A vocal group, including the pastor, opposed the scheme that had the support of some lay leaders. The pastor opted for tithing and other more traditional forms of stewardship. The anti-lottery forces prevailed in a congregational meeting.

The Reverend Mr. Henry is skillful in dealing with the political realities that exist in any church. He is described by members as having a congenial, even jovial, style; as being direct without forcing himself or his views on the people; as knowing when to take a firm position and when to compromise, although a few members think he is too willing to "circumvent controversy." One member attributes his authority in part to an ability to deal with controversy while preserving members' freedom to disagree and to draw their own conclusions. "One of the reasons he is so popular," she notes, "is just because he does bring social and political issues into his sermons and keeps them in the forefront. But he seldom directly says you should do this or not do that; he lets you know in a more round-about fashion."

The pastor is admired and respected, is described as "gracious" and "kind," and has endeared himself to the people. In return, he is given broad authority, a fact reflected in his call to Carmel's pulpit for life (unless three fourths of the members vote him out). He is an ex officio member of every organization of the congregation and chairs the church's Executive Committee.

Sunday morning at Carmel is a mixture of the formal and informal, the scholarly and the revivalistic in worship. A devotional service, led by a deacon, takes place in the sanctuary before the 11:00 A.M. worship. The atmosphere is informal; the style, personal. Testimonies are offered and songs are sung, songs affirming the grace of God in lifting one "out of the miry clay" or declaring, "If anybody asks you who I am, say I'm a child of God."

At the 11:00 A.M. service the style shifts. Worshipers are met at the door by formally attired ushers, who move with smooth, almost military, precision, obviously taking pride in their task. Ushers make no small talk as they escort people to seats; all they extend is a warm smile. Strangers are not welcomed verbally at the door; rather, they are recognized individually during the service. The close of the service is time for conversation and many extend hands of welcome.

The 11:00 A.M. service is a mix of "typical middle-class New England Baptist and typical black." The parts of the service—hymns, readings, sermon, lessons, and the covenant—follow standard Baptist practice. The

138

amount of music and the colorful robes of the clergy bespeak the black heritage.

Sermons combine contemporary illustrations, scholarly references, social concern, and evangelical zeal. There is always a call to make a specific decision to follow Christ. For the most part, the chorus of amens characteristic of black worship is low, almost perfunctory. "There is little vocalization." Only a few elderly members occasionally call out in dialogue with the preacher.

A typical Sunday morning service lasts about an hour and a half, two hours when holy communion is celebrated. The pastor is not concerned about the length so long as there is "progression." The standard practice is to allot five to fifteen minutes to a member, a visitor, or an invited guest to bring before the congregation a special concern. Communion, which is open to all believers—including children—is highly formal, even "high church." White gloves on the hands of clergy and deacons keep the trays from being touched directly, and the containers are never put into the hands of the worshipers.

The preaching of the Word is clearly the central activity of the congregation. As the pastor notes with a smile, "white folks arrive no more than five minutes late for church. But black folks are what we call a 'waiting congregation.' They place such emphasis on the Word that it's enough if they arrive in time for the sermon." Carmel, nevertheless, also places considerable emphasis on Christian education for both children and adults, although the latter is more limited than the pastor would like because of the demands on his time. The Sunday school proper is only for children and youth; it stresses biblical teachings, black history, and social awareness and meets at the same time as worship. The students begin the morning in the sanctuary and are excused to classes after a children's sermon. Attendance averages about sixty persons, which is "not very good" in the estimation shared by most church leaders, perhaps a reflection of displeasure with the facilities or with the time, or a result of the commuting nature of the congregation.

Despite low enrollment the Sunday school and youth program feature many special activities, including observation of Black History Month, a Christmas pageant, vacation Bible school, programs on "political awareness" and "spiritual development," and even a trip to Walt Disney World. On the second Sunday of each month young people conduct the 11:00 A.M. worship, and during the month of February they present a "black nugget" (a piece of black history or statement on a black issue) at each service. There are also several youth choirs and the annual banquet honoring high school and college graduates. Implicit in all the activities is a stress on leadership development, as adult members seek to give back to a new generation of young people one of the most valued gifts they themselves received from the church. One member recalls:

The young people's services I went to were tremendous. They gave you so much opportunity to develop leadership. Much of the training I received was right there; it not only developed my potential, but also gave me a chance to demonstrate it. It has helped all through the rest of my life, one thing building on another. An awful lot of the leadership ability I have been called upon to use really grew from seeds that were sown back there in those meetings at the church.

Other activities of the congregation are varied, suggested in the listing from the church newsletter:

Weekly: *Rehearsals for five choirs or chorus, midweek prayer and Bible study, and Sunday school*

Monthly: *Missionary Society, Flower Club, Church Aid Society, Senior Usher Board, Hospitality Club (a men's study group), Baptist Youth Fellowship, Pastor's Aid Society, Board of Deacons, Joint Board of Deacons and Trustees*

Carmel Baptist also has various auxiliaries, a couples discussion club, a fine arts committee responsible for an extensive series of programs, a building committee, and a newly formed committee to oversee outreach programs. As is typical of black churches, Carmel's members—particularly the deacons—also spend considerable time visiting other churches.

Carmel holds one revival a year in its own facilities. It cosponsors another through the Hartford Ministerial Alliance, and members participate freely in the revivals held in other area churches. Carmel's revival runs Sunday evening through Friday night. Its main thrust, according to the pastor, "is to strengthen the faith of those already in the church and to offer an invitation of acceptance of Christ to those not in the church." As one deacon noted, "the revivals draw people from the community—from other churches, but not too many unchurched. We sometimes have problems getting enough from our own church." Agreeing that the revivals draw few, if any, nonmembers, the pastor also added, "But those not in the church are not coming to the church for anything; you have to go to them, you have to get some sort of an outreach ministry." Despite the social distance, Carmel does try to reach out to the community, but little, if any, of this is evangelistic. For example, no door-to-door canvassing has been done for years.

Carmel's Public Presence

Whether preached in sermons, taught in classes, read responsively, or printed in publications, the needs of the community are brought before the members of Carmel Baptist Church regularly. This is done "primarily through the professional ministry," note several laity, "but not exclusively so." "To alert the membership to what is actually happening in the community—that's the first step," a member observed, "and then to bring in experts who will help us learn how to deal with them. It's an educational process that has to begin in the congregation." Although some would prefer that spiritual needs be addressed first, there is a general recognition that "you can't bring a man to God if he has a hungry stomach."

How does Carmel respond? If it begins with the pastor, to paraphrase one of his favorite expressions, does it end there too? The pastor candidly admits that a great deal of the congregation's social outreach is really "inreach," directed to the needs of the members. "That may sound selfish," he said, but it is "realistic and necessary." Benevolences are needed to help the members themselves: "scholarship aid to our young people or travel money or other support for those who need it." It is the same sentiment the pastor expresses in describing his ministerial priorities. After listing more than a dozen of his involvements with the larger community, such as Urban League and Human Rights Commission, he paused and then continued: "Then again I have to remember that I am called as a pastor. That doesn't mean I am not expected to be involved in the community. But my primary thrust must be in terms of meeting the needs, the multitude of needs, within the church. You have to visit, you have to take time to study, et cetera."

"Calling ourselves Christians and being Christians—there's a great gulf between them," the pastor said.

A woman on the street who does not belong to Carmel put it more bluntly: "The minister there gets up in the pulpit and speaks about the neighborhood, but speaking about it and dealing with it are different."

Carmel's deacons hold a different view of their actual outreach efforts. Although acknowledging that they could and probably should be doing more, they asserted that Carmel is "the most liberal church" in the area in what it does for people. They cite a food bank, a fuel fund, and a voter-registration program as examples. Furthermore, they noted that individuals who are members work for community betterment through such organizations as the NAACP, the Urban League, Operation PUSH, and the Community Renewal Team (a municipal agency), and that many of these involvements were directly traceable to the influence of the church. The chairman of the Board of Deacons, for example, at the pastor's urging, has become involved in developing plans for a federally designated Enterprise Zone in the North End. Another member, who declined a church assignment because he was on a committee in his suburban town nevertheless said, "I felt this was an example of carrying my actions from the church to the community and carrying my Christian commitment along with me." Still another described his post as chairman of a college board as "a ministry." He said, "I see it as a way of using my religion because I am trying to function in such a way that benefits come to the people."

Several members are indeed actively involved in social and justice causes, often in neighborhoods other than those around the church. But not all see this as directly tied to their involvement at Carmel. As one member noted in response to Carmel's possible influence on his involvement in suburban politics, "I never think of it directly, but it probably comes in through the back of my mind someplace, according to what I had been taught in childhood; it goes back to the home, and of course my family has been closely related to the church, this church."

Specific social service projects include:

- A *low-income housing project* sponsored jointly by Carmel and a white suburban church
- A *farmer's market,* where surplus produce is available free of charge to any who need it, including some Carmel members. The produce comes from growers who are members of a Congregational church in an outlying area. Carmel is the distribution point.
- A *fine arts series,* mainly concerts at which young artists in the region perform. Seen as "our most unique program" by the pastor, this series apparently has limited appeal but offers experience to youthful performers and a cultural opportunity for those who want to take advantage of it.

Carmel Church provides *space* to the Hartford NAACP and staff services for the Connecticut Myasthenia Gravis Foundation. Involvement with the foundation dates to the illness of a member. The staff services are real, if minimal. The church secretary takes calls for the foundation and maintains certain records.

In theory, Carmel's building is available to community groups; in practice, few calls for space seem to be received, possibly because the many churches in the area provide more than enough meeting rooms for organizations. But Carmel has responded positively to a small, Southern Baptist Hispanic congregation's request to use its facilities.

Recollections differ on how active Carmel Church was in the black struggle of past years. The church's historian does not think the congregation is as active today as it once was. Others (as noted in the case's introduction) do not remember the congregation as ever being that involved.

The pastor reflects over the past quarter century:

> In the sixties we were trying as churches and as individuals and as leaders to get the implementation of certain laws that worked—laws to provide opportunities and privileges for blacks. The next phase was economic. There was no sense in just being allowed to go into a

hotel to sleep if you couldn't pay for it. More recently, I think, it's been political, including forming coalitions with groups that agree with you and your goals.

The pastor sees his personal role in justice issues as being related to the forming of coalitions. He has been active in a broad range of organizations, including the Urban League and the Hartford Ministerial Alliance, and recently was elected president of the regional council of churches. He is perceived by many community leaders as an elder statesman of Hartford's black community.

Public demonstrations and marches are not the Reverend Mr. Henry's style. His absence from public demonstrations precipitated by the shooting of a black youth by suburban police, for example, stood in contrast with the high visibility of many black pastors. He did go to the housing project where the incident took place "to be supportive of the people." He also met with Hartford's chief of police and with representatives of the state attorney general's office. He preached about the shooting incident to his congregation and provided time during a service for the protest leader to address the congregation.

The behind-the-scenes role was typical of the Reverend Mr. Henry's public presence on issues involving the black community. "He is more the diplomat," notes one Carmel member, "visiting and calling on people of influence, not marching in the streets. Nor does he ask members to do that."

Recently, the pastor has been stressing his sense of the political nature of the current black agenda with the congregation. Although he "usually" does not engage in partisan politics, he does admit involvement in several recent political campaigns. "I did urge people to vote for Mayor Milner because his outlook on the welfare of people was much the same as ours," he said. "We encouraged him, sent him a mailgram celebrating his first anniversary as mayor. We also have gone to see him to pledge our support. But we want our people to understand that Milner is not 'the black mayor of Hartford' but 'the mayor of Hartford who happens to be black' and who is responsible to every citizen of Hartford."

Pressed on the "we" in his comment, the pastor conceded that it was he who thought of the mailgram and signed it. "On things of that sort the congregation leaves it to the leadership of the pastor; they have no problem with it."

But at least one member found a problem with it.

I'm glad our pastor meets with the police chief and goes to City Hall; that's part of his job. But that's not enough. A few people speaking for the institution—is that the church? The church should have some influence in the community, but the church is the whole congregation,

*not just the pastor or some other leader. When pertinent issues come
up the members themselves should get involved.*

But speaking specifically to the pastor's urgings in regard to the Milner
campaign, another member had a slightly different perception of the
congregation's response:

> *There was no organized involvement, but the information certainly
> came through the pulpit, and not just there through the pastor. And
> even though many of us live in the suburbs and therefore could not be
> actively involved, through friends and other contacts at work in the
> city I'm sure we had some impact on the importance of the matter.
> About the closest we came to an organized effort, however, was the
> voter-registration drive, which was set up in the parish house on
> Sunday mornings so that people could go right from worship to
> registration.*

Such a divergence of opinion about the effectiveness of a church's social
outreach is not surprising for a congregation that has chosen a strategy
oriented to service and education and, at best, individually oriented to
activism. Carmel Baptist has its share of activist members, to be sure.
These are the members that the pastor calls "yeast." They benefit society
and the church in broad, if quiet and indirect, ways; how much of it
reaches the ghetto outside Carmel's sanctuary, however, is difficult to
measure.

What of the future? The pastor's response is theological and social, local
and universal:

> *In the next ten years I would like to see the church lay great emphasis
> on the church members becoming New Beings in Jesus Christ. We
> need to reach out and change structures in our society creatively. We
> need to help bring about the kingdom of God. The church should
> concern itself with third world countries that are hungry. We need to
> address all contemporary issues from the Judeo-Christian perspec-
> tive. There needs to be much more training and Christian education
> than in previous years. Group training and work for mission must be
> stressed. If religion begins with the individual, it begins; if it ends
> with the individual, it ends.*

Parishioners respond with the phrase "an untapped potential." At the
same time they recognize that, as one put it, "it won't be easy to project
ourselves quite to the extent that we're going to have to."

CHAPTER 7

THE CONGREGATION
AS ACTIVIST

In the discussion of the four mission orientations in chapter 2 it was noted that activist congregations are the most likely to bring public issues and controversies directly into the worship and program life of the church or synagogue. Civic congregations also give attention to public concerns, but as we have seen, they generally do so in the form of education and service programs; there is hesitancy to involve the congregation corporately in what appear to some members to be "political" issues.

Congregations whose primary mission orientation is activist are more likely to blur the line between education/service and political action. They are willing to risk criticism from members and neighbors in the interest of social and economic justice and see the pursuit of justice as an integral part of their ministry.

The two activist cases in this chapter come from Hartford itself. Downtown Baptist Church is in the center of the city; its "neighbors" include department stores, major insurance companies, and city, state, and federal office buildings. The residential character of its neighborhood is varied and is undergoing significant changes as young white professionals discover the attractions of downtown living. Downtown Baptist's staff and members are proud of their liberal activist reputation but remain sensitive to the pastoral needs of their mainly middle-class suburban members.

St. Margaret's Catholic Church is also located in the city, but in a poor, mainly Hispanic residential neighborhood. Of the cases in this book, this is the one in which liberationist theological themes are most evident. The church's pastor and many of its younger members have come to identify with Latin American liberation movements, although older members remain fairly traditional in their beliefs and understandings of the church's social role.

Although Downtown Baptist's activism is somewhat genteel, emphasizing its institutional leverage in dealings with real estate developers and city officials and its ecumenical strategies for social service and social action, St. Margaret's members are more likely to "take to the streets." It is difficult to imagine the members of Downtown Baptist Church protesting at a Republican fund-raising rally, as did St. Margaret's members in an incident discussed in the case.

Nonetheless, despite differences in cultural background, theological point of view, and style, both churches see themselves as actors on the city's political stage. They represent two good examples of the activist orientation as found in Greater Hartford.

DOWNTOWN BAPTIST CHURCH

ON A COLD, blustery February day in Hartford, looking out from the Federal Building at a signboard across the street, one was confronted with this message:

Downtown Baptist Church
THE NUCLEAR ARMS RACE IS INSANE! IT THREATENS OUR LIVES! WHAT CAN WE DO BESIDES PRAY?

At a City Council meeting three months later it became evident that the question put to the city was more than rhetorical, at least for the members of Downtown Baptist Church. At the meeting, with a large contingent of Downtown Baptist members in attendance, the mayor of Hartford proposed a resolution calling for a bilateral nuclear freeze between the United States and the Soviet Union. The resolution, initially brought before the mayor by the church's members, passed by a vote of six to three.

The excursion into the public arena was not unusual for Downtown Baptist Church. Concern for justice in international affairs and for the city's poor and disenfranchised is important to this church. As the signboard read on another day, "Woe unto you who lie on beds of ivory and forget the poor!"

"Justice," for Downtown Baptist, is not an abstract or complicated theological concept. It is "doing for others what you want for yourself." Neither is "justice" a theological "option." Rather, it is held to be the "pilgrimage" by means of which one "seeks and finds God."

Setting

Located on Main Street in the central business district of Hartford, Downtown Baptist is well situated for its ministry to the city. It stands across the street from the Federal Building and City Hall. Within a few blocks are major banks, department stores, and one of the nation's largest insurance companies. Two blocks west is the State Capitol.

People still live in the neighborhood around Downtown Baptist Church, but the residential character has changed dramatically over the years. In the nineteenth century, downtown was a choice neighborhood in which to live. Some of that era's great houses remain, reminders of the wealth once clustered a few blocks from the church. In those days the general area also included middle- and lower-income housing for various ethnic groups, particularly Italian and Polish, newly arrived in the United States.

In the 1920s, 1930s, and 1940s wealthier families moved to the suburbs. The neighborhood around Downtown Baptist gradually filled with poor people who were living several families per housing unit. Home ownership fell; currently nearly 90 percent of housing units are renter occupied. Population density rose as ethnic group followed ethnic group. The most recent arrivals have been mainly black and Hispanic, with Spanish-speaking people the most numerous since the mid-1970s and now constituting just less than half the neighborhood's population.

Now a new movement is very much in evidence, further complicating the housing situation and residential mix. "Gentrification" has come to the near South End of Hartford, as young professionals and former suburbanites have moved into the area and refurbished many of the older, Victorian-style homes. Some of this is as immediate to Downtown Baptist as across the street. Most of it, however, is a bit more distant, such as the 540-unit Congress Square project. As touted in the City Planning Commission's "State of the City" report for 1983, the project "was the first public redevelopment project to promote preservation of historic neighborhood character as opposed to demolition." The report also notes that the project "set a precedent by requiring that 20 percent of the units be made available for low- and moderate-income households and 10 percent be barrier-free units for persons with disabilities."

Congress Square notwithstanding, there is little evidence that the gentrification of the area will have much positive impact on the housing problems of Hartford's poor. Against this pessimistic assessment, Downtown Baptist hopes and believes that its strategic location and property holdings can provide leverage toward channeling at least some of the city's redevelopment energies more directly toward needs of the neighborhood's current residents. For example, the church has cooperated with a local developer in the restoration and renovation of a large nearby building. This building has been divided into luxury condominiums priced from $65,000 to $250,000. Downtown Baptist made the restoration possible by selling the developer part of a parking lot it owned directly behind the renewed structure. In doing so, however, the church extracted a pledge from the developer to convert a nearby apartment building to low-income housing. Downtown Baptist used part of the money it received from the sale of the parking lot to help initiate the low-income housing effort. Members cite this incident as an example of the creative use of economic clout on behalf of its poor neighbors.

The church's hope for the neighborhood is that, as one active member put it, "it will become economically and socially heterogeneous—rich, poor, and middle-class people—people all living in harmony. It is a faith commitment. No one knows whether such a community is really possible." The church is pledged to work toward the possibility, seeing its heavy commitment to housing as a key component and using other key pieces of real estate it owns in the area as further leverage toward that end.

History and Public Perception

Downtown Baptist was founded near the turn of the century and shortly thereafter merged with a smaller congregation. The present church building was built in the mid-1920s, constructed in such a manner that it could be converted to an opera house and office building if the congregation should fail. Despite hints of self-doubt, the congregation flourished. Its building proved an important asset. The new sanctuary, with a balcony, could seat 1,100 persons. The remainder of the new structure consisted of 120 rooms wrapped around the sanctuary in three stories. A full basement contained a massive kitchen, a fellowship hall, and a bowling alley, which remain in use today. The church once used the bowling alley for youth and community programs. Now the center of its youth recreation program is the basement gymnasium. Many of the original 120 upper-story rooms have since been combined by removing partitions and most are used to house a job-training program and a day-care center. Although expensive to maintain, the building and its space have been and continue to be a major resource put to work in outreach programs.

Downtown Baptist's period of greatest growth followed the construction of the building. Membership reached a peak of 1,400 in the late 1930s, with 1,800 in the Sunday school every week. The pastor of this era of growth retired in 1942, after a forty-year tenure. Since World War II, membership has dropped steadily, not unlike most of the mainline Protestant central-city churches in Hartford.

Although Downtown Baptist has always drawn a majority of its members from middle-class and blue-collar ranks, a few wealthy families have contributed to an endowment that now enables the much smaller congregation to offer an extensive ministry in its neighborhood and to civic and corporate structures. But relative to other old city churches, Downtown Baptist has never understood itself nor been known as a wealthy church.

The founding members of Downtown Baptist were Anglo-Saxons. The merger brought an influx of Italian families, some of which remain today. The largest ethnic minority at present, however, is composed of Jamaicans. Hartford experienced an influx of immigrants from the island of Jamaica in the 1940s and 1950s, and many persons of evangelical and Baptist backgrounds began attending the church. Of the church's current active membership of 350, some 200 are white, 50 Jamaican, 20 American-born black, and the rest Hispanic, and Indian and other Asians. The racial and ethnic mix is apparent on any Sunday morning and has a special appeal to the membership. As one white suburban member said, "I go to Downtown Baptist because it takes my children and me out of the homogeneous isolation we experience living in the suburbs." Or, as one black member put it, "this church lives out the Christian proclamation of the unity of all races and nations."

Several Jamaican members hold key positions of leadership, but most church officers are white. Almost all the whites and a substantial number of black members live in the suburbs. Downtown Baptist is keenly aware that it does not attract many new members from its immediate neighborhood, and some uncertainty is expressed about the future. Doubts are voiced that the new people buying the high-priced condominiums in the area will become churchgoers; the doubts are reinforced by the fact that none of the first wave of buyers can be seen among Downtown Baptist's worshiping congregation. Can the church devise programs that might capture the interest of the new urban gentry? So far, Downtown Baptist has resisted altering its priorities to mount a special appeal.

Nevertheless, Downtown Baptist's ministry is highly visible in the community, and the church works to make this presence more widely known. It is especially visible to several distinct groups, including the following:

• *Street people.* The numerous vagrants and transients in the area know Downtown Baptist as a place where they can go for direct assistance. The church has food and funds to give in emergency situations. The pastor in charge of outreach spends forty-five minutes to an hour each day handling requests for such material assistance.

• *Passersby.* Downtown Baptist uses various methods to contact people who regularly pass by its Main Street location but who might not otherwise notice the church. One is the signboard with its weekly message to the community. On Thanksgiving and before Easter the church also serves coffee and doughnuts to people waiting at a bus stop directly in front of the building. This gesture has made some new friends, but it has been greeted with suspicion by others. Many people refuse or insist on paying for the refreshments. But Downtown Baptist doubts that it is really effective in reaching the thousands of commuters who work in the banks, insurance offices, and other businesses in the area. The church is currently considering ways of becoming a stronger presence in the lives of the nine-to-five crowd. One proposal involves a program of art and music during the weekday noon hour.

• *Neighborhood people.* Area residents, especially poor families, are familiar with the church as a result of its advocacy on issues affecting their welfare. They feel free to approach the congregation for help in addressing community problems, and they know that the building is open to them. Many community groups use the building for meetings. Neighborhood youngsters are welcome in such church programs as Arts and Fellowship, which indeed was organized for them. The gymnasium is open to neighborhood youth on a regular basis. A day-care facility draws heavily from the surrounding area.

• *City Hall.* Downtown Baptist lobbies regularly at City Hall, so much so that one city official said publicly that he would "toss out" his pastor were he like Downtown Baptist's senior minister. The quip was taken as a compliment by the congregation. Public officials are frequent speakers at church forums.

Membership

True to its denominational heritage, Downtown Baptist understands membership as an adult "decision" for Christ followed by baptism by immersion. A few new members are received by transfer of church letter. All those who join, unless they come through the confirmation class, are required to take a six-week course of preparation, taught by the minister of social ministries. The course focuses on the structure and theology of the church and on its social ministry. The diaconate officially accepts or rejects new members, and those who are accepted (in recent memory, all who desired) are then presented to the congregation.

Expectations conveyed to members, new and old, include both participation and financial support. Each person who joins is visited by a lay delegation that presents a church directory and a pledge card, and every member is visited annually by a representative of the stewardship committee. In addition to financial support, pledge cards also seek to know how each member plans to invest himself or herself in ministry during the coming year. Pledges of time and talent are passed on to appropriate committees and are taken as seriously as financial commitments.

The involvement of members in the internal life of the congregation is high, especially for a "commuter" church. Average worship attendance is slightly more than 200. Sunday school and youth groups average a total weekly attendance just under fifty. Adult education averages about the same, and special series, such as during Lent, draw 100 or more. The monthly diaconate and committee meeting draws between forty-five and sixty. This meeting is held at the church, but because the membership is mostly suburban, study groups and women's organizations tend to meet in private homes. Relatively few night meetings take place downtown. Many members are hesitant to come into the area after dark and report that automobiles have been stolen from the parking lot. Guard service is now provided whenever night meetings are held and also on Sunday mornings.

A continuing question for Downtown Baptist is just how active the laity really are in the church's outreach ministries. Although the membership approves of the social action ministry, the staff appears to do most of the work. Laypeople sit on the outreach board and endorse plans; several also serve as volunteers in various programs, and a few are active in lobbying/advocacy efforts, particularly around the rights of the handicapped. But it is the dynamic, hard-driving staff that is most often out front. The church has asked itself whether this is (1) because the laity would rather sit back and let the professionals do it, (2) because time and distance do not permit it (many members are active in community concerns in their suburban communities), or (3) because the staff does not want or encourage help. The answer is unclear, but the situation is of concern to many members, in part because "it makes the programs dependent on such a small group."

A related concern shared by the staff and at least several lay members is that the church has not made a more significant impact in changing members' "life-styles." There is a feeling that long-term solutions to such issues as hunger, poverty, and housing in the city will necessitate changes in the personal and family life-styles of those who live in the suburbs, but as one concerned member confided, "while we've done a lot of 'educating' in this regard, I don't think we've had much effect, even on our own members."

Lay involvements in community ministry and in personal/social transformation are not the only membership concerns of Downtown Baptist. On a different level, the church is concerned that its congregation is aging. This is most evident in the Sunday school, which currently has only twenty to twenty-five children from kindergarten through eighth grade. Junior high youngsters number twelve to fifteen; senior highs, six to ten.

Young adults, single or married, are also few in number. The "graying" of its membership translates into a concern about membership numbers in the years ahead and, ultimately, survival. As previously noted, affluent newcomers to the neighborhood are not seen as likely potential members, and little headway has been made in attracting low-income residents into the full life of the church. Neighborhood youngsters participate in the church's Youth Center programs, but hopes that this would contribute indirectly to membership growth have not been realized.

In the late 1970s several area children began attending Sunday worship without their parents. They were rowdy and disruptive, creating considerable consternation among some members, notably those of Jamaican background. A staff member tried to work with the visitors, calling on their parents to invite them to church services and devising various approaches to discipline. Nothing worked; the disruption continued. An adult member became so upset that he called one of the black children a nigger. The child's mother responded by saying she could never attend a "racist" church. Only one neighborhood youth in recent memory has ever become genuinely active in the regular church life of the congregation.

Failure on this front has caused the congregation, in one member's words, to struggle with "the question of whether it is possible for people from lower socioeconomic backgrounds to be integrated into Downtown Baptist. The problem does not seem to be race, since we are already a multiracial congregation; the problem seems to be that of class."

Despite its community outreach, Downtown Baptist remains an aging, middle-class, suburban congregation worshiping in a building located in the inner city but having little spiritual or communal interaction with the people it seeks to serve. "An active ministry of outreach, advocacy, and service," a deacon concluded, "does not always mean that common worship and fellowship will follow."

Theological Self-understanding

Like many mainline Protestant congregations, Downtown Baptist encompasses a variety of theological currents. Most of the minority members tend to be theologically conservative—not biblical fundamentalists—but evangelical in their stress on religious experience and personal salvation. The present staff, most of the white majority, and a significant number of the black and Hispanic members can perhaps best be described, as one member put it, "as Social Gospel liberals emphasizing a commitment to justice, the expression of personal faith by active involvement in the world, as much, if not more, concern for structural change as for individual transformation." The Social Gospel orientation clearly dominates church life. It is evident in Sunday school and youth group curriculum. It undergirds the church's approach to adult education, which concentrates on pragmatic social issues rather than on abstract theological topics. It is the operative hermeneutic of most sermons, and it is the predominate "language" laity use to express their faith and faith struggles.

In a typical Sunday adult forum the discussion focused on the meaning of the morning's sermon as it applied to the church's recent efforts to engage City Hall around the issues of housing and peace. The sermon had taken Amos 5:4–15 as its text, with its themes of seeking the Lord to live and doing justice at the gate. As one lay participant observed in the discussion, "part of the fear of the holy is the call to pilgrimage. The pilgrimage is doing justice every day; taking the road 'less traveled by.' And the gate is the door of the powers and principalities." The discussion moved on to consider the similarities and differences between Amos at the gate of the house of Israel and Downtown Baptist at the door of City Hall. One difference noted was that Amos had the advantage of at least enough belief in the Lord among those in the house of Israel that Amos' invoking of the name of the Lord had some meaning and power. The members of Downtown Baptist did not feel that such a level of belief was evident in society today, and that, consequently, merely invoking the name of the Lord in the name of justice was no longer, if ever, an effective strategy toward change.

The senior pastor at Downtown Baptist is self-consciously liberal in theology. When asked about certain Christian doctrines, such as sin and salvation, he quickly interprets them in Tillichian language: sin as alienation and separation, salvation as wholeness and growth toward maturity. He acknowledges that traditional language might communicate more effectively with segments of the congregation, yet the liberal cast to his vocabulary and his message does not seem to cause tension within the congregation. A key factor in his seeming ability to bridge potentially divergent traditions is suggested in one member's observation that "although sermons always relate to contemporary and social issues, since the pastor is such a well-grounded biblical scholar, the issues are always sensitively and decidedly related to the biblical text."

Traditional Christian virtues (along with justice-oriented life-styles) are lifted up as ideals, to be sure. But matters of personal morality, discipline, and belief are left to the individual. There is no memory of sanctions ever being employed by clergy or the congregation for people who did not conform to church teachings or positions.

Downtown Baptist has had no aggressive program in evangelism of the kind that is aimed deliberately at increasing the membership. Although no congregation in the same situation could ignore the need for new members, the church seems to understand growth more in terms of quality than quantity, as, for example, is suggested in a recent annual report from its Executive Committee:

In December the Executive Committee voted to make church growth our theme for 1981. We mean by growth all of us bringing other people to Downtown Baptist to join the church of Jesus Christ by Baptism or church letter of transfer. But more importantly we mean by church growth, growth in one's spiritual life. This means becoming more like Jesus and doing ministry in the world.

Structure and Organization

The congregation itself is the final authoritative body at Downtown Baptist, but as in many Baptist churches, most decision making is delegated to an executive committee. An annual meeting of the congregation approves the budget and the general program and elects officers.

The Executive Committee is made up of the church moderator, the vice moderator, the clerk, the historian, the chairpersons of all boards and special committees, and the professional staff. This body serves in a review capacity more than it initiates program. Programs generally are proposed and carried out, with committee approval, by boards, which include churchmanship, worship and fellowship, Christian education, outreach, stewardship, and trustees. A staff person works with each board, and there is some feeling that most of the program ideas come from the staff. Yet there is no overt hostility toward the staff or impression that the laity are "run over" by the staff.

Procedures for reaching a decision on a new program or a change in congregational life are informal. Considerable data usually are gathered before formal discussion takes place. For example, when a change in the Sunday worship hour was being considered the Worship and Fellowship Committee polled members for several weeks to see how they felt about such a change before making a recommendation to the Executive Committee.

On another occasion a local group representing the Metropolitan Community Church (a predominantly homosexual congregation) requested space in the Downtown Baptist building. The request was circulated among all the boards to obtain reactions. Considerable opposition was expressed, particularly by black and Hispanic members. Consequently, the Executive Committee denied space to the gay congregation despite support voiced by the staff as well as many members. The risk to unity was considered too great.

Downtown Baptist has a senior pastor, who is responsible for worship, preaching, and pastoral care and nurture; an associate pastor, who is referred to as the minister of outreach; and an educational director. By church policy, all three staff members are charged to spend more than half their time in outreach ministry. In actuality, for the minister of outreach this can amount to as much as 80 percent. The education director works thirty hours a week for Downtown Baptist and ten hours a week for Center City Churches, an ecumenical coalition of downtown churches and partners through which much of Downtown Baptist's social service ministry is conducted.* A fourth full-time professional staff member is the pastor of a Spanish-speaking congregation that meets in the building. The staff is rounded out by a part-time organist-choir director, a part-time parish visitor, two office workers, and a substantial janitorial staff.

The Hispanic congregation, numbering about eighty members, is organized separately. Nevertheless, it does receive some financial support from Downtown Baptist, and its pastor is considered a full member of Downtown Baptist's staff. The Spanish-speaking church emerged largely through the efforts of the state Baptist association, whose executive initially proposed the idea, encouraged Downtown Baptist to act as host, and recruited a pastor from Puerto Rico for the congregation. It is the only mainline Protestant Hispanic congregation in a city with nearly 30,000 Hispanics but struggles for members because most Hartford Hispanics are Catholic, because many who are Protestant are more evangelical and charismatically oriented, and because of the transiency of many people in the Hispanic community.

The Spanish congregation once worshiped on Sunday afternoons but moved its service to 10:00 A.M. to coincide with the English-language worship service. It now uses a chapel next to the main sanctuary. The two congregations share a coffee hour and other social events. Relationships between the two groups are good, and they are working their way toward increased interaction.

In addition to the Hispanic congregation, a small Ukrainian Baptist church also uses space in the building but is not involved in the larger activities of the church.

The senior pastor, associate pastor, and director of education seem to have a good working relationship. They regard themselves as a creative, well-coordinated team and are perceived as such by the laity. The senior pastor has been at Downtown Baptist for six years; the associate, slightly less. The senior pastor's two closest colleagues say that he is occasionally "controlling," especially when his own anxiety level is high. This potential cause of tension, however, is discussed openly and levels of trust are high.

Both the senior minister and the associate are active within the denomination—the American Baptist Churches—at both the state and national levels. Downtown Baptist has always been strong in its financial support of the national denomination and state organization, last year contributing more than $25,000.

As noted earlier, Downtown Baptist is intimately involved in Center City Churches. The coalition came into existence fifteen years ago with

*See chapter 4 for further information on Center City Churches.

eight churches as members. Downtown Baptist's previous senior pastor played a key role in those beginnings. Center City Churches currently has ten member churches representing seven different denominations; has a budget of close to $600,000, much of that from federal grants; currently has eighteen full-time and thirty part-time staff; and has become known throughout the country as a model for the ecumenical possibilities of urban ministry. In the words of its director, "downtown Hartford is our parish, and we are comfortable working with and for and beside the residents and the institutions in the parish. We feel responsible for all ages, sizes, shapes, and incomes, with a special focus on the needs of the poor and disenfranchised."

One of the unique features of Center City Churches is the commitment by member churches to channel their own community involvements through the ecumenical coalition. This is not only an ideal toward future program initiatives but has also included the turning over of existing programs established by the various individual churches' own initiative, to Center City Churches. "It makes good sense," according to Center City's director,

> both from a supervisory standpoint and also because it frees the churches to do other kinds of things. But it's not just been giving the whole responsibility [for social ministries] over to Center City Churches so that they can get on doing "parish work." What we've found as things have grown, especially in the past few years, is that the individual churches are giving over not only program and cash, but also a considerable amount of staff time.

Much of Center City Churches' ministry is direct social service. It is direct service, however, as a staff member notes, "on the basis of responding to someone as a member of our family, our parish, as opposed to a we-they kind of thing." Primarily using facilities in the various member churches, Center City Churches' service programs include three different meals programs; classes for senior citizens seven days a week; tutoring, recreation, and summer job programs for youth; a drop-in center for street people; two overnight shelters; an adult job training program; and a recently begun counseling-referral program.

Center City Churches has also begun to be more intentional in dealing with structural issues underlying the more immediate needs it addresses in its social service programs. In the director's words:

> One of the things that I had to push for was that in the future as part of our either establishing new programs or recommitting ourselves on an annual basis to existing programs, advisory councils working with each of the programs also identify a systemic issue related to that direct service issue. We realized that we undermine our own best efforts if we don't do this, and we certainly do not contribute to the

long-term betterment of the people that we're serving on a daily basis. The idea has been well received. But it remains to be seen how well we work at it, because it will inevitably call into question our life-styles, our style and comfortableness with using political persuasion, and so forth.

Center City Churches focuses primarily on outreach ministries, but it does offer a few more traditional parish activities, such as study and spiritual growth retreats and special lenten series. Public worship, however, is "turf for the individual churches, the one exception being the annual ecumenical service."

Downtown Baptist is one of the most involved and committed members of Center City Churches. All its major social service ministries, many of which have a long history at Downtown Baptist, are now run under ecumenical auspices; in fact, laity and staff make little distinction between "their" and "our" programs. In addition to space for coalition programs, Downtown Baptist contributes considerable staff time and $15,000 annually to Center City Churches.

Despite its large budget and relatively small membership, Downtown Baptist is in a comfortable financial condition. Its annual budget is just under $350,000, of which $170,000 comes from endowment, $55,000 from pledges, and the remainder from rents and contributions for the use of building space and parking facilities. Some $62,000 is spent each year to operate and maintain the building, a dollar amount greater than the $45,000 given directly to outreach (including contributions to the American Baptist Churches), but the congregation feels strongly that its building is one of its major mission assets; as one member put it, it is "a house of God highly visible in and ministering to the heart of the city." When both direct and indirect contributions (staff time, building use, etc.) are considered, Downtown Baptist estimates that well over 60 percent of its budget goes toward outreach.

Downtown Baptist is well aware that its financial health is due to rather extraordinary circumstances. Its current comfortable position, however, is tempered by an awareness that as membership has decreased, so has pledge income (down from $65,000 in the mid-1960s), and that rising utility costs in particular have rapidly escalated the cost of maximizing the use of its building (it paid almost $20,000 for heat and water alone in one year). But at least for the present, where the money is going to come from appears to be less of a concern than how to be in mission to the city more effectively.

Program

Downtown Baptist is known for and has a long history of community-based social ministry, a ministry strongly supported by and identified with its current members. The positive lay attitude has been promoted, especially since the late 1970s, by a carefully developed balance between social outreach and the nurture of the congregation itself. Downtown Baptist would describe it as balance between "in-house" and "out-house" ministries. The in-house ministry includes pastoral care, counseling, visitation, and other programs addressing the needs of the membership. The senior pastor has primary responsibility for this and does most of the preaching, parish calling, and development of care and counseling groups. This contrasts with a previous senior pastor, who gave less attention to pastoral concerns and social involvement and action (at least as perceived by the lay leadership), failed to generate significant commitment, and was sometimes disruptive. In response, the in-house/out-house strategy was devised through lay initiative during the interim between senior pastors and served as the informing model during the search process. Division and alienation have not been common since the dual-focus pattern of ministry was introduced.

The 10:00 A.M. Sunday worship service is the major gathering of the membership at Downtown Baptist. The service is plainly Baptist (e.g., no vestments). Ritual, style, and tone are Baptist, although an attempt has been made to integrate the black Baptist religious experience, especially hymns, into the predominantly and historically white congregation. It is not uncommon for worship leaders, both lay and clergy, to alter masculine pronouns and references in reading scripture, creeds, and prayers, although there is no formal policy that this be done.

A full range of Christian education programming is offered. After Sunday worship and a short coffee hour are Sunday school for children, groups for youth, and an adult forum. Although sometimes the sermon is discussed in the adult forums, more typically they focus on a major social issue—local, regional, national, or international. Such consciousness-raising forums often include an invited public official. Recently, for example, these have included several members of Hartford's City Council, the lieutenant governor of Connecticut, members of Hartford's Board of Education, and several people who are nationally prominent in the peace movement. There are also several Bible study groups for adults meeting at various times throughout the week, one convening weekly to go over the next Sunday's scripture text with the senior minister. A half-dozen women's circles and other organizations combine study with fellowship and service projects.

Downtown Baptist has an active program of member visitation headed by the senior minister. Adapting an idea developed by a neighboring church, the pastor has trained two dozen laypeople to visit regularly. The church also has the usual variety of social gatherings, including an annual picnic.

Most of the social service ministry programs housed in Downtown

Baptist's building are now run under the auspices of Center City Churches. These include the Center for Youth and Community Resources, offering tutoring, counseling, and recreational services; a daycare center serving 100 children; the Church Academy, designed to both train and develop skills for women who are trying to enter the job market—usually thirty to fifty women are enrolled in each fifteen-week course; and a food pantry. In addition, a number of community groups use the building for meeting space.

Downtown Baptist has intentionally directed a major part of its mission toward issues that are troubling or affecting its community. It understands the major local issues to include housing, poverty, education, health care, and employment. Its programmatic efforts, through Center City Churches, speak to these needs on an immediate, individual basis, and as previous noted, Downtown Baptist is well known to city officials for its lobbying efforts on matters of public policy. Of the issues listed above, however, Downtown Baptist chose housing as its priority for the early 1980s. It intends to continue using its significant downtown property holdings as leverage toward increasing housing opportunities for low-income and working-class people. The associate pastor has also devoted a significant portion of his time to helping form a coalition of downtown churches to work together on the issue.

Conclusion

Downtown Baptist has six major assets making its strong social ministry possible:

1. A highly visible location in the heart of the city
2. A large building with usable and flexible space
3. Leverage over strategically located property
4. An endowment enabling a relatively small congregation to support a sizable budget
5. A creative staff of multiple talents and high commitment
6. A membership supportive of social action.

But for how long? Will the laity continue to back a ministry in which few are involved directly? Will membership continue to decline to the point that Downtown Baptist is left with a big building, a big endowment, and an activist staff but few worshipers? Is there a new constituency on the horizon? If so, will a new membership approve of such intense social involvement?

These questions are currently unanswerable. For the time being, the blend of in-house/out-house ministry is working well. And quite apart from its own programs, the church seems to be training its members for active Christian involvement in the world.

Is Downtown Baptist's social ministry effective? All indications point to "yes" in terms of direct service to people in need. The activities at the church building, the expenditure of funds, the cooperation with others trying to improve the human lot is impressive. There are notable gaps, to be sure. Staff and lay leadership, for example, bemoan the fact that they haven't been able to develop an overall strategy for linking the efforts the church undertakes for the welfare of the city with the heavy involvement of members in civic activities in their own suburban communities. The quality of life in Hartford is intimately connected to life in the suburbs and vice versa; Downtown Baptist appears as well situated as any church to make the city-suburb connection but has thus far been unable to do so—as have others. Related to this is the fact that Downtown Baptist's efforts in the city have been less effective in terms of changing the social, corporate, and governmental structures than in meeting immediate human needs. The church does not include in its membership the local power brokers, and its lobbying efforts notwithstanding, it is just beginning to learn how to influence them. With the housing priority, in particular, the congregation has edged in that direction—slightly.

St. Margaret's Roman Catholic Church

"President Reagan swept into Hartford for a three-hour visit Tuesday to pitch his policies to the centennial convention of the Knights of Columbus," the front-page story in *The Hartford Courant* proclaimed.[1] "He left as their echoing endorsement was still resounding through the Civic Center arena." The story continued:

> *It was vintage Ronald Reagan: patriotism, piety and old-fashioned values proclaimed before an enthusiastic audience.*
> *"The President told us what we wanted to hear," said Archbishop John F. Whealon of Hartford. "One point after another was what we believe in."*

But not all Catholics in Hartford shared their archbishop's assessment, and many, including members of St. Margaret's Church, were present at the convention to protest what they perceived to be Reagan's insensitivity to poverty and the threat of nuclear war.

St. Margaret's is a Hispanic parish located in the inner city of Hartford, where, in the words of its senior priest, "only the poorest of the poor live." "The Reagan policies are affecting our parishioners directly," a member commented, "for many are qualified to receive aid from the programs that his administration is reducing the most." The idea to participate in the Reagan protest originated with the staff and was announced at all Masses. Forty-five adults from the parish joined in. The group first attended the Tuesday morning Mass at the convention. After the Mass they joined more than 600 demonstrators outside the Civic Center, voicing their concerns and passing out leaflets. St. Margaret's members then returned to the convention arena for the President's speech, silently rising and walking out just as he began.

The Knights of Columbus incident is but one of many public demonstrations in which St. Margaret's leadership has involved its membership, symbolizing the worldly implications of its sacramental theology. As one member put it:

> *The Mass is the reenactment of the moment of Redemption. In every Mass, the Cross of Calvary is transplanted into every corner of the world, and humanity is taking sides, either sharing in that Redemption or rejecting it, by the way we live. We are not meant to sit and watch the Cross as something done and ended. What was done on Calvary avails for us only in the degree that we repeat it in our lives. All that has been paid and done and acted during Holy Mass is to be taken away with us, lived, practiced, and woven into all the circumstances and conditions of our daily lives.**

St. Margaret's current active membership of approximately 800 adults and children worship in an early-twentieth-century structure at the end of Samuel Street, surrounded by industrial buildings and dilapidated housing, some of which is slowly being remodeled through programs initiated by the church. Many of the tenements have Hispanic-owned stores on their ground floors. Many of the others are burned-out and boarded-up.

St. Margaret's complex of buildings is one of the few bright spots in the neighborhood. The white-brick sanctuary is relatively well maintained. Between two sets of front steps on a small lawn is a statue of the Virgin Mary. The rectory is behind the main building and nearby is a wooden youth center that is gaily decorated with peace-inspired murals. One mural is of a dove of peace. The most recent addition is of people holding hands in a field of flowers, inscribed with an antinuclear warning and incorporating a rainbow and a school, representing the good life. It was painted by the church's youth group under the guidance of an artist the group met at a peace rally.

St. Margaret's is officially designated as a "national parish," meaning that its ministry is not confined to a single geographic neighborhood; Catholics living anywhere can be registered there. This designation is not unusual for a Hispanic congregation; the city has five other Hispanic Catholic parishes.

The parish was organized in the 1890s by German Catholic immigrants

---

*Interviews were conducted both in English and Spanish. Translations were made by the case writers.

who felt uncomfortable in the then predominantly Irish and Italian churches. Completed in 1914, the building has warm-toned stained-glass windows imported from Germany that depict scenes from the life of Jesus. The original ornate altar of marble is seldom used any more, functionally replaced by a simpler altar at the end of the long nave. Side altars near the main altar are dedicated to the Holy Family and to the Sacred Heart of Jesus. A large crucifix hangs over the altar.

Until the end of World War II, St. Margaret's remained ethnically German. As blacks began to move into the community in the late 1940s, the German population relocated in new suburbs. Few of the blacks were Catholic, and many of the Germans continued to commute to St. Margaret's.

People of Spanish background began moving into the area in the early 1950s, and it was in 1956 that the church was designated a "national Hispanic parish." One Spanish Mass was introduced. By 1972 two Masses were being said in Spanish and two in English. In 1975 three Masses were in Spanish, one in English. The last English Mass was dropped in 1981, during a time when the parish temporarily had only one priest. The forty communicants—almost all Anglo—who attended the English service agreed that they could find churches in other communities.

Presently, three Masses—9:30 A.M., 11:00 A.M., and 1:00 P.M.—are said each Sunday. Attendance is best at 9:30 and 1:00. Daily Masses are no longer held on a regular basis, although the two current priests try to offer three weekday Masses at noon.

The Mass

Life at St. Margaret's, in the words of a deacon, "begins and ends with the Mass." Priests and parishioners share a common eucharistic theology. "Mass is the center of everything," the senior priest states emphatically.

> The eucharist is the living presence of Christ. In sharing that presence, the call is to go out to make that presence operational, living in the world. That going out wears us out, so the eucharist is both the beginning and the end: It draws us to it, pushes us out into the world, and then draws us back. It is an overflow of the Lord's presence. The Mass is part of the world and the world is part of the Lord.

Laity share a clear understanding that the Mass is the substance of life—personally, in the church, and in social interaction within the world. Typical lay comments include:

> The Mass is the most important part of my life. If we didn't go, we wouldn't be anybody.

The Mass dispels the shadows that can bring me sorrow; it gives me hope and I can smile.

It enables me to do whatever I am asked to do, or feel the need to do.

The Mass unites all people on a journey together.

It is a constant reminder of our obligation to fashion a society with Christian values.

Mass helped me see that in a nuclear war nobody gains, we all lose; instead of constructing a beautiful world, we destroy it. That was not the message of the cross.

Members of St. Margaret's are encouraged to develop an active prayer life in response to the Mass. A charismatic group exists within the parish. But under the influence of the priests' refusal to draw a distinction between the sacred and the secular, the group has made a conscious effort to keep its fellowship from becoming too introspective. Several members are involved in an active parish council and in the various social service programs of the church; several have participated in the church's public protests. As one active member of the group put it, "our prayer deepened and we deepened. We gained strength and confidence in ourselves and in what we could accomplish."

St. Margaret's Sunday Masses are warm and celebrative. Families sit together, and most communicants are members of extended families. No one is bothered when toddlers run about during the service. The singing has gusto. Music at St. Margaret's has the distinct flavor of that familiar to many from Puerto Rico, the home island of many members. Each regular Mass has the accompaniment of at least two guitars. On feast days there can be six guitars, drums, and a cuatro (double-string guitar).

Informal sermons deal with personal morality, domestic relations, Christian responsibility, and justice. According to the deacon, a Puerto Rican who often delivers the homily, St. Margaret's tries to encourage a response to God in the forms of "actions serving people."

The exchange of "the peace" in the Mass is a time of genuine fellowship, and visitors—both Spanish- and non-Spanish-speaking—are made to feel welcome. The people linger after the service. "I have come here for seven years because I feel at home," said one layman. "I like the feeling at the Mass and afterwards. I like to talk to my friends and socialize."

"There is an openness," said another layperson.

"The feeling of sharing with everyone as a family brings me here," said still another.

Reflecting on the role the parish plays in social action on behalf of Hispanics, the deacon said of his personal involvement, "I gain spiritual strength to be able to walk with my brothers in their shoes and help them get to the end of the road."

The Congregation

Those who participate in St. Margaret's seemingly do so because they want to, not because they feel social or traditional pressure. Communicants from the immediate community are numerous, and a significant number drive in from the suburbs and surrounding towns, some to maintain ties initially established when they formerly lived near St. Margaret's and others drawn to the parish's program and style. On a typical Sunday, attendance at the 9:30 A.M. Mass is just over 225; at 11:00 A.M., just under 100; and at 1:00 P.M., nearly 250. The priests believe that this is impressive in a state in which only 5 percent of the Hispanics are said to attend religious services regularly.

The senior priest, who is Anglo, would like to engage more Hispanics in the life of the parish, especially in the Masses, but he takes a positive view of those Spanish-speaking Catholics who rarely attend worship. "St. Margaret's is a family church," he says. "There is one part of the family that comes to church and shares in the liturgy every Sunday; and then there is the 'larger family.'" He is adamant in his belief that the non-churchgoers in the larger family have not abandoned the faith. He believes that most are deeply religious Catholics who are historically conditioned by a religious community, or "pueblo" (town).

The senior priest's positive attitude toward the religious participation of the larger family is not fully shared by all staff. Some think that the noninvolvement of Hispanics in organized Catholicism is a problem to be confronted more directly. They maintain that U.S. society is not conducive to spirituality in isolation from a religious community. U.S. cities are not "pueblos" of support. When Hispanics in the United States do not attend Mass and stay in touch with the faith community, they find few religious support mechanisms.

St. Margaret's assistant priest and its deacon are particularly sensitive to the erosion of faith that can take place in fast-moving, individualistic, and materialistic U.S. culture. Partially in response to this sensitivity, the assistant pastor, who is fairly new to the parish, has initiated a program of visitation to reach people in the larger family. The senior priest channels his pastoral perspective largely through his investment in St. Margaret's multidimensional program for young people. In his eyes, the mix of spirituality, activism, education, service, and recreation that is embodied in the program is one of the church's most important attempts to inculcate religious values in danger of being lost and to integrate the bicultural experience within which St. Margaret's youth find themselves.

A strong concern within this program is the preservation of Hispanic culture. As is true throughout the United States, many Hispanic teenagers in Hartford do not want to speak Spanish at home, a rebellion that many believe may have as much to do with "authority" as with language. St. Margaret's tries to address this issue through educational programs that emphasize the value and beauty of the Spanish language. The programs try to give the teenagers pride in the language of their parents and to motivate the parents to learn English. The philosophy is that increasing respect between traditional language and values and new language and values will build stronger bonds between the generations.

Integrating the youth's own bicultural experience is also held as an important goal in its own right. As the senior priest observes, "the kids are living right here, not in a barrio on the Island. We attempt to bring together the strengths of both Spanish and American cultures." The youth at St. Margaret's are also taught black history, both because of the many blacks in the immediate neighborhood and to further develop an appreciation for other cultures. "Our program," an adult member notes, "gives them [our youth] a richness that other kids don't know." St. Margaret's bridging of Spanish and English CYO (Catholic Youth Organization) activities initially brought protests from Hispanic traditionalists in other parishes. But acceptance has grown as St. Margaret's youth have proven their ability and comfort in moving freely between them.

Most of the adults at St. Margaret's are traditional, rather conservative Catholics on most issues, reflecting in large part their Island roots. They are more sanctuary oriented, for example, than are the youth and, with some exceptions, are more likely to think of the priests as "the boss" (a view they would like to change) rather than as friend or teacher.

Awareness of the Church in the Community

Almost everyone in the immediate neighborhood is aware of St. Margaret's. Many residents—especially "the poorest of the poor," who seldom attend Mass—avail themselves of parish social services, such as food, clothing, or help with housing, and most Hispanic youth in the area have been touched in some way by the parish's tutoring, counseling, and related youth programs.

But the parish is known not only for "being there" for people in need, but also for seeking out the needy who might have too much pride to request assistance. The latter, in particular, represents St. Margaret's efforts at visitation among the larger family.

Relatively little financial support for either religious or social programs is available from the immediate community, however, partly because the local residents are poor and partly because the local merchants do not seem to have a philanthropic inclination. Invitations extended to merchants to both participate in parish life and support it, for example, have largely gone unanswered. A letter requesting donations for Thanksgiving baskets that was sent to merchants brought only one check. At the same time the merchants maintain a high regard for the parish. More than one noted that "the church is respected by all." Another said, "It has done a lot to keep the kids in school."

"The summer program is very good; it keeps kids out of mischief," said still another.

Keeping "kids out of mischief" is a major concern in the neighborhood among virtually all adults. St. Margaret's is in an area in which street gangs are common, and some incidents have occurred that cause adults to be afraid to go out after dark. The priests downplay the danger. "Kids in gangs are kids," they say; they believe that much of the problem arises from a communications media that exploits gang-related incidents and from the unnecessary fear of adults. They do not think it is the church's job to try to break up the gangs; rather, they want to work with them as they might with other community groups.

A few gang members have taken part in church-related tutoring programs; some come to talk with the pastor when problems arise, but none is known to attend church. The parish staff does not fear the gangs. After one particularly troublesome incident that frightened neighborhood adults, the priests and deacon organized a group to walk the streets for two weeks. When nothing further happened during that period, normal going and coming was resumed.

St. Margaret's staff views the gang members as alienated, misunderstood youth for whom society—Anglo society—has too little tolerance. To decrease the alienation felt by most gang members, therefore, would imply changing the Anglo society.

St. Margaret's reputation extends far beyond the immediate neighborhood, and on this larger scale the views are somewhat mixed. The parish has done a remarkable job recruiting friends and supporters in the suburbs, in governmental agencies, and in major corporations, thanks in part to a now-proven track record.

At the same time the policy of encouraging St. Margaret's teenagers to take part in the English-speaking CYO was opposed in other Hispanic parishes more comfortable with the Spanish religious group, as noted earlier; and the question of St. Margaret's balance between spiritual formation and social activism is raised from time to time in the larger religious community in Hartford. A priest in another inner-city parish, for example, wonders how deeply a commitment to social action has penetrated the adult ranks at St. Margaret's.

Parish Structure and Administration

The parish staff administers day-to-day activities, but all major decisions are made with the advice of the Parish Council.

The staff (at the time of our study) consisted of two priests, a full-time deacon, a part-time deacon who handles accounts, a religious education coordinator, an assistant in education, and two full-time tutoring program coordinators. Seminary interns sometimes complement the staff. St. Margaret's has no parochial school.

Teamwork is the key word in the relationship between the senior priest, the other staff members, and the Parish Council. All have an awareness that they must work together.

The senior priest was on the staff when St. Margaret's was in the process of becoming a thoroughly Hispanic parish, and he, along with a colleague who has since left, is largely responsible for the social consciousness and the youth focus of the parish. Laypeople use such terms as fighter, patriarch, and boss to describe him. He clearly sets the tone of the parish and is perceived by the people, to quote one, as "demonstrating a deep preoccupation about all aspects of life." He is given special credit for the youth program. To the extent that there are some misgivings, they are that his heavy involvement with the youth and his extensive non-parish commitments afford too little time for pastoral work among adults.

St. Margaret's senior priest also commands considerable respect among the other clergy of the archdiocese and greater religious community. As one fellow priest describes him, he is a man of integrity who "does not accept any separation between the secular and the sacred." He is also highly regarded by most community leaders, even those who may disagree with his activist orientation or be occasionally frustrated by his outspokenness.

The second priest is fairly new to the parish. To prepare himself he spent two months in Puerto Rico. Community outreach and evangelism are among his particular interests and complement the more activist thrust of the senior priest.

The full-time deacon, a Puerto Rican who has belonged to the church for fifteen years, plays a prominent role in all aspects of St. Margaret's life. He and other staff members who are not priests deal with the constant stream of people coming to the rectory for assistance. People—usually nonmembers—come for food, clothing, money to get home or pay the rent, help with the police, consolation at time of bereavement. They come asking for places to sleep. It is not unusual for him to be aroused in the night to respond to some human need. Once he arrived at the church to find that a mother, on her way to the hospital for an operation, had left her six children at the rectory for the deacon and his wife to attend.

The deacon does marriage counseling, engages in evangelism, and assists with the Masses. He helps prepare individuals for baptism and advises young families on the importance of the Sacraments. He also has a Sunday religious program on a local Spanish radio station. His messages are of love and of the importance of attending church.

In the deacon's view, St. Margaret's is "the house of everybody"—the center of life in the community. He has a special devotion to the parish's educational work with young people. "If the church weren't here, there would be many more school dropouts," he said.

He also does extensive visitation among the larger family, finding this an invaluable means of identifying the human and material, as well as the spiritual needs of those who seldom, if ever, cross the church's doorsteps. It is not uncommon for someone he has recently visited to be called on again by a member of St. Margaret's, bringing food or other assistance, not asked for, but which the deacon perceived as an urgent need nevertheless.

The coordinator of religious education has only a high school diploma and a few undergraduate courses by means of formal preparation. But she has considerable experience and skill, having been a volunteer in the program for ten years before taking her present position in 1979. She and an assistant oversee the religious education of some 300 young people, preparing them for Confirmation, First Communion, and Confession.

Because St. Margaret's has no parochial school and because a public school-oriented tutoring program uses the church basement in the afternoons, religious instruction takes place in homes scattered throughout the community and city. Fifteen groups meet weekly. The education coordinator likes this arrangement because she sees it as an opportunity to take the gospel to entire families. Parents who have been inactive in the parish sometimes return to the Mass when they are exposed to the religious instruction being offered to youngsters in their homes.

The teachers for these groups receive three years of special training through the archdiocese and a Hispanic commission. This training helps prepare them to explore the spiritual and material needs of the homes into which they go. They make referrals to physicians or social services.

Religious instruction at St. Margaret's does not end with First Communion but extends through the teen years. The number of children and teenagers enrolled has grown substantially since 1970.

The Parish Council, which meets monthly, is composed of twenty-one members, of whom five are ex officio. The lay members serve on various parish committees, such as those concerned with liturgy, finances, and education. The council does not make policy; it is advisory, but at St. Margaret's it is taken with great seriousness. Virtually all new program proposals go through the council, which itself often initiates new forms of witness and service.

Funds for basic operations represent a problem at St. Margaret's. Sunday collections amount to about one fourth of the operating budget, another fourth coming from contributions from suburban churches. The archdiocese provides the remaining funding through an urban parish subsidy program of Catholic Charities, paying the salaries and for the utilities and making building repairs. Ten years ago there was no subsidy program, and as one priest in the diocese put it, there was the attitude that "if you can't make it on your own, then maybe you ought to close." But several urban parishes, including St. Margaret's, impressed their "mission" value on the archdiocese, and the policy of no subsidy was reversed.

St. Margaret's organizational structure includes various associations, such as the following:

The *Holy Name Society* (men) and *Our Lady of Providence* (women) members visit the unchurched and assist with services to members and nonmembers. For example, they raise money when a family has difficulty paying for a funeral. Although these groups are small, they are linked to counterparts in parishes throughout the state.

Members of the *Saint Vincent de Paul Society* assist with social services (see the next section). They number less than thirty.

Teenaged girls are encouraged to join the *Daughters of Mary;* some forty belong. Both boys and girls may join the *Teen Center.*

The most impressive programs of St. Margaret's are those for children and teenagers. Reflecting the staff's refusal to separate the sacred and the secular, it is not easy for an outsider to distinguish programs for parish youngsters from those offered by, or through, the church to the community at large, although formal distinctions do exist. The entire ministry to children and youth is covered in the next section.

Relating to the World

At least three fourths of St. Margaret's formal programmatic witness and service to the community beyond its sanctuary walls involves education for children and teenagers, and in many cases, the youngsters are also part of the worshiping parish. Some programs are combinations of general and religious education (the latter in addition to church membership preparation) and are ecclesiastically related in a strict sense. Others are technically secular in design and funding. Education through St. Margaret's is carried by the following programs.

1. *Head Start,* which is funded by the federal government, is a preschool program emphasizing skills that are needed to be successful in kindergarten. Basic socialization and language skills are included in the curriculum. Breakfast and lunch are free. Six full-time staff members are assisted by parent volunteers. Bilingual education is available. Head Start is held in the church basement, which has a kitchen.

2. *Elementary Education: Rio Piedras Tutorial* is an eleven-year-old program that provides extra academic tutoring to students of local elementary schools. Tutors are college students, often recruited by the pastor. Each child is tested on entering the program, and strengths and

weaknesses in reading, writing, and mathematics are diagnosed and a remedial course outlined. Tutoring is given in English and Spanish. An average of between 150 and 200 children enroll each term, coming three times a week for one-hour sessions in the church basement.

One feature of this program is the parent advocate, who has been trained to represent Hispanic parents in case problems occur with their children at school. For example, if a child is to be tested to try to determine the cause of learning difficulties, the advocate will accompany the parents to meetings with school personnel to make sure the parents understand why the test is being given and that they are treated fairly. The current advocate is a parent who was previously assisted by the church.

3. *Secondary: Rio Piedras Tutorial* is a four-year-old program to provide remedial assistance and an atmosphere that is conducive to study for high school students. It stresses good study habits and motivation. Between 200 and 250 students participate during a school term. The high school program also attempts to identify students who show a potential for college education. For example, two juniors at a nearby college are there because the director of the program recognized their potential, approached the college, and was able to arrange scholarships through an order of Catholic sisters. During their freshman year the girls were visited weekly by the director and another staff member, who helped them understand assignments and build self-confidence. The young women had a difficult time adjusting to the college environment, but their hard work and the encouragement of their sponsors paid off.

4. *High School Equivalency Program (G.E.D.)* prepares individuals to take the standard examination for what amounts to a high school diploma. To qualify, a person must be nineteen or older, or his or her high school class must have graduated. Arrangements for taking the test are made with the help of a counselor.

5. *The Learning Center* is a new program of intensive remedial help for students who are two or three years below grade level in language and mathematics. Each student has an individualized program taking personal learning style into account.

The school year tutorial programs at St. Margaret's are funded by grants from the state and from foundations, corporations, banks, and utility companies in the region. The Rio Piedras tutorial center is legally a distinct entity from the parish. It uses church space and receives some advice from church members through its Board of Directors but is without an organic connection. However, this distinction is not readily apparent to an observer, since what the center does is in harmony with the philosophy of education held by the church staff and the Parish Council. The leadership of St. Margaret's values consciousness raising, especially regarding the expectations of young people from economically depressed areas. As one priest notes, "if young people are going to be committed witnesses to the Lord in the future, they have to be aware of the context of the real world." But along with awareness, there must also be hope, he quickly adds. Hope for achieving a better life must be instilled before education means much; Hispanic youngsters must come to believe that they can have a good future and then gain the skills to make hope a reality. As a former tutor puts it:

> They need to gain the skills that will enable them to work and have a respectful life. They must also know that the circumstances they may be in at the moment can be surpassed through education and perseverance in true Christian virtue.

The program has had an impact.

"I feel that the program at St. Margaret's has helped me to be sure of my future," said one student. "It gave me hope that if I study and go out and work, one day I will have a better life."

"My experience is that it helps a person by giving him more energy to start thinking about the future," said another.

In addition to these personal testimonies, members of St. Margaret's also tell with pride any number of stories about kids who have "made it" with the help of the church. One is of a former youth who, as a young man was

> offered a big salary to go work at City Hall. But this young man chose to work with C.H.A.N.E. [a community organizing project] and help the community instead, earning a meager salary as compared with the City Hall offer.

Although the tutoring is technically secular, some teachers and volunteers find a religious mission in the work. One teacher remarked, "I help the youth under God's guidance, who gave me some gifts I am using to help them reach out to others."

In addition to the school year tutoring program and Head Start, St. Margaret's sponsors a summer program, using, in part, federal CETA funds. For fourteen years it has given daily summer instruction in English, Spanish, mathematics, arts and crafts, and swimming and sports to children in grades one through six and to youths between ages fourteen and eighteen. Some 250 enroll each year for the six-week program.

The summer program has ten certified teachers and a staff of forty-five teenagers, each in charge of a group of five or six children. The small groups spend the days together, beginning with breakfast. They move on to academic subjects in the morning and after lunch engage in arts and crafts and sports. Many of the teenaged group leaders have moved up from being summer students in their childhoods. To qualify as a group leader, a teenager must be from a family below the poverty level, as required by CETA regulations.

Youth in the summer high school program combine study and physical activity. Those enrolled are divided into crews that have done a considerable amount of work renovating buildings used in the church's outreach programs. The project in 1983 was winterizing the wooden Teen Center on the church property, a task in which they were joined by volunteers from a suburban Catholic parish. In 1983 *The Wizard of Oz* was produced. A free lunch is served with federal funds.

6. *Youth program/social action.* Eighty young people come together each Sunday evening for a more directly church-related program that includes strong emphasis on social action. The first hour is a discussion of the Gospel lesson for that Sunday. The objective is to get the teenagers to relate the biblical passage to their lives. A second hour is devoted to a specific contemporary issue, often centering on justice issues. (The staff believes strongly that youth must become aware of the social, political, and economic realities of the world in which they live.) The second hour usually involves a speaker, followed by a question-and-answer period.

These Sunday evening sessions have provided primary motivation for several direct action efforts undertaken by St. Margaret's youth, staff members, and some adults. Programs on peace, with speakers from the antinuclear weapons movement, prompted participation in a rally in New York City, a protest at a nearby shipyard, and a vigil outside the Pentagon. The trip to Washington (in 1982) served three purposes, according to a young person who took part: "It heightened public awareness of the connection between the arms race and poverty, helped us admit guilt for not stopping the arms race, and gave an opportunity to pray for forgiveness and relief for the poor."

Five adults and thirty-five young people went to the Pentagon vigil, which took place on the Feast of the Holy Innocents. The group found a connection between King Herod's order to kill the male children of Bethlehem and the threat of nuclear war. "As Christians, we have the right and the obligation to stand up for the right to live," said one participant.

The demonstration at the shipyard had unexpected results. Ten adults and fifteen young people responded to the priests' prompting to protest the U.S. Navy's launching of the nuclear submarine *Corpus Christi,* whose name alone was considered a sacrilege in the religious antiwar movement. The homily on that Sunday was titled "To Construct, Not to Destroy."

The group from St. Margaret's went by bus, singing hymns and reading the Bible en route. Five people went inside the base, and although none took part in the spraying of paint on Navy property, the five were arrested (along with others), refused to cooperate with the officers, and were carried out. All were released and promised to show up for trial.

At the trial, attended by a group from the parish, the charges were dropped. Some observers claimed that this happened because one of the defendants, a priest from another church, came wearing his clerical collar. He had not been in clerical garb when arrested. "The judge did not want to sentence a priest," said a witness to the incident.

On another outing in 1981, members of the youth group went to Washington to protest President Reagan's policy on El Salvador, particularly the presence of U.S. troops there. "We went," said one young person, "because we are the ones that will have to fight if the United States gets more involved. We don't want to go and kill our brothers in El Salvador or Nicaragua. They are Hispanics, like us. Let them decide their future."

Housing is frequently a topic at the Sunday evening youth sessions. The problem of housing in the immediate neighborhood was taken by the young people to the Parish Council, and out of that concern has come the Roberto Clemente Housing Corporation (described below).

Educational achievement is another issue addressed by St. Margaret's teenagers through the youth programs on Sunday nights. Part of the emphasis is on self-help. Many of the young men and women of the parish are below grade level and know it. They are all too familiar with the high dropout rate among Hispanic students. They have become concerned with overcrowding in schools, low teacher expectations, and the frequent moves of Hispanic families. Guest speakers on Sunday sometimes stress the students' own responsibility in pursuing an academic or technical education.

Members of the youth program have responded by setting up their own tutoring service to assist one another. They meet four nights a week. An annual Christmas retreat is planned to examine academic situations halfway through the school year. Students who are failing or having problems with particular subjects are identified and offered individual help.

To participate in the youth program centered in the Sunday evening sessions, a young person must attend Mass regularly and take part in the first hour of religious discussion. The program frequently considers religious vocations, and at least two young men have entered seminaries as a result of the program.

The youth program is perhaps the best example of St. Margaret's "wholistic" approach to ministry. The spiritual dimension of life is addressed through the Mass and discussions of the Gospel lessons and Sacraments. The intellectual dimension is considered by developing awareness of social reality and a sense of Christian responsibility for selves and others. An active concern for justice is fostered through personal involvement. The "play" dimension is met by recreational activities after the sessions and at other times.

Roberto Clemente Housing Corporation

The Roberto Clemente Housing Corporation is a nonprofit urban homesteading program with origins in the youth program. In the mid-1970s the youth group became concerned about the sad condition of housing in the immediate community. The issue was taken to the Parish Council, which decided that the parish should assume a role in upgrading the tenements. An abandoned building was obtained from the city and the youth group did most of the renovation. The program is now a corporation dedicated to providing decent, affordable, multifamily cooperatives.

The corporation has renovated three buildings. Members of the parish staff and the Roberto Clemente board raised the money to purchase the buildings and locate families to buy into the cooperatives. The down payment is "sweat equity"—working on the remodeling. Workshops provide training in money management, and low-interest mortgages are arranged from the U.S. Department of Housing and Urban Development, other government agencies, and private businesses.

The housing corporation now has a small paid staff to work with the families in setting up the cooperatives and in arranging for contractors to do work the people cannot do themselves. The people who are to live in the renovated buildings are involved at every stage of the planning and remodeling. Part of the purpose of the corporation is to build pride in self and community, to develop incentive and skills.

"This is a wonderful thing," said one new co-op member. "We are strangers, but we work together and now we are friends. It's so good to know that after all the work is done the house will be ours."

The senior priest is very proud of the corporation and wants it to remain independent, despite suggestions that it become part of the city's housing program. He argues:

> We have proven how poor people can turn out very good housing without overhead. Why isn't it more popular? Because it doesn't make money. It is seen as "dangerous" because . . . it could eliminate all the middle people in construction. But it is good because it is an anti-welfare program. It says that poor people are strong, intelligent, hard-working, and dedicated to building and managing their own housing. The Roberto Clemente Corporation teaches them how to keep books and manage property. The people would learn nothing if the city managed it.

The housing corporation, according to the pastor, emerged from the Mass:

> The program is good because it is building something without the government's initiation. The work is done with the ingenuity of the

*people, their labor, and God's help. That power came from the Mass.
The Lord gave the people talents and abilities and strengths to help
themselves.*

Food and Clothing

St. Margaret's helped start and continues close working relationships
with a soup kitchen—the House of Bread—and a thrift shop—the St.
Vincent de Paul clothing store—in a neighborhood building bought with a
no-interest loan from the archdiocese. These facilities use only part of the
building. The remaining space was remodeled into fourteen rental apartments, with revenues devoted to maintenance and retirement of the loan.

The clothing store and soup kitchen are run primarily by volunteers
from the parish and their friends in the larger community. Adults and
youth from the archdiocese help in keeping the store stocked.

The Future: Needs and Goals

St. Margaret's is successful in tending to the human needs of the community, but some of the people interviewed worry that the parish is seen
primarily as a social agency rather than a spiritual renewal center. The
staff recognizes that this may be the perception of outsiders and acknowledges that social and educational needs have been stressed in recent
years, at least in the ministry to the wider community. The staff does not
have that feeling about ministry to the communicants.

To insiders, the Mass is at the center of everything being done at St.
Margaret's. "The Mass is a renewal," said one of the staff, "the strength to
help adults accomplish their mission in life; an ever constant reminder to
be fully human, to serve others, as Christ served us."

"Among the young people," he continued,

> *the Mass is where life starts. If the church wants to teach values that
> are not paramount in the society, then the team of the parish must
> teach them to look at life as the Lord does and utilize their talents for
> more than themselves. Then they will have a real sense of the gifts
> they have been given, gifts being developed by the support system of
> St. Margaret's, so they will not only have happy lives as individuals
> but can also be of service to the Lord. This is countercultural, because
> it is not what the culture around us teaches.*

Many parishioners expressed a hope that soon St. Margaret's can have a
priest on duty at the church day and night. The senior priest is so busy
and the assistant so new to the situation that the deacon or other staff
members usually deal with the stream of people coming for spiritual or
material comfort. The members think it would be more appropriate for a
priest to deal with the human problems brought to the church. With the

full integration of the recently arrived assistant priest into St. Margaret's strong team ministry, this "hope" should become more of a reality.

The expressed goal of the leadership—clerical and lay—is to work within the world to make it Christian, a world in which love toward God and neighbor is the maxim. Energy for this task, in the St. Margaret's view, comes from the Mass. The model is Christ on the cross, and there is a firm belief that human nature can be shaped into the formations of love.

CHAPTER 8

THE CONGREGATION AS SANCTUARY

Providing opportunities for people to set aside their day-to-day problems and join together with fellow believers is an aspect of the life of most congregations. We have seen in chapters 6 and 7 that this "sanctuary" function is expressed in congregations whose principal mission orientations are civic and activist. At River Plain it finds expression in the reinforcement of Jewish identity in a gentile culture; at Carmel and St. Margaret's it is expressed in programs emphasizing black and Hispanic roots.

In the three cases representing the sanctuary orientation, the withdrawal themes are much stronger than those seen in chapters 6 and 7. These are congregations that understand their primary mission to be the provision of a special space outside (or, more precisely, alongside) a community whose character is somewhat suspect.

In some respects the three churches are very different. St. Felix Catholic Church is a relatively new parish in a blue-collar community "east of the river." Its life is centered around its founding pastor and the Mass. There is some concern for community problems and issues, but this concern finds limited expression in the life and program of the parish. Indeed, as one member puts it, "I look at my religion as my own personal thing, and I look at the educational role I have as a public thing. I try not to—and have been successful, I think—in not mixing the two." The contrasts with St. Margaret's Church, also Catholic, are striking.

Faith Episcopal and Cristo Pentecostal Churches are located within two blocks of each other in Hartford's Holtville neighborhood. Both draw their members from outside Holtville.

Faith Episcopal Church has become *the* Anglo-Catholic parish in Greater Hartford and takes some pride in its stance "over against" the diocese and modernizing trends in the Episcopal Church. One sees in the case a tension between wanting to be a "good citizen" in the Holtville community and the desire to preserve its distinctive theological character and cultural heritage. Perhaps more than any of the other cases, Faith struggles with its community and its role in it. In a sense, the character of the community reinforces its sanctuary leanings.

Cristo Pentecostal Church presents the sanctuary themes most dramatically. It is the most explicitly otherworldly of the three. Cristo could be located anywhere in the region and it would make little difference to its life and program. Its priorities are clear, and community involvements are not among them. Cristo exists to prepare its members for new life in Christ and a world to come in which the cares of this world will be absent. It is the "purest" of the three sanctuary cases.

St. Felix Roman Catholic Church

THE SIGN AT THE CORNER of Maple Avenue and South Street points up the hill and reads:

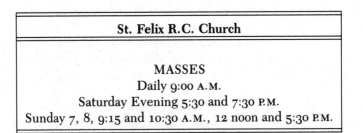

St. Felix R.C. Church

MASSES
Daily 9:00 A.M.
Saturday Evening 5:30 and 7:30 P.M.
Sunday 7, 8, 9:15 and 10:30 A.M., 12 noon and 5:30 P.M.

Six times each Sunday the cars follow the sign and wind their way up the hill for about a half mile through a modest, blue-collar residential neighborhood, until they reach the attractive white-masonry sanctuary nestled among the trees and shrubbery that surround it. The cars' occupants, upward to 1,800 a week, gather for the Mass.

Historical Factors and Facilities

St. Felix Roman Catholic Church is located in the southeast corner of Green Haven, one of Hartford's older, first-ring suburbs. Originally a mission of the adjoining Green Haven parish, St. Felix has had the same pastor since it became independent and dedicated its building, in 1964.

Today that priest, an associate pastor, and a director of religious education serve some 1,200 families, or a total church community of between four and five thousand persons.

The attractive white-masonry sanctuary stands within spacious land-scaped grounds, bounded on two sides by residential streets of closely clustered houses and on two sides by Perry Glen Village, an aging housing project. The church's sixty-five-foot spire supports a twenty-six-foot cross. The total effect, according to one member, "is an uplifting experience for everyone who passes by."

The sanctuary's square interior is of sand-finished concrete; the nave, with a free-standing altar, is in one corner. A quarter-circle seating plan can accommodate 600 worshipers. The vestibule and balcony, each of which can be closed off for meeting rooms, can seat another 200. During Mass the vestibule often serves as the "cry room."

Side walls in the sanctuary are decorated with murals. Two bronze figures, one of St. Felix, stand in the front. The ceiling of the nave is of striated wood panels in a driftwood tone. Pews also have a driftwood finish. The altar is of walnut, the rails of wood and wrought iron, and the Crucifix is an adaptation of the "crux gemmata," or jeweled cross. Lighting is indirect.

The front altar rail was removed after Vatican II, to bring greater unity to people and priest at Mass. Parishioners like the symbolism of open access to the Host. However, the altar's side rails, initially removed with the front rail, have been replaced, at parishioner request, to provide support for those who choose to kneel to receive the sacrament of communion.

Building and grounds are well maintained. Parishioners do much of the cleaning and repairs themselves. As one puts it, "maintaining our property is both an extension of our respect for Almighty God and an inspiration to the neighborhood to keep their property in good condition." The members' pride in their building is noted by their priest. When asked what he felt they would be most proud of, he replied:

> The first thing, I would think, is the edifice they have created and we maintain for the glory of God. I think the edifice is a real indication of their love for God.
>   Second, I think, would be our liturgical services. . . . The music in particular is light and airy and conducive to congregational participation. . . . All in all, they are extremely well done.

The sanctuary and Mass are clearly the focus of St. Felix's ministry, in part because space for anything else is problematic. The sanctuary has no usable basement. A parish house located nearby is really nothing but offices for the staff and St. Felix's food pantry and thrift store. At one time

St. Felix had use of the Perry Glen Village community center, which it rented for one dollar a year. But with the decline of the Village, that building has now been boarded up. Small groups can meet at the parish rectory, about a mile from the sanctuary. St. Felix has no parochial school. As a result, a parish of nearly 5,000 persons has essentially no fellowship or educational facilities. They would like to build such a facility, but so far the archdiocese has not responded to that interest.

Neighborhood and Image

The parish's service area falls into two parts. To the north and east are small but comfortable single-family houses owned by stable, relatively affluent, blue-collar families. The vast majority of the people who live here are white, middle-aged, married, and Catholic; two thirds are native born, but with close Italian, Irish, and Polish family ties. Well over half have lived in the area for longer than ten years.

To the south and west is Perry Glen Village, a series of monotonous duplexes, a number of which are run-down. They house younger adults, transients, and low-income families. Outsiders comment that residents have a sense of acute social isolation. They certainly are alienated from St. Felix, even though almost half are Catholic in background.

The overall population of the St. Felix parish has not increased to any appreciable extent since the 1970s, nor has the church's membership. Most land for housing is already developed and little future growth is anticipated. At the same time the population is slowly changing as more young families and single adults move in.

Most of the people in the area work in the inner ring of Hartford County, east of the Connecticut River. They work as clerks, craftsmen, foremen, and operatives in manufacturing plants, and in retail trade, finance, insurance, real estate, and educational services. More than 50 percent of the women are employed.

Businesses in the immediate vicinity of the church include small shops, restaurants, and service establishments. They seem prosperous.

Residents in the area know that St. Felix is there, but the sense of its presence is greatest among the longer-established residents; after all, many of them are members. (Ninety-five percent of the communicants live within one mile of the church building.) The younger and newer residents in the area seem to have less awareness of any religious institution, St. Felix included. As one commented, "the younger adults seem to have, at best, a rather casual relationship with Christ."

Some non-Catholics in the area view St. Felix as a close-knit parish that enjoys "celebrating"; others think of it as a church of devout, elderly men and women who seem to need one another. There is virtual consensus, however, that members are hard-working, conservative, and family oriented, and that they take great pride in their church.

Green Haven community leaders are well aware of the parish. Several leaders, including the police chief, the school superintendent, and the chairman of the Board of Education, are members. Familiarity also comes from the parish's use of public school facilities for its large youth education program and from the fact that prominent leaders of two of Green Haven's more publicly active community organizations—the Citizens' Voice and the local chapter of Connecticut Pro-Life—happen to be members.

St. Felix is not known for its outreach evangelism. "We don't go in much for publicity or advertising," notes the pastor. In fact, the parish has done little evangelism in recent years, except for a community religious census currently in progress. Preliminary returns indicate that about 40 percent of Perry Glen Village families are Catholic. Of these, two in five said they were active at St. Felix, two in five said they were not very active, and the remaining 20 percent of the self-identified Catholics in the village recorded no interest whatsoever in the church. Of 358 families contacted beyond the village—that is, in the area of single-family residences to the north and east—68 percent registered as Catholics, and of these, 77 percent indicated St. Felix as their parish of active involvement.

Nor is St. Felix known locally for being a social service center, although it has a thrift shop, a food pantry, and a senior citizens' organization that is open, in principle, to the entire community. The church itself takes no stands on public issues, despite some members' involvement in the Citizens' Voice, in the prolife movement, and in the leadership of the town's school system. The church and its members seem to operate with the clear sense of separation between the religious and the public, as evidenced in the following statement from a St. Felix member who also serves on the town's school board:

> I look at my religion as my own personal thing, and I look at the educational role I have as a public thing. I try not to—and have been successful, I think—in not mixing the two. And you know, the people from the Citizens' Voice keep things pretty well separated too. There really has never been a problem. I might receive a comment from the leader of the Citizens' Voice organization about what I am doing in the church, and that is her concern then. And I might receive something from her to the Board of Education, which is an educational thing. Actually, I don't have a problem separating the two, because one is personal and one is public.

Neither do residents think of St. Felix as a place for quiet meditation. The sanctuary is locked most of the time. There is not even a sign outside that announces St. Felix's name. "If it weren't for the steeple and cross," one neighbor noted, "you'd have to be a member to even know it was a church."

What St. Felix *is* known for is its Masses—thirteen a week. Particularly important are its Saturday and Sunday evening Masses, which are attended by people from near and far, including many who are not members of the parish.

Membership and Expectations

Technically, the members of any parish are those Catholics who live in its service area. Practically, the members of St. Felix are any Catholics who attend, regularly or occasionally, who are not involved in another parish or who call on the priests for sacramental ministry. For this reason St. Felix does not give a specific membership figure, only the estimate of between 4,000 and 5,000 persons.

The major expectation of members is acceptance of Catholic beliefs and practices, expressed through observances of the Mass and the other Sacraments. Although communicants are not asked to make pledges to the parish budget, they are expected to contribute and some do, in fact, make a yearly pledge. The pastor considers member contributions to be "generous."

Attendance at Mass has decreased slightly in recent years. Members of the Evangelism Committee think that this is because the community has many young adults, who are more indifferent to organized religion than are their elders. Only a small percentage of the communicants take part in any aspect of church life apart from Mass, an occasional social event, or, if they have children, the CCD (Confraternity of Christian Doctrine) program. The pastor estimates that between 100 and 150 members are "regularly involved in extending themselves to help others, to share their talents with others by being in the choir, teachers, ushers, ministers of the eucharist, deacons, etc."

Regular attenders look to St. Felix for solace, inspiration, education, and counseling. Some also note that they find there a sense of community and the foundation for friendships. Many feel closer to their church since the liturgical and theological reforms of Vatican II; they sense a new emphasis on a loving God rather than a legalistic God. They like the downplaying of mortal sins. "The church doesn't tell you everything that's right or wrong," said one member. "People have got to be more responsible for themselves."

St. Felix has realized the need for a greater stress on evangelism, both to newcomers in the vicinity and to its own people. The community religious census is one strong step in this direction. According to the Evangelism Committee, the census is intended "to bring the message of the parish to the people and to hear their complaints, to learn of their needs and learn how they might help the parish." According to the pastor:

*A census is the best way to reach parish families, of going to them. It
is somewhat problematic, however, because many families would like
the priest to visit the home. But because the parish has only one or
two priests this is extremely difficult, especially because in many
families both spouses are working and therefore the time of visitation
is further limited to a few hours in the day.*

Members of the Evangelism Committee and a seminary student assigned
to the parish are doing the visitation.

St. Felix is also preparing to participate in a diocesan-wide program
called "Renew" that is currently under development. The program will
seek to increase lay involvement in parish life through networks of small-
group experiences.

Theological Self-understanding

"Church is all about our relationship with God and God's relationship
with us," says the pastor of St. Felix.

*Our most basic purpose is to bring a knowledge of God to people, a
personal knowledge of Jesus Christ. In this sense we help people know
that Jesus Christ teaches that they are worthy of his efforts and
therefore that in the sight of God they have great dignity.*

*Our people also appreciate that they do sin, and when they sin they
readily know and believe that God our Father is a forgiving God, a
compassionate God. He knows their weakness and appreciates that,
and when they turn to him to ask forgiveness he readily grants that
and they readily accept it because they want to be restored to the
friendship of God. They want to bring out the best in themselves. This
is why we celebrate the confession nowadays. It is over the idea of
reconciliation, the happy return of the sinner to almighty God.*

The number of Masses at St. Felix, particularly the eight weekend
Masses, are an intentional "accommodation" to the large number of members, according to the pastor, "to help to make it easier for them to
nurture their relationship with God. The church is right in the midst of
our community . . . and we try to help people have a relationship with the
church."

The pastor sees his ministry as specifically focused on the immediate
community; that, he believes, is his calling and obligation. He is there to
offer the Sacraments, to guide and counsel, and to exhort. He wants,

*to uplift and inspire people; to make them good citizens of the church,
state, and country; and to bring God to the world and the world to
God. God has made us great. If we would follow God's plan for us,*

183

this greatness that's in each one of us would be developed and would bring good to ourselves, to the neighborhood, to the country, and to God.

Conversations with members indicate a high level of lay agreement with the pastor's theology of the church. Communicants view their parish as a place to help them grow spiritually, to reach for personal holiness, to learn to be more concerned for neighbors, and to receive advice, counsel, and support. They see practical Christianity as loving, listening to, and caring for other people—characteristically, people nearby.

"I am inclined to just take care of the local situation and try to handle that to the best of my ability," says the pastor. At the same time he readily acknowledges that the extent to which a congregation reaches out to its community and world "does depend on the pastor, the leader." In his own words:

> *I try to do a good job in the locale I'm in and to let the good effects from that flow to others. . . . In that sense once they [St. Felix members] go beyond our own community and into the larger community, they certainly bring their talents and abilities and faith to play. One has to go about doing good to the best of one's ability and let God handle the extended effects.*

A small number of laypeople, however, especially those who have taken part in various diocesan workshops, show signs of a somewhat larger view of the church's ministry. A few have moved toward an ecumenical theology; "anyone who has accepted the Lord and proclaims his message is a believer," said one member.

As individuals, some people within St. Felix believe that Christian service must go beyond the parish. They have gotten involved in programs that respond to the needs of the poor in the large municipality and in the Greater Hartford area. "They are searching, they want to be dynamic, they want to progress; they're willing to try new things," one man stated.

A variety of practical theological trends can be detected among the laity of St. Felix. Some are exploring the meaning of church membership in family life and on the job, weighing their witness in day-to-day encounters. Some are concerned about the dignity of the laity within the church and are trying to increase lay participation at St. Felix. Most of their activities, however, are self-initiated and take place beyond the "official" scope of St. Felix's programming, often involving participation in diocesan-wide programs. The latter is facilitated at St. Felix by an extensive weekly bulletin that includes a comprehensive listing of such programs.

Structure and Organization

The Catholic Church is hierarchical and priest-centered in governance, and so it is in St. Felix parish, although the pastor has shown a willingness, even a desire, in recent years to share certain nonsacerdotal responsibilities.

The pastor is careful to observe the chain of episcopal authority. He takes his cues from his immediate superior, the bishop. "I'm not inclined to be a maverick and to go out and plow new fields," he said. He describes his role as that of an administrator.

> We have and people want Christ's teachings and the church's teachings, so I administer that.
>
> We also have directives from the archbishop. The archbishop is the real leader of the diocese and we are just his extension in the parish. Now we do have a great leeway, but you generally take your cue from him. What he wants stressed and what he wants emphasized, you try to go along with. Our Catholic program is pretty well set for us. I solicit ideas from the bishop so as to be in line with the church's teachings.

St. Felix functions around the pastor. Nothing happens without his approval, seldom without his participation. He is always at work, saying Mass, visiting the sick, counseling, helping members in physical need, overseeing education, conducting the financial affairs, and preparing sermons. The pastor considers it his duty to maintain continuity, elicit interest, balance the budget, instruct the children, and keep people happy and harmonious.

Some members think that the pastor tries to do too much, that he should learn to delegate certain tasks and spend less time on administrative details. He is not in basic disagreement. "We've been brought up to think that the priest does everything," he said. "But now we're coming to the idea that he should divest himself of certain things and concentrate more on spiritual matters." Although some members find the pastor authoritarian, others have found him open to suggestions, even willing to move toward a more open style of decision making. But the movement is slow.

Perhaps the most significant sign of greater lay involvement was the introduction of a parish council in 1979. St. Felix was one of the last Catholic churches in the area to organize such a council, which had been a possibility since the late 1960s. "The big reason for going along without it was that we thought all the bases were being covered, that all the work was being done," the pastor said. "It seems there was no need. But on the insistence of a group of people in the parish we started one." The council mandate is "to help guide the parish in the mission of Christ."

Council functions, as stated in its constitution, are:

> to foster unity and to encourage a more prominent lay involvement in the spiritual, material, social, and cultural life of the parish community; to establish and serve as a medium of communication between the pastor and assistant pastor(s), the pastoral minister(s), and the director of religious education in determining and administering parish policy on spiritual, material, social and cultural matters; to encourage involvement with other churches and organizations in Christian service to all.

The council is made up of the clergy (which have no vote), representatives of various parish organizations (see below), and members elected at large. Candidates for the at-large seats are solicited through the weekly bulletin. A representative announcement, appearing in the bulletin, stated:

> Within a few weeks, we will be electing members to the Parish Council. The council has an important part to play in the life of the parish, but this part can be more successfully fulfilled if more and more people can become involved in its work. All members of the parish are invited and encouraged to seek election to these positions so that council membership can be representative of the entire parish in the truest sense. ARE YOU CALLED BY THE LORD TO SERVE THE NEEDS OF OUR COMMUNITY? WHY NOT PUT YOUR NAME UP FOR ELECTION? WE NEED YOU. DO IT NOW.

Response to such announcements is not overwhelming. According to the pastor, "there just isn't that much interest in the council. They don't have the time." According to some members, however, time isn't the real reason. As they see it, it is either because the notion of a council is so foreign to the kind of thinking most members grew up with in the church, or because, particularly at St. Felix, the council's decision-making role is clearly advisory to the pastor.

Any member of the parish may attend council meetings. The agenda provides opportunity for any parishioner to express opinions or offer suggestions.

The Parish Council operates through seven standing committees: Christian service, evangelism/ecumenism, education, family life, finance, liturgy, and parish activities. (The work of these committees is discussed below under "Program.")

Just how far the council has gone in accomplishing a redistribution of power within St. Felix is a matter of speculation. Still relatively new, the council does not seem to have developed a sense of cohesiveness. In terms of program, it discusses more than it proposes, but in terms of parish morale, it provides a positive outlet for likes and dislikes. Some members see the council as a real beginning of parishioner involvement in decision making at St. Felix; others are not so sure. Those with doubts say that the council does not function effectively as a lay voice. The pastor is equally ambivalent in his assessment: "I don't know if it's been really beneficial. Some good ideas have come through it. But then again we've had to check them on a few."

Of particular note in the latter regard is the following announcement that appeared in the parish bulletin:

SPECIAL NOTICE

Because current financial income is less than current financial expenses the refugee resettlement family will not be coming to our parish at this time. Father Melley exercised his veto power over a seven to six acceptance vote by the parish council [*emphasis added*].

This came after several months of work by the Christian Service Committee in polling members as to interest and support, and negotiating arrangements with the archdiocesan refugee settlement agency. Needless to say, it strained already ambivalent feelings on both sides as to the role and meaningfulness of the Parish Council, strains that are still very much in evidence today.

In addition to the Parish Council and its related committees, the pastor has the advice of two trustees, required by state law, whom he appoints; a building committee; an assistant priest; and the Christian educator.

Program and Activities

Parish life and activities at St. Felix can best be summarized around seven headings corresponding to the Parish Council's standing committees, although these committees do not necessarily conduct the programs.

1. *Liturgy.* The Mass is the most important event in the life of the parish. The pastor is known as a good liturgist who brings a sense of celebration and joy to worship. The music is "light and airy," conducive to congregational participation, and the sermons are well prepared and well rendered. "People are happy when they attend our ceremonies," notes a member, "in fact, we are particularly known to people outside the neighborhood through our Masses."

The thirteen weekly Masses follow the order set forth in the *Monthly Missalette* and include singing and other acts of congregational participation. Most are well attended, and a Sunday afternoon service, one of few in the area, is especially popular.

187

Both men and women may serve as lectors, and eucharistic ministers (male only) help to distribute the elements. Parishioners are invited to bring gifts of bread and wine. Altar boys were dropped along the way but will most likely be reinstated at the request of communicants; the question of altar girls is under consideration. Members of the congregation enthusiastically "pass the peace" among themselves at the proper point in the service.

Sermons are important to the pastor, who usually preaches, bringing messages built around the Gospel lesson and directed toward more God-centered parish, family, and personal life. He rarely addresses political or social issues, except to read diocesan-approved statements on moral matters. The pastor does use sermons to encourage people to be responsible citizens, to exercise their right to vote, and to express themselves to legislators.

The hesitancy, or at least the carefully considered use of the pulpit, to address political and social issues at St. Felix stems partly from an incident that happened a number of years ago. As recalled by a long-time member, it involved a visiting priest preaching during a local election campaign. "He made an unusual move by taking a side in a political discussion, favoring one candidate over another." The parish's response was "the most that we've ever seen in terms of fireworks." In part, the outrage stemmed from the fact that the particular candidate the priest endorsed "was not in the prolife camp." But also at issue was the priest's use of the church, and more particularly the pulpit, to convey a personal conviction. "Let's face it; he is a priest and he has the opportunity to speak to our congregation, and he abused it. It hasn't happened since, and I don't know if it will ever happen again."

Indirectly, however, the parish does use the Mass as an opportunity to confront its members with significant social and political issues. Specifically, this is done either through making petitions on public policy issues available in the rear of the church for people to sign voluntarily, or through notes, announcements, and letters that appear in the bulletin. A recent bulletin, for example, contained both a letter from the archbishop encouraging support of the diocese's Campaign for Human Development and a letter from a parishioner urging people to write to the Federal Communications Commission to oppose the elimination of all religious television.

The parish goes all out with decorations and special celebrations at holidays. For example, at Thanksgiving the altar may be banked with cornstalks, pumpkins, and bags of food.

Except in summer, the 9:15 Sunday Mass honors residents of a particular street, with a banner indicating where the special group is to sit. This plan is designed to encourage attendance at Mass and to help parishioners who are neighbors come to know one another. There is another purpose.

Those being recognized are asked to bring an item or two of nonperishable food or a monetary donation for the food bank. A coffee hour for residents of the street being honored follows in the Parish Center. This program has been successful in encouraging active communicants to seek out inactive parishioners on their street.

The Liturgy Committee of the Parish Council helps to plan special services and prepare new lectors and tries to assess member response to worship.

2. *Education.* St. Felix has never had a parochial school. It has no Sunday school—partly because it has no space for one—and little adult education, a lack decried by many members. Yet it has a full-time director of religious education and a program of instruction for 600 elementary school-aged students.

Religious education for kindergarten through eighth grade takes place after hours in two neighborhood public schools, one serving families in Perry Glen Village and the other serving families from the area of single-family houses. This split, which corresponds to economic and sociological realities, is not universally applauded within the parish.

The students, only 65 percent of whom attend Mass regularly, receive thirty hours of instruction a year from volunteer teachers. The curriculum is described as "faithful to the rich heritage of Catholic tradition" and also "sensitive to recent developments in theology and the social sciences." Courses are progressive, each grade focusing on specific aspects of belief in keeping with the child's level of maturity. The program, according to the director of religious education,

> is designed to prepare the students for their roles in everyday life and for their future roles as adult members of God's people. Our aim is to present the basic tenets of Catholic teaching in an atmosphere that will foster realistic and sound Christian attitudes and convictions and to awaken in the students the desire to work for Christ and to identify with Christ in every facet of their daily lives.

The religious education director would like to see more educational programs for adults and for youth. There is an awareness in the parish that a dearth of programs may explain why young adult attendance is low. One developing initiative, mandated by the diocese, will set up sessions in which engaged couples may evaluate future mates and strengthen their relationships.

St. Felix's Catholic Youth Organization is extremely weak. About a dozen high school students participate weekly in discussions and activities guided by a volunteer couple. Conversation is about the meaning of Christian faith, individual self-image, sexuality, and peer pressure. Sometimes an outside speaker is present. The group has social outings and sponsors fund-raising events, especially for a senior citizens' program.

3. *Christian service.* The task of the Christian Service Committee of the Parish Council is to study, recommend, and execute programs responding to human needs in the parish, the local community, and the global community. Actually, most efforts are parish and local.

St. Felix's food bank is open to anyone in the town. A municipal social service organization keeps in touch with the parish repository and sometimes recommends recipients. Members are frequently urged to make contributions of goods or money to the bank. Money contributions to the bank amounted to $670.95 in 1980, and a year-end announcement in the bulletin noted that food had been provided for "300 people for 550 days in 1980."

Money raised in a thrift shop, The Recycle, run by volunteers, is used to buy clothing for the needy, and merchandise from the shop itself is used in emergency situations. Recycle's income in 1980 was $818.30.

An effort to raise funds for a city fuel/energy bank did not spark significant response. Collection boxes were placed in the vestibule and notices appeared in the bulletin. Announcements were made from the pulpit urging people to contribute toward the $1,000 goal. The amount given was $99.06.

One recent fall at St. Felix the Office of Urban Affairs of the Archdiocese of Hartford presented a three-part seminar on social justice. The seminar covered theology, needs assessment, research, education, and action strategies. Approximately twenty-five parishioners attended, and afterward some reported a renewed call to a social ministry. But plans within the Christian Service Committee to follow-up the seminar did not materialize.

St. Felix parish sponsors a monthly senior citizens' group that is open to anyone, regardless of church affiliation. Programs are social, spiritual, and recreational. Activities include bingo, card games, crafts, musical events, prayer services, and parties.

A group of women in the parish take part in a municipally organized Meals-on-Wheels program for the elderly.

4. *Evangelism/ecumenism.* The Parish Council committee charged with duties in evangelism and ecumenism has a huge challenge at St. Felix. This committee is charged with "renewing and deepening the faith of believers, taking the gospel to non-Christians, and fostering a spirit of unity with other religious traditions."

The recent community religious survey is part of the emphasis on parish renewal; however, the Parish Council was not prompted to act by the discovery that many newcomers in Perry Glen Village were unaware of the church. Again, part of the problem in proposing new programs to shore up parish life is the lack of space for social or community events.

Ecumenics is equally problematic at St. Felix. The pastor takes a particularly parochial view, declining even to belong to a local clergy association. Invitations to take part in city ecumenical events are universally declined, although a few members attend ecumenical services and are developing a broader Christian outlook.

5. *Family life.* Programs promoting Christian family life are few, although the Parish Council would like more, including activities and education for the single, the divorced, and the widowed. Again, space is a problem. A Christian singles club, divorced and separated group, and widow-widowers' organization have used rectory facilities for their gatherings.

6. *Parish activities.* St. Felix has its complement of parish organizations and churchwide activities. There are suppers and an annual festival with booths, contests, and recreation. The parish prepares and delivers food baskets to the poor at Christmas and Thanksgiving.

The Men's Club seems to have stopped functioning in 1979; the Ladies' Guild continues, attracting a dwindling number of women to help with church suppers and, as a group, take trips and arrange educational programs for themselves. The women's group also collects funds to support an American Indian child.

A weekly prayer group meets in the Parish Center. The pastor describes it as "adults seeking better understanding of scripture in order to appreciate the life and teachings of Christ." This group, begun in 1975, is lay-led. In earlier years, when the parish had nuns serving as pastoral associates, study classes were more numerous. The present group has developed a deep sense of commitment to study and to the needs of members.

7. *Finance.* St. Felix lives within its means. It has no debt and follows the accounting procedures prescribed by the archdiocese. There is no endowment.

The Finance Committee of the Parish Council is there to offer advice; the pastor determines most expenditures, which, in 1980, amounted to $151,827. Of the total, $13,515 was received in special collections requested by the diocese for its work, and $1,890 went for charity. The parish gives $100 a month to a struggling parish in Waterbury and a similar amount to an inner-city parish in New Haven. The remainder of the expenditures apparently went, in 1980, to run the church and its educational program for children.

Money comes from member donations; fund-raising events, such as the annual festival; and bingo.

St. Felix does not ask members to pledge; no specified financial commitments are requested. The "envelope system" of contributions is used by about half the families, but it is not mandatory. There is a move within the church to replace the "basket collections" for diocesan work with yearly pledges. The special diocesan collections number about a dozen a year.

The pastor does not seem anxious to change the informal system of financing. "What I like to think is that all the bases are being touched and that they [the parishioners] are happy and content. I think they show this happiness by their generous contributions."

Bingo games are held every Tuesday evening in a nearby hall. Admission is $1.50. Money taken in is spent on the parish at the pastor's discretion.

A handful of members are unhappy with the pastor's approach to finances. They would like a more detailed breakdown of expenses and income and more say in organizing a budget. These members do not miss the fact that an annual outlay of $151,000 for a parish of perhaps 5,000 does not represent a high level of stewardship.

Into the Future

St. Felix parish is in a period of slow transition, gradually moving toward greater lay participation and toward an enlarging vision of ministry and service. But things are not likely to change rapidly, particularly as long as the founding pastor is in charge. His ways are basically traditional; he is parochial, seeing his task as serving the Catholic Church by helping people achieve "a knowledge of God . . . through helping them know Jesus Christ more fully as a person who is present and who is constantly interceding for them." And at least for the moment, the vast majority of parishioners are comfortable with his approach.

The pastor is aware of the fact that he should know the people of the parish better. To him, the best way toward that end is census taking. He wants to be, and considers himself, open to people's needs and complaints. In particular, he would like to employ a social worker with knowledge of local, state, and federal assistance programs to work with the Perry Glen Village people.

Parishioners see the church as primarily responsible for the spiritual and physical needs of members. They are not articulate about how this is done. A sense of lay ministry is beginning to develop but is not refined or widespread. The most immediate and deeply felt need, as perceived by the laity, is for a parish hall, but at present the dollars are not available. Ecumenical ministries and justice ministries in a broad social sense are not central.

For the time being, whatever happens in St. Felix parish depends on the attitude and wishes of the priest. The pastor listens to the Parish Council and other voices, but he is, in final analysis, very much in control.

FAITH EPISCOPAL CHURCH

TURNING LEFT FROM Holt Street onto New Holt Avenue, one's eyes are drawn to the fading, white-brick elementary school that stretches south for what seems to be the entire west side of the block. In the background one sees the steeple and heavy stone architecture of St. Mary's Roman Catholic Church. One can easily miss altogether the small, red-brick church building tucked in between. The church's sign, hanging just inside the iron fence that rings the carefully manicured property, reads: "Faith Church, Episcopal." The words are in English and in Portuguese.

Faith Church is a small, elderly congregation of, to use the language of the community, "Americans." It is set in the ethnically mixed Holtville area of Hartford—Spanish to the east of New Holt Avenue, Portuguese to the west. In a literal sense, Faith is "in but not of Holtville." That the church continues to exist at all is testimony to its dogged commitment to maintain an Anglo-Catholic presence in the Greater Hartford area. In comparison, community involvement and even membership growth are secondary concerns—not so much from not wanting as from lack of energy and vision.

Following their Anglo-Catholic heritage, most of Faith's 150 parishioners and their rector have a sacramental view of life, focused at the altar and carried from there into the home, the workplace, and civic affairs. Members, individually, are community oriented, especially active in charities, but chiefly in the suburban communities in which they live—all at considerable economic and social, if not geographic, distance from Holtville. Faith is open to ideas on how it might become more significantly involved in predominantly Catholic Holtville, but members are not encouraged or enthusiastic about the prospects. Recent efforts have had little effect on Holtville or the church. Perhaps as a result, Faith's resolve to preserve the richness and beauty of its Anglo-Catholic liturgy has become an even more central part of its identity than it had been in the past.

"In a way," as one observer summarized Faith, "it physically and liturgically resembles a beautiful but hidden garden, tucked away from the working-class neighborhood surrounding it . . . unsure of its future, prepared to die if it must, a distinct entity in the place where it was born a century ago."

History

Faith Church began as a Sunday school established in the 1850s by another Episcopal parish. The land on which Faith stands was donated in trust in 1863 by the rector of the parent church. At the time there were no other churches, of any denomination, within a two-mile radius. With no public transportation, the people of the industrial neighborhood took advantage of the new Sunday school, which soon became a mission and in 1912 was recognized as a self-sustaining parish.

Its official history describes Faith Church in its early years as "a truly neighborhood church." In the late nineteenth century "the congregation was mainly a mixture of English, Scottish, German, and Scandinavian, with a few Irish and French," reflecting the then ethnic makeup of Holtville. The history goes on to say that Faith Church has never been "a socially prominent parish, distinguished by the presence of many wealthy persons. Over the years a large proportion of the members could be described as lower middle class."

Historical records also show that although Faith was able to pay its own way through the mid-1960s, there was never much money to spare. The rector's salary was low and often paid late. In fact, the parish was so economically marginal that from the late 1930s through the 1960s the thought of selling the land and building and merging and moving in with the nearest parish was constantly in the air. But selling proved to be difficult; the land was held in trust by the estate of the rector who had originally bequeathed it, and the legal instrument provided that it would revert to his heirs should the property be used for other than religious purposes. The Episcopal Society of Donations and Bequests, which held the trust documents, refused to consider withdrawing the reversion clause. Had Faith really wanted to merge and pressed its case, the legal obstacles to the sale of its property may have been overcome. But even in its days of greatest financial insecurity, the parish's desire to maintain its distinct identity carried the day.

Merger talks ceased in 1962, when Faith received an endowment of $200,000. Affluence seemed to breed affluence, as other bequests followed. The parish's financial woes were over. The building was expanded, structural improvements were made, and a few years later, a new organ was installed. Faith flourished, and although membership remained stable at around 200, the parish had a blossoming of organizations and activities, including a Sunday school of fifty to seventy-five children, and was able to provide generous support to Episcopal charities in the diocese and region.

Faith's endowment has continued to grow, to the point that members are no longer asked to pledge to the budget. Giving today is totally voluntary, and if nothing were contributed, the rector could be paid and the building maintained from endowment income alone.

Member loyalty is and always has been remarkably intense. So have been its conflicts, such as that occasioned by the process that eventuated in the selection of the current rector. One faction of the parish wanted a rector who would give primacy to the spiritual nurture of members; another faction wanted a rector who was concerned with social action and community affairs. The heated debate stretched on for longer than a year and a half, and more than a few members left the church. The present rector was chosen in an attempt to heal the split by calling someone who was interested in both the "inward" and "outward" aspects of ministry. Today, there are few visible scars from the confrontation, except, perhaps, the diminished number of members. The "healing" that there has been seems to have resulted from the efforts of the new rector and from the fact that many of the more social-action-oriented members were among those who left.

Few of those who left have been replaced. Faith Church attracts few new members, especially from among the young. Parishioners say that the most dramatic change in the life of the church since the early 1970s has been the decline of youthful participants. The Sunday school, for example, no longer exists. When asked why the decrease in children and youth at Faith has been more dramatic than that of other Episcopal and mainline Protestant churches in the area, members begrudgingly admit that it may be Faith's Anglo-Catholic emphasis. The theology, liturgy, and accompanying pastor-centered style of leadership, they are aware, has become increasingly out of favor within the Episcopal Church, especially among young adults in their childbearing years.

Faith's members believe that their Portuguese and Hispanic neighborhood is an unlikely source of new members. In fact, they readily admit that they do not know how to relate to Holtville, although they continue to try. They maintain a food pantry for needy people in the neighborhood and provide space at nominal cost to community groups, including the Community Renewal Team (CRT), a secular social service agency whose Holtville branch offices are located in the basement of Faith's fellowship hall. The rector makes a personal effort to be visible in the community, and he or women from the Vestry often attend a weekly meeting of community leaders at the Senior Citizens' Center, which is housed in the elementary school next door. Parishioners occasionally help at bazaars and social events held in the parish house by the CRT. And Faith's weekly bulletin always carries a section of "Holtville Notes." One issue, for example, noted the CRT's job placement program for youth and asked for donations to an upcoming tag sale sponsored by the Bilingual Education Center.

But in general, members of Faith seem to have neither the time, the energy, nor the will to comprehend and minister to the neighborhood around their building. Holtville bewilders them. At a Vestry meeting, for example, the Senior Warden asked, "Suppose this church had the budget to do anything. What would we do? What kind of community activities would we be involved in?" His question was met with silence.

The Community

Holtville, like most of the neighborhoods in Hartford, has changed from "Anglo" to something else across the years. The original white residents, mostly of British or northern European background, gave way to blacks and Hispanics in the 1950s, with an accompanying period of social and economic decline. The overall population of the area continues to decline; according to the latest census figures, the population decreased by 17 percent from 1970 to 1980. But with the arrival of a new immigrant group, the Portuguese, beginning in the late 1960s, community leaders have noted a slight upturn in the area's social and economic fortunes. Today, Portuguese and Hispanics dominate the area. Enrollment at the public elementary school, for example, is about 48 percent Hispanic and 29 percent Portuguese, and at St. Mary's School, about 30 percent Portuguese and 20 percent Spanish origin.

The Portuguese in Holtville are a hard-working, family-oriented people, striving for the upward mobility that will bring them into the mainstream of American life. At the same time, social service agency staff note that they show little inclination to abandon their language, traditional religion, or culture. They put guarded emphasis on education as a means of "getting ahead" but emphasize instead the financial remuneration coming from hard work in menial blue-collar jobs. Men and women often work multiple jobs in construction, domestic service, or unskilled factory positions. Savings go toward the purchase of a home, perhaps one of Holtville's large Victorian structures, which, when renovated, can provide space for more immigrants from the "old country."

Holtville's Portuguese are as independent as they are hard-working, especially the elderly. The older Portuguese have difficulty accepting any "free" public or private assistance, according to local social service representatives.

> Getting them to accept Medicare cards or publicly subsidized housing is no easy task, even if they are in great need. They do not respond easily to anything new outside the immediate family. . . . To provide any services at all, agency personnel must visit homes, most often several times, to win their trust.

Besides the clear needs of the elderly Portuguese in Holtville, social service staff also point to the critical needs of the children. Because both parents, and often resident grandparents, work long hours outside the home, the young people must fend for themselves, receiving minimal parental guidance after they start to school. And because education is not held in notably high regard in many homes, teenagers frequently quit school at the legal age in hopes of getting blue-collar jobs similar to those of their parents. Portuguese families that break out of this mold typically leave the neighborhood.

Crime exists in Holtville, mostly perpetrated by children and youth in the form of petty theft and malicious mischief, but is no worse here than in other parts of Hartford. In fact, several long-time community residents say that the upward mobility of the Portuguese families helps to stabilize the area and keep the crime rate from climbing.

In general, area social workers and other community leaders offer the same two insights into the religious participation of Holtville's Portuguese:

1. They are not interested in "Anglo" services, be they Catholic, Pentecostal, Episcopal, Lutheran, or whatever, partly because of the language factor and partly because the music and style of worship do not fit their values and standards of inspiration. "They are 'different.' They are and they know it, and they do not want to be judged by an alien culture."
2. Any group or organization, religious or secular, that wants to "reach" the Portuguese in Holtville to serve them, include them, or just get to know them must do so on the Portuguese turf—going to them and talking to them in their own language.

What about the religious or other characteristics of Holtville's Hispanic population? This question isn't even raised at Faith. Commenting on this apparent gap in Faith's community perception a friend of the church observed:

Although Hispanics are still a significant factor in the area, one nevertheless has the sense that the future now belongs to the Portuguese. When the Hispanics were the new wave in the neighborhood's ethnic history—back in the late sixties and early seventies—Faith was flourishing. It had all it could handle just to keep up with its own membership. It didn't "need" to turn to the immediate neighborhood in search of members or service projects. Today that's different and in a sense its community sensitivities missed an entire generational change in the neighborhood—namely, the Hispanics.

Faith Church and Its People

Most of Faith's parishioners are over age fifty; half are older. "Young adults" are people in their middle to late forties. Two thirds of the members have full-time or steady part-time jobs or do volunteer work outside the home. A majority are white, professional people: lawyers, business executives, engineers, surveyors, teachers, and social workers. A few communicants could be considered "working class," but Faith is today a middle- and upper-middle-class congregation. Most commute to the church from Hartford suburbs, a one-way trip from home to Faith taking anywhere from a quarter hour to forty minutes. There are two black families of West Indian origin in the parish.

Most present members originally came to Faith because they wanted a church that offered an Anglo-Catholic liturgy, based in an Anglo-Catholic world view. They are typically conservative in theology and social perspective. Lay leaders point with pride to Faith's liturgy and its commitment to "theological truths." They like the idea of the two Sunday morning Masses and the regular weekday services, despite the fact that neither of the Sunday Masses is well attended, and five persons constitute a large crowd the other six days of the week.

The majority of the active parishioners are aware that the missals (prayerbooks) used at Faith are no longer sanctioned by the Episcopal Church. There is even a sense of pride expressed in defying the ecclesiastical authorities. Some laity only half-jokingly boast that "we are stubbornly holding to the old tradition . . . we are clinging to an outdated way of doing things." Being somewhat of a liturgical "outlaw" gives the parish, as one member said, "the courage of convictions. It is a binding force."

The smallness and familylike nature of Faith are noted with fondness by many members. Communicants speak of themselves as a family, helping one another in times of sickness; joining in personal celebrations, such as birthdays (birthday greetings are a regular part of the fellowship hour between Sunday services); and generally "helping out." The caring is genuine, if a bit haphazard, since the members rarely see one another except on Sunday. But they are willing to, and do, assist when they know assistance is needed.

Of the membership of 150, slightly fewer than 100 persons are active; this number is divided between those who attend the 8:00 A.M. Sunday Mass and those who elect the 10:00 A.M. service. Seeing one another on Sunday is no sure thing.

The early Mass on Sunday relies heavily on the spoken word. It has no music, no singing, no incense, no processional. The emphasis is on prayer, the sermon, and the eucharist. Some twenty to thirty persons typically attend this service, many because they consider it the "pure" Anglo-Catholic observance, others because they prefer the early hour. The 8:00 A.M. Mass tends to attract the older members, especially the women. A coffee hour follows, for which most worshipers remain.

By contrast, the 10:00 A.M. Mass is permeated with music, drama, and incense. A retired priest usually assists the rector, as do acolytes. The thirty to forty persons who usually attend this service say they like the music and the congregational participation through singing. Some find the hour more convenient, and there is more variation in age, race, and sex than at the 8:00 A.M. Mass. The coffee hour after the second service is attended by about half the worshipers.

All that remains of a once highly structured parish organization are the Vestry and an Altar Guild. The Vestry, composed of six men and six women, meets monthly in the evening, moving from home to home. The Guild has only two or three members. In winter months, five to ten persons participate in a Wednesday morning study group led by the rector. A few potluck suppers are held during the year, and fifteen to twenty persons typically take part in semiannual retreats.

The scattering of members in different suburbs is blamed for the demise of most parish organizations and for the low level of social contact. The lack of interest in social and educational activities was recognized fifteen years ago. A 1969 parish survey reported:

> We seem to be split almost in half on the question of social life for adults beyond the Sunday morning coffee hours. Distance is a factor, although one or two termed this a "tired excuse." . . . The general feeling seems to be that those who want a social group should take the responsibility, but that it is not an essential part of parish life.

The references to Faith Church as a "family" do not seem to fit the facts. Social life is even less important today than it was in the late 1960s, gauged by the comments of the present members. Only a few persons indicated that they see other members on a regular basis beyond Sunday morning. Those who did tended to work with or live near other members.

Theological Identity and Expectations of Members

Anglo-Catholicism—its liturgy and, to a lesser degree, its underlying theological values—is the major force binding the members of Faith Church together. And perhaps appropriately, given its altar-centered tradition, the visible reminders of the tradition are nowhere more in evidence than in Faith's sanctuary. It is rich and colorful. Wall carvings depict scenes from Jesus' last days. Over the main altar hangs an almost life-sized figure of Christ in white robes. A small altar on the right features a large, painted Madonna and Child. A smaller figure of Jesus on the cross hangs opposite the Virgin, on the left. Highly polished mahogany pews can seat some 250, and behind them is a huge organ and a choir stall. Colored glass windows are all around.

The application of the tradition to contemporary life is left mainly to the rector, who has made clear his disapproval of women priests, the new Episcopal prayerbook (twice removed from that used at Faith), divorce, and abortion. Communicants who disagree with his views may do so privately, but they are expected not to challenge openly the conservative liturgical and theological stance. Some deviance would most likely be tolerated among new worshipers showing an inclination to join, most Vestry members concur, but since new faces rarely appear, such openness has not really been put to the test recently.

The operative theological values are prescriptive as well as proscriptive and are not necessarily conservative in form or result. Members of Faith are expected to minister to people in the world and that includes participation in political and economic structures. Said the rector:

> Theologically, we hold to an incarnational theology. Jesus Christ came as God and man to save and redeem us. If redemption is begun,

we show that in the way we live and what we believe about the sacredness of human life. That gets expressed in the belief against divorce and remarriage, against abortion but also in support of the hunger fund and our involvement in housing. Our theology is expressed sociologically in the things we do, but it comes from a theology of the altar. That is, we do what we do in the world because the altar, the communion—our relationship with the Sacraments, with the Lord—is first in our lives. . . .

This is different from starting with social things and then coming into the church. If you consider the history of the Anglo-Catholic movements for the past hundred years, you see Anglo-Catholics going into the slums of London to care for plague victims and the poor. . . .

It is because of the Anglo-Catholic concept of Christ's redemption of all people, not just the rich and the middle class, that we must be concerned about the poor.

The rector added that although he exhorts members to put faith into action, he almost never preaches on particular social issues or instructs the people directly on their actions, not even on such an issue as abortion, on which his and the Anglo-Catholic position is well known. His preaching style is to use the Gospel or Epistle lessons of the lectionary as the basis for suggestions on how faith relates to life in the 1980s. The closest he would come to an antiabortion sermon would be a homily on the value of human life, emphasizing that baptized people do not have a "right" to their own bodies, since in baptism "our bodies become the temples of the Holy Spirit and belong to God."

The needs of others—locally and around the world—are a frequent theme in sermons, the weekly bulletin, and Vestry meetings, but the rector does not offer specific suggestions for meeting these needs. Christian action, in short, is a private matter motivated by a community (church) awareness. On a more concrete level, however, Faith does contribute 10 percent of its offerings to the Episcopal Church's Hunger Fund.

The rector is clearly in charge at Faith. He is the "supreme commander"; always so in spiritual matters, most frequently so in organizational and financial areas. The role of the Vestry is primarily that of concurrence. If there is displeasure with the concentration of power in the rector's hands, it is only among the few younger members, who would like more lay participation in the social dimensions of parish life. But the younger members do not control the Vestry, and even they indicate no interest in challenging the rector's prerogatives in liturgical and religious affairs.

However, members of Faith do not expect the rector to carry the full load of Christian ministry in terms of service and witness. They acknowledge their responsibility to live demonstrable Christian lives, and many believe that they do express their convictions in dealings with family, friends, and business associates. They say they would welcome greater stress in parish life on the day-to-day ministry of the laity in normal human contacts. Less enthusiasm was expressed for ministry to those with whom they have no daily contact, such as the Holtville Portuguese.

Church and Community

Faith Church knows it is not a neighborhood church and is not likely to become one. It is what it decided to be in the 1960s, namely, an Anglo-Catholic "magnet church" for high church Episcopalians in the Greater Hartford area. The parish history explains:

> By the early 1960s the parish had reached the conclusion that its center would have to remain where it had been for a century. All proposals to move to another location, the effort to have the property deeded to the parish, and the merger plan had failed. It had become a case of "make the best of what you are and what you have become." Since Faith Church was not a neighborhood parish and drew attendance from a wide area, it seemed to make little difference where the building would be located. It became the accepted idea that Faith Church would be the Anglo-Catholic parish of the Hartford region.

The current membership thinks the decision was sound. The location remains central; besides, the property cannot be divested easily, and no Episcopal parish can decide to relocate in a territory served by another. By choice and providence, Faith Church is where it is, and although it is not of Holtville, it finds it difficult not to look at the immediate neighborhood and wonder what it should, or could, be doing there.

Two major attempts have been made to relate to Holtville. Both involve social service agencies—the Senior Citizens' Center and the CRT.

In 1969 Faith decided that it could help the community by allowing its space to be used free or at a nominal fee by neighborhood groups. Such organizations as Alcoholics Anonymous accepted the offer, and in the mid-1970s the Holtville senior center came to be housed in the parish hall. The space was donated. The center's meetings and recreational activities took place at the church, the kitchen was made available for the Meals on Wheels program, and the rector shared his small office with the center's director.

The church liked the arrangement, feeling that it was good for the parish and for the older citizens of Holtville—at least the "Americans" among them, since the Hispanic and Portuguese elderly seldom participated. Said one member, "Although the seniors, being mostly Catholic, seldom attended any services at Faith, they showed their appreciation for what Faith was doing for them." Another commented, "All the seniors were very nice to us." Parishioners became so enthusiastic about the center that they donated a minibus to deliver meals.

But the church was too small for the growing senior citizens' program, and the center moved into more spacious and modern facilities in the public school next door. Relationships between the church and the center cooled with the move and grew quite cold when the center decided to sell the minibus. Although the vehicle had been given on a no-strings-attached basis, the sale was a blow to Faith's pride and was perceived as a rejection of its beneficence. The center, it seems, found the bus too large for the Meals on Wheels program but too small for carrying people to and from activities. It was sold to the grounds keeper of the neighboring Catholic Church. Because Faith occasionally "borrowed" the minibus for outings, some members wondered why the center did not offer to let the church buy it. The Vestry's anger made the center's staff angry in return, since they had considered the sale good stewardship. Bruised feelings over the bus effectively terminated the association between the church and the center.

After the program for seniors vacated, Faith rented a large basement room under the parish hall to the CRT. The Holtville CRT focuses on two groups: the Portuguese-speaking and the Spanish-speaking. Staff members attempt to help people find jobs, low-cost housing, and adequate medical care. CRT also sponsors social, educational, and recreational events and must raise money to pay for these. Among its fund raisers are tag sales in the Faith parish hall or on the lawn, with many of the sale items donated by Faith members. Parishioners occasionally assist at the sales and at CRT-sponsored social events held at the church.

Largely through these efforts, the rector and members of Faith have come to realize that they "are not adept at relating to the Portuguese community." What is more, they candidly admit that they do not find it rewarding to act as salespersons or hostesses at activities held in a foreign language. They also doubt that the Portuguese really appreciate their presence or their building.

A proposal that Faith provide teachers for a CRT program to provide English instruction to the Portuguese did not get off the ground. Faith's people do not know Portuguese and showed little interest in learning it—as little as the Portuguese seemed to show in learning English.

Today the CRT and Senior Citizens' Center do much of the local social service work that the churches once did. They even use techniques pioneered by churches and religious settlement houses. Community leaders, including the clergy, are convened weekly by the senior center. But neither program has developed much skill in recruiting volunteers from the local churches, especially from an Anglo parish like Faith. And churches always seem a little hesitant, according to the social agency people, to become too strongly committed to efforts they did not initiate.

Perhaps typical of Faith's involvement is the following exchange that occurred at a Vestry meeting:

> The rector turned to two Vestry members and asked for a report on the last community meeting. They admitted that they did not go, but that they would be at the next one. The pastor noted that the senior center is sponsoring a shut-in picnic. The two representatives to the community meetings agreed that maybe they could donate some cakes, but "no," they certainly did not want to go to the picnic.

Constantly hearing about their responsibility to the surrounding Portuguese, Faith Church has decided to set aside income for a part-time Portuguese-speaking social worker of its own. Other community agencies do not like the plan; they see it as potential competition and duplication. The Senior Citizens' Center suggested that the money be spent on a church worker for Meals on Wheels, with the food delivered "in the name of Faith Church." Meanwhile, the CRT would like free rent in the church. It has paid $150 a month and thinks its future would be more secure if a neighborhood institution were to house it at no charge.

The Future

Faith Church has little confidence in its ability to relate to or work with the surrounding non-Anglo community; nor does the non-Anglo community express much interest in relating to Faith. "We are elderly Anglicans in the middle of a Hispanic and Portuguese neighborhood," said one Vestry member. "Parishioners are frustrated and bewildered by overtures to 'do something' for the area and by all the talk of our needed 'presence.'" Faith does not want to live entirely to itself, and it will keep trying to find some way, however small, to be part of Holtville.

The parish is in no danger of closing because of finances. It has a loyal, if small and aging, membership, stable at present but unlikely to grow. Many of the elderly hope the church lasts as long as they do, providing spiritual nourishment as they prepare, as one said, "for crossing the River Jordan." Members in their forties and fifties hope for a change of fortune. "We are at the bottom of a curve, something is bound to happen if we just wait," noted one. Others are not so sanguine. They see little future for Faith, certainly not by outreach to the Portuguese. A member explains: "If Faith attracted the Portuguese, it would grow; however, if it did attract them, it would change the character of the church. . . . There is a fear of what it might actually mean to Faith to have Portuguese here."

Faith is in a difficult position; it has been for years. The 1969 parish survey stated:

> Faith Church seems to mean a great deal to its parishioners as a source of strength to them and as a source of Anglican continuity in

the community. There was some feeling that we have become too self-centered at the expense of those who might need us, who are presently outside the Anglican Communion. We seem almost equally divided between a feeling that we should reach out to those who might not presently be in the church and do more to cure the social ills of our time, and a concern that in so doing we would lose the central meaning of Christianity and become secularly oriented "do-gooders." Some people feel the major effort should be to bring people into Faith Church, rather than to spread our energy too thinly in the community. . . . The overwhelming response is that we at Faith Church have something very valuable that we want to preserve and that the world needs very much. Our dilemmas lie in the area of how to share it with the world without losing ourselves [*emphasis added*].

What was true in 1969 remains today, and the rector looks forward to an upcoming sabbatical.

CRISTO PENTECOSTAL CHURCH

IT'S ALMOST 10:30 on one of those warm, springtime Sunday mornings in New England that seem to call people out of their homes to walk in the park, to work in the yard, or at the very least, to "hang out." But these are not the options for members of Cristo Pentecostal Church. The light blue buses and vans have been going and coming for at least an hour already, and the best the riders can hope for in terms of enjoying the sun is to tarry a few moments between the bus and the church. And most do, especially the kids. In fact, quite a few linger just inside the fence, on the walkway leading to the fellowship hall. The children are dressed in their "Sunday best." They are extraordinarily well behaved, the most venturesome among them daring at most a brief swing on the fence gate, out to the public walkway, and then quickly back into the churchyard. Walking by, a few people turn and smile, but the kids hardly notice, engrossed in their play with one another.

At 10:30 the last of the children are beckoned inside for a day of prayer, study, and worship that will last well into the evening.

Cristo Pentecostal Church is located in Holtville, an older industrial district in the city of Hartford, at the junction of two rivers.* Many small, ornamented houses, built at the turn of the century, have been preserved and give the residential streets a cohesive, villagelike appearance. The neighborhood's commercial life is centered on Holt Street and New Holt Avenue, thoroughfares that tie the area to a business center in West Hartford, a mile to the west, and downtown Hartford, a mile to the east.

*Cristo Pentecostal Church is located about three blocks from Faith Episcopal Church, also in Holtville.

Some homes along Holt and New Holt have been turned into markets and other retail establishments. Apartment buildings with storefronts at ground level typify the early-twentieth-century urban pattern combining businesses and residences.

Holtville has kept part of the industry that spawned it and retains a working-class character. Many residents work in nearby factories. A Portuguese community, which began to grow rapidly in Hartford in the mid-1960s, is now an important presence. In fact, the majority of people living within a few blocks' radius of Cristo Pentecostal are ethnically Portuguese.

Holtville is known locally as "Little Portugal" and features a proliferation of Portuguese restaurants, bakeries, and fish and meat markets. A large number of French Canadian and Hispanic families also live in the neighborhood, and in the past five years Puerto Ricans have replaced Cubans who settled there in the 1960s.

History

Cristo Pentecostal is a new church, begun in the late 1970s. Its pastor, after encountering a number of problems in his previous Pentecostal congregation, was inspired to organize an autonomous church that first met in Colt Park. Perhaps responding to the pastor's radio advertisements, about thirty persons attended the first meeting marking the beginning of Cristo. For three months members prayed and praised the Lord outdoors, "where the grass was their floor, the air was their walls, and the sky was their roof."*

From the park, the congregation, then composed of forty members, moved to a small storefront on South Main Street. The storefront was soon outgrown. After months of searching the pastor found the present building, the group's "temple"—the former United Methodist Church of Holtville. The temple has given the congregation considerable stability, as well as a sense of security. Members are proud of what they have accomplished in a short time. Working and praying together has enabled them to find a place where they can worship the Lord peacefully as they choose.

Cristo Pentecostal has some 200 members (excluding children under age twelve). Almost all are Puerto Ricans. Services, classes, and all other activities are conducted in Spanish. The congregation is young both in years and in the age of adult members, the majority of whom are between eighteen and thirty-five. Newness and youth contribute to a dynamism and intense level of participation.

Almost all the members come from outside the neighborhood. Five

*Because interviews with members were conducted in Spanish, quotations are translations.

percent or less live within walking distance of the temple. Cristo Pentecostal is thus a commuter congregation, a Hispanic Protestant church in the heart of a Portuguese Catholic community.

Although the ethnic composition has changed, Holtville looks and functions much as it did a half-century ago. Most community activities are concentrated in one block, where the old has given way to the new in a large, one-story building housing the elementary school, the branch library, the senior citizens' center, day-care facilities, a recreation room, and a community conference room. The complex contains many neighborhood associations and serves as a focal point of community life. Within the same block is a CRT office, which was established in the mid-1970s with one worker and has now expanded to four full-time professionals.

Within two blocks of the school/community center are the area's three churches: Faith Episcopal, St. Mary's Roman Catholic, and Cristo Pentecostal. Faith Church, made up of commuting Anglicans, appears to be losing both its members and its impact on the community. St. Mary's is maintaining its vitality and an involvement in the neighborhood. Through its parish activities and parochial school, Portuguese and Catholic Hispanic communities are in contact, although the area's Portuguese Catholics, in particular, seem to favor their small national parishes to the larger and more inclusive St. Mary's.

Perception of the Church by the Community

Cristo Pentecostal has little involvement in the immediate area. Neither its pastor nor most of its members live or work there, nor do they feel any special sense of responsibility toward Holtville. They focus completely on their own group. Consequently, few residents of Holtville know much about the church aside from its building and the light blue buses and vans that fill its parking lot. Even neighborhood leaders know little of its purposes and programs. Typical comments by area residents include:

> I know where the church is but I never came in contact with the pastor or any other Pentecostal member.

> I only see the buses go up and down Holt Street whenever they have a service or activity.

> I hear them singing when I drive around the church, mainly during the summer months.

> I have known the pastor for several years but I am not familiar with the programs and activities of the church. I don't think it has much impact on this community.

> When they first moved to the area a member used to come to our [community] meetings but that lasted a very short time.

To look at Cristo Pentecostal's building is to see a Methodist church that was built in 1900. The sanctuary is Romanesque and follows a multipurpose design that is common among urban Protestant churches of its era. One interior wall opens to connect with a large parish hall. Another, separate hall was a later addition.

Architecturally, the structure is complementary to the neighborhood and has not been altered significantly by the Pentecostal group, although much painting and some restoration was required after Cristo Church moved in. The building had been vacant for a number of years, but immediately before being purchased by Cristo Pentecostal, it had housed the local CRT office. Perhaps the only external change is a fence that was built in part to provide a security parking area for the five buses and vans used to transport members. This fence effectively blocks street access to two front (Holt Street) doors, which the Pentecostals do not use. Many residents like the fence because it has put a stop to the corner being used as a teenage hangout.

Conception of Membership

Members of Cristo Pentecostal are given clear guidelines on what is expected of them once they become active, and the process of becoming a member begins at the moment of conversion. Conversion, which may take place at any time in adult life, is understood as both internal and external. The converted personally experiences repentance, and this experience manifests itself externally in a change of life-style. The convert comes to the sanctuary and, prostrated before the congregation, offers himself or herself to the Lord, promising to disavow anything displeasing to God. The pastor prays and lays hands on the individual, beginning the preparation for membership.

The period of preparation usually lasts for three to six months. Each prospective member is closely supervised by the pastor and is monitored carefully to assure that the change (the "conversion") is real, expressing itself in lasting commitment to Jesus Christ after the initial emotional experience passes.

Baptism by immersion signals active membership, but there is no timetable for baptism after conversion. Some people are not baptized for many months. These "passive members" can attend worship and some church activities but may not participate fully in the life of Cristo Pentecostal. Passive members may not receive the "Santa Cena" (Lord's Supper), hold positions of responsibility, or take part in certain associations.

The congregation has 140 active and 70 passive adult members. Children under age twelve may attend church and, after their twelfth birthday, become candidates for baptism. Infant baptism is not practiced, since the Sacrament implies a commitment to the Lord within the church and young children are not felt to have the ability to make such a commitment.

Members consider themselves consecrated to the Lord, separated from the world although living in it. As people who are chosen and set apart, members show no interest in entertaining the ideas, values, or life-styles of those outside their church. Most active members look on themselves as "holy people," "servants of the Lord." As one member put it:

> Pentecostals consider themselves a people set apart, people that the Lord has chosen and separated from the rest. "Separated" not humanly or physically, but in the sense that we worship the Lord. We are holy people, set apart. The word consecration means separation. We are separated from the type of life we used to live before. Our life is different, and light and darkness should never be forgotten. The world outside, with its sin and carnal life, we cannot participate in once we become new creatures. We love that world because many of them are our parents, children, husband. But we are unable to go along with what they do.

Within the group, members take responsibility for one another if there is physical need. In practice, calls for physical or material assistance are relatively few, since most of the members are employed. Dependence on welfare or any other form of government assistance is rejected. As a relatively recent convert elaborated:

> Many come to the church receiving some help from the government, but as soon as conversion takes them and they accept Christ as their Savior, they have to change in certain concrete aspects of life, and this is one of them. Cheating the government is not accepted and a person has to change.

Members, once converted, are expected to find a job if they do not already have one. Work is a sign of the new life in Christ. It is also a part of Cristo Pentecostal's felt responsibility toward society. As the pastor notes:

> Persons may be dependent on welfare and without work. They don't have the motivation to look for a job. But when they receive the Lord, the Lord moves them and encourages the person to look for one, to realize that he has a responsibility to his family, to society. And he starts looking for a job right away.

Active members are expected to worship regularly and frequently and to participate in educational, spiritual, and outreach programs. Services are held four times each week. Work is one of the few acceptable reasons for missing a weeknight service. On evenings when there are no services, active members are expected to meet together in their homes for prayer and study or to evangelize by making house calls. This daily involvement seems to maintain individual interest and to develop a sense of self-worth among the members, most of whom are working-class people who rent their houses or apartments and take no role in civic affairs. Although the church schedule is demanding, the pastor and the adult members say it is possible to maintain because of the joy produced by complete commitment to the Lord.

Theological Self-understanding

Individual acceptance of Christ as Savior is the foundation of Pentecostal theology. This acceptance, beginning at conversion, opens the way to a new life. "Christ is the solution to all our troubles, pains, and sufferings in life," said one member. The new life in Christ means seeing life from a different perspective; it means doing new things, and although it is described in spiritual terms, there is also an underlying belief that the material aspects of life also improve. Members of Cristo Pentecostal like the biblical affirmation from Matthew's Gospel, "Set your hearts on his Kingdom first, . . . and all these other things will be given you as well."

Salvation in Jesus is an individual matter. Church members can help others by prayer, preaching, and fasting, but finally, conversion requires individual response to the crucified and risen Lord. God, in divine mercy, touches the individual. A resulting positive response is closely linked with the Second Coming of Christ. On that day the "saved" will go with their Lord.

The Second Coming—the end of the world—is near in the theology of Cristo Pentecostal. This rubric of faith is repeated in services of worship, in classes, and in preparation of new members. The "end" is expected before the year 2000. Believers must be ready and waiting for the first sound of the trumpet. "Soon" is the message of the signs of the times: catastrophes, wars, oppression, crime, drugs, prostitution, disintegration of family life. Firm dedication to the Lord is required to be ready and to witness to others who might be saved. The sermon delivered at Cristo Pentecostal's recent anniversary "celebration" is typical of how the themes of future prosperity, the centrality of the "temple," and the coming of the end of the world are intertwined. Based on a passage from the prophet Haggai, and lasting for longer than an hour and a half, the forcefully delivered message included:

> We are the house of Jehovah and our prosperity is a sign of our faithfulness. But greater will be the future glory of this house. Better and more glorious things will be seen by Jehovah's people. . . .
> Jehovah is always faithful and fulfills his promises. The Lord will

always be with us. In the new times the Lord Jehovah made a pact with his people, "Take courage because I am with you.". . .

The end is coming. It is very near. This is why we have to work very hard to prepare ourselves for this moment. The Lord will come before the turn of the century. Don't be discouraged, any of you. "Do the work for I am with you." In a short time all powerful institutions— even religious systems—will be shaken. "Before long I'll shake heaven and earth, land and sea. I'll overthrow all the nations. Only the temple will remain. . . . At that time the church will be the owners and possessors of everything. "The treasures of the earth will be brought to the Temple and it will be filled with wealth. All the silver and gold of the world is Mine."

The main mission of the church, according to the pastor, is to work for the spiritual nurture of members through their personal conversions. "I believe the church has a certain responsibility toward the community and its problems," he said. "But the greatest responsibility is to the soul, to the spiritual aspect of the person." He sees two purposes being served by helping people to accept the Lord: "We help the person to become good and at the same time we help society. By changing the hearts and minds of people we indirectly change society." For example, a converted drug addict not only becomes a better individual, but also stops being a threat to society.

Divine healing plays a significant part in the life of Cristo Pentecostal. Strong faith makes for miracles in the theology practiced at the church. "Faith is powerful enough to stop any kind of sickness," say the members, and virtually every person in the group has a story about the miraculous healing of some friend or family member.

Prayer and fasting on the part of the congregation is one of the principle contributions they believe that they can make toward healing, the healing not only of physical illnesses, but also of problems of all kinds. As a member elaborates:

> *Prayer campaigns are planned by the pastor whenever he feels the inspiration. The congregation is told what we are praying for, and all together we start a campaign. For example, there may be an internal problem in a family. We pray and fast so things will become better and more peaceful. We know the strength of our prayer can change things. It can change problems of all kinds—related to our people; related to the community; and related to international problems, like the peace around the world, like in El Salvador.*

The Bible is held to be true in every literal respect. Therefore, members must give the biblically sanctioned tithe of 10 percent of their annual earnings to the church. Tithing is the major reason the relatively small congregation could pay for the old Methodist building in a year and a half and can maintain the rambling structure.

Based on the experience of the early Christian church, as recorded in the Acts of the Apostles, Cristo Pentecostal places great reliance on the guidance of the Holy Spirit, individually and corporately. Decisions and plans are dealt with in an atmosphere of prayer and fasting so that the Lord's speaking to the heart through the Spirit can be heard. The Spirit is believed to manifest itself to any adult member or the pastor. Revelations to an individual may be taken as messages for the whole group, and consensus is understood as the action of the Spirit and a sign of God's presence.

The presence of the Holy Spirit is sought in preaching. Members believe that the Spirit inspires and guides the pastor in the pulpit. The pastor is a forceful preacher who, in Pentecostal fashion, repeats the same message again and again. Repetition of selected themes also occurs in Sunday school classes, in which lessons tend to be strong lectures on Christian values, attitudes, and actions required by the Word of God.

Members speak knowledgeably about their beliefs, their moral code, and what is expected of them. They know the contents of the Bible and are in close agreement on theological issues and the implications of church membership. They seem to think alike and give surprisingly similar answers to common questions. The people of Cristo Pentecostal can explain what they believe and why they believe it. Their concern is singular: Christ as Personal Savior.

Structure and Organization

Cristo Pentecostal Church is an autonomous religious organization following the basic doctrinal tenets and practices of American Pentecostalism. It has its own constitution. The pastor belongs to the Confraternity of Christian Ministry, a federation of Pentecostal congregations in voluntary association. This membership is strictly fraternal. In a time of need a congregation may seek assistance from the confraternity, but there is never outside interference. The confraternity is chiefly a means for Pentecostal pastors to keep in touch and to foster unity within the movement.

The pastor is the leader of the congregation, according to the constitution. He leads the people under the inspiration of the Holy Spirit and should be a man of God to whom the Lord speaks frequently. To assist the pastor, the constitution provides an executive board comprising a missionary, the deacons, and sundry church officers, such as secretary and treasurer. This board, guided by the pastor, helps the congregation to be informed and to reach decisions after prayer and discernment.

Although the pastor is clearly the leader, the final decision on many issues is with the congregation. The pastor may present a plan as inspired by the Holy Spirit, but if the membership does not reach a consensus, or particularly if they think it does not follow the Bible, the proposal is dropped. If the said plan is truly inspired, the congregation will receive messages similar to that of the pastor. When conflicts arise, issues are dropped or postponed until after a time of prayer and fasting.

The office of missionary was established for and is filled by a woman, who is the right hand of the pastor, a man. The missionary represents the pastor when he is absent and may substitute for him at any church function.

At the behest of the founding pastor, the financial authority of the pastor is carefully defined. The pastor may not, on his own, expend any amount of money exceeding $200. Larger sums must be approved by the Executive Board. At Cristo Pentecostal the money belongs to the people, and in keeping with stipulations of civil law, if the church should be dissolved, any funds remaining after debts are paid would go to a Pentecostal charitable institution.

Financially, the church is in a strong position. In addition to the tithe, members make freewill offerings to cover the expenses of the Sunday Bible classes, and some volunteer to help pay for a weekly radio program the pastor sends to a Spanish-language station. About economic matters and church administration, the members evidence a spirit of cooperation and common purpose. They take seriously the biblical admonition "The Lord has given you to share with others what you have. Everything belongs to the Lord."

Program and Activities

A member of Cristo Pentecostal could easily be involved in church activities every night of the week. Services are held on four evenings, and the other three evenings could be devoted to home visitation or to participation in "Sacred Hours" in members' homes.

The worship on Sunday night is the major weekly gathering of the community. Sunday is a most holy day, the day of the Lord, and members are not allowed to work or entertain on the Lord's day. "Sunday is the day of the Lord and we have to praise him," said the pastor. "We cannot go to parks to play ball, watch a game, and drink cold beer. It is a sin for us to be at the park on Sunday."

The Sunday night service lasts for about three hours. The event begins outside as the people gather and visit with one another. Inside the temple the atmosphere becomes serious. Members prostrate themselves when they enter and remain bowed before God until the worship begins. The opening segment of a typical service is conducted by a lay member, chosen on a rotating basis. For twenty minutes to a half hour the member encourages the community to praise God. Some moments of silence occur, but for the most part the worshipers pray aloud, praising the Lord with their whole being. They sing with great enthusiasm, accompanied by a band composed of six men. Many members also bring tambourines. The songs are mostly short verses, easily memorized and oft-repeated.

The period of spontaneous prayers and songs is followed by a time of intercession led by the paster. Petitions are offered for the needs of the world, of the congregation, and of particular members, including those who are sick or away. Members then offer prayers of petition, frequently most personal, after being individually acknowledged by the pastor. Outpourings of praise may interrupt these prayers. During intercession, new members, those who have been away, and visitors are given special greetings, indications of the congregation's joy that they are present.

Money is collected at every service. Within a prayerful attitude, the people are asked to contribute generously to cover church expenses and to bring the *good news* to others. The congregation sings and the pastor prays as the plates are passed.

Toward the middle of the service the pastor discusses the church's activities and programs. Members volunteer to visit homes on certain nights. Other responsibilities are assigned or confirmed. This business meeting (held during the Sunday night service) seems to interrupt the flow of the worship, but members find it important because it encourages people to show their dedication to the Lord by assuming work for the church.

The pastor may also deliver a short talk on practical matters bearing on the life of the fellowship. For example, there might be a reminder to notify the bus driver in advance if a member does not plan to attend worship and does not need a ride. Or he might admonish parents to instruct their children on proper behavior in the church building.

Then comes the "preaching of the Word," beginning with several minutes of praise. Sermons are long, always based on biblical texts, and make specific application of the theme to concrete life situations. The language is forceful and repetitive.

Services end with an opportunity for conversions. An invitation is extended to those who have not accepted Christ as Personal Savior. The "saved" may come forward for forgiveness. The people pray for one another and, in a special way, for any who are that night accepting Christ.

Bible classes take place on Sunday mornings. The pastor presides at an assembly in the sanctuary and introduces the common theme for the day. Children, youths, and adults receive the same message. The group then divides according to age, sex, and degree of preparation. After the lessons the Sunday school reconvenes for praise and songs, and conversion is encouraged.

In the future, Cristo Pentecostal would like to be able to afford its own day school, so its children and others could have the opportunity to receive a "Christian education." As several members put it:

> *Education is a means to get better prepared in the secular fields, but at the same time our own school would help remove persons from the outside forces—no bad language, no stealing, no dancing, no smoking. Our bodies are temples of the Holy Spirit. We would like a Christian atmosphere for our children.*

The Sacred Hour, which is held three nights each week, serves the purposes of both evangelism and strengthened Christian commitment. These sessions, part of a sustained "reach-out" and spiritual development program, take place in the homes of present or prospective members and consist of Pentecostal prayer and praise.

Three or four times a year the congregation observes "Santa Cena," a remembrance of Jesus' Last Supper with his disciples. Only active members may receive the bread and grape juice in a ritual of commemoration.

Renewal weekends *(campañas)* are part of church life, as are occasions with other Pentecostal congregations. The renewal sessions often take place at the church but in good weather may be shifted to a public park for an afternoon of preaching, singing, and praying. Cristo Pentecostal is ecumenical only to the point of associating with churches that share its doctrinal values and beliefs.

Virtually all the activities are geared toward reinforcing Pentecostal community ties. Members devote a great deal of time to the church, an indication of the importance of "belonging" to the group and being accepted by it. The programs go hand in hand with the theological understanding; everything is close-knit, one of the strongest assets the congregation has in keeping members active, enthusiastic, and dedicated to the Lord's cause.

The World Outside

Characteristically, Pentecostals believe that Christians are in but not of the world; likewise, Cristo Pentecostal Church is in but not of Holtville— or even of Hartford. The temple is a spiritual oasis where members go to find shelter from the struggles of daily life and affirmation in their "true" life as children of God. The congregation reaches out primarily to draw others into its special community. Ties to the immediate neighborhood or to the city are almost nonexistent.

Direct ministry to society, except through proselytization, is not part of the congregation's understanding of its mission. The main purpose is to change the hearts of people, to bring them to the Lord. "Indirectly," members concur, "consecration to the Lord cannot fail to improve one's worldly status." According to the pastor:

> By helping other persons to come to Christ we kill two birds in one
> shot. We are helping the person become good and accept the Lord,
> and at the same time we are helping society by changing the person
> who may be a real detriment to it. By changing the heart of people we
> change society, family, etc.
>
> In any program planned by the government we can say that it does
> not help at all. Millions of dollars are wasted because nothing will
> change until the heart of one changes and receives conversion. You
> have to go to the heart of the matter. Christ can solve all kinds of
> problems. In Christ is the solution.
>
> The purpose of the church is for the spiritual nurture of members
> through or by means of their individual conversion. Yes, the church
> has certain responsibility toward and within the community regard-
> ing social problems and social issues. But the greatest responsibility is
> to the soul. Members have to proclaim the Word of God and be
> witnesses in front of society. This has to be manifest by a complete
> change of life: change in obedience to civil as well as ecclesiastical
> authorities [emphasis added].

There is complete agreement at Cristo Pentecostal in response to what members would do if on the same evening they had services at the church and an important meeting in their neighborhood: "I'd come to the services. It is more important to serve God's blessing than people's blessing. Prayer can really change things, and I am sure the Lord would help at the other meeting. God is above all things." Such an attitude perhaps explains why the representative of Cristo Pentecostal—even though he attended the first interagency meeting of the local community social service network on the church's move to Holtville—did not show up again.

Consciousness of being a group set apart encourages members to support one another and to work within the structures and programs of the congregation. The "holy people" do not mix with the corrupted and the corrupting. Outsiders can be loved but never joined. The unsaved are possible candidates for the joy and tranquillity the members say they experience. "I have such a joy since I accepted Christ and I would like for other people to feel the same," said one member.

Because expectations and obligations are clearly stated, members have no problem knowing when one of their number begins to stray, to lose enthusiasm, dedication, or the Pentecostal pattern of behavior. On such an occasion a member's duty is to offer a loving reminder of the proper belief or deportment. If a deviant should continue on a false path, the pastor would be notified and strong action might result. Said a member: "If you see your brother not following the way of the Lord, you are responsible to report him; otherwise, you are an accomplice in his sin and condemnation."

Individual social involvement in the immediate or broader community is neither encouraged nor discouraged vocally. Any member of Cristo Pentecostal could become active in civic or political life without violating any stated belief. But active membership does not leave much time for anything beyond church, home, and job. Especially, there is no time for anything beyond the Lord's work, and that is defined in terms of the congregation's beliefs, programs, and worship.

CHAPTER 9

THE CONGREGATION AS EVANGELIST

The fourth pair of congregations see their mission in evangelistic terms. They believe that God has given them a message that *must* be shared with their friends and neighbors, and the message itself—the need to respond to God's saving action in Jesus Christ—is at the center of congregational life.

Most of the congregations we have examined to this point have shown concern for evangelism. Downtown Baptist, for example, set "church growth" as a congregational goal for 1981; St. Felix's Evangelism Committee has conducted a community census and is concerned about "lapsed Catholics" in its parish; Cristo Pentecostal members witness in Hartford's parks in the summertime. For Grace Assembly of God and Mountainview Evangelical Baptist Church, however, the emphasis on the congregation as evangelist is even more explicit, and the focus, as one Mountainview member puts it in the case, is on "bringing people to *Christ*," not just bringing them to their congregation.

In some respects the congregations are quite different. Grace is located in the city and, although it has little relationship to the neighborhood in which its building is located, defines itself as a "city church." Its biracial membership is solidly working class. The congregation has a long history and has adapted effectively to the changing composition of the city's population.

Mountainview Evangelical Baptist Church is a new congregation in one of Hartford's western suburbs (quite close, in fact, to East Town, in which

First Church and River Plain Jewish Congregation are located). Its members are upper-middle-class professionals, many of whom commute to the city to work. Mountainview is our third Baptist case, and although it is not affiliated with the American Baptist Churches (as are both Downtown Baptist and Carmel Baptist), it illustrates the diversity of mission orientations found within a single "denominational" tradition.

GRACE ASSEMBLY OF GOD

AROUND CHRISTMAS or Easter one sees them at the Hartford Civic Center. On sunny summer days they are in Bushnell Park. They stand out because they're talking quietly with all who will listen, and passing out Bibles to those who are interested. They are members of Grace Assembly of God, a Hartford church whose purpose is, in the words of its pastor, "to worship God, to convert the unsaved, and to train believers in Christian living and service." The members say simply that their purpose is to "win the lost for Christ." Above all else that means the practice of personal witnessing: "the ability to explain and introduce persons to the same kind of faith experience oneself has had, identifying it in the Word of God and the preliminary steps of what it means to be a Christian."

Grace Assembly of God is a fundamentalist Protestant church of charismatic leanings. It is housed in an old mansion, to which a sanctuary has been added, and located in a quiet, gracious, residential neighborhood just inside the western border of Hartford. Neighborhood residents are middle to upper middle class, white, and aging. Few children are seen on the streets, which are lined with large single- and two-family homes. Several buildings containing expensive condominiums are scattered throughout the area. The governor's mansion is nearby, as is a Seventh-Day Adventist Church, which meets in another old home two doors away from Grace Assembly.

Few of Grace Assembly's members live in the immediate vicinity; rather, they come from surrounding communities, mainly to the east and north. They converge on the more or less centrally located facility, lining the streets with their Chevrolets and Fords, many with bumper stickers proclaiming that "Christ Is The Answer." The congregation is strong and vital but does not show the rapid growth that is characteristic of many of its Assembly of God sister churches in the suburbs.

History and Setting

Grace Assembly was formed a half-century ago, when forty-three charismatic members broke away from a Swedish Baptist Church to form a gospel tabernacle. The group did not feel that its experience of the Holy Spirit was understood or appreciated by the Baptists, although most of the breakaway members were themselves of Swedish background. The congregation first worshiped in a home and then moved to a West Hartford building now used by The Lutheran Church of the Deaf. The mansion was acquired twenty-five years ago, and the sanctuary was added later to the building's rear and side.

Evangelical zeal has always been part of Grace's tradition. In a letter of greeting sent to the church on the occasion of its fiftieth anniversary—its "year of Jubilee"—the wife of Grace's second pastor recalled:

> My husband had always said that he was as definitely called to the mission field of New England as anyone was ever called to Africa. . . .
>
> We remember so well the revival that we had there with Brother and Sister Johnson and so many received the Holy Spirit. As I remember forty-two people received the Holy Spirit in that revival, and some went from there to Bible School.

Occasional revivals notwithstanding, until a decade ago a conservative Swedish mind-set prevailed, not overly adventuresome in style of worship or in evangelism. Today, 40 percent of the members are black, most of them Jamaicans, and there is a sprinkling of Hispanics. Opening the church to "all God's children" is one of the accomplishments the pastor is proudest of.

Purchasing the mansion and adding the sanctuary represented a challenge to the membership, but not a strain. The old house has been renovated to accommodate church programs, but it retains much of its original elegance. Oak and mahogany paneling, silver chandeliers, tapestries, and fireplaces have been kept and maintained; the congregation likes and works to preserve the homelike quality. Within the mansion are a fireside chapel, a church office, studies for two pastors, a nursery, Sunday school rooms, and a common area containing books, magazines, and an announcement board.

The stucco house stands near the street. The sanctuary alongside seats 500 persons on the main floor and in a recently expanded balcony. The focal point of the sanctuary is the central pulpit, which is situated on what may best be described as a stage. During services the pastors sit to the side of the pulpit; to the back of them is the choir, to the front, are a piano and an electric organ. An outside tower has a lighted cross on top, and a modest sign hangs, colonial-style, from a post on the front lawn. With the possible exception of the lighted cross, the entire setting so fits the surrounding neighborhood that few passersby even notice that this mansion is different in function from the others that line the street.

The grounds are well kept, and the congregation occasionally considers future plans for a rather large backyard. A parking lot is sorely needed; the possibility of putting one in has been investigated a number of times but no action has been taken. The senior pastor also entertains dreams of using the space—perhaps augmented with the purchase of another lot—for a day-care center and housing for the elderly.

Because the house fronts the sanctuary on the street side, any sense of the openness and accessibility often associated with church buildings is lost. Members, for the most part, enter and exit through the house rather than use the sanctuary doors. Although this arrangement may discourage some strangers from entering, it contributes to the family nature of the congregation and perhaps symbolically represents the church's conviction that one enters into the kingdom only through the narrow gate.

Self-image and Perception by the Community

Grace Assembly defines its purpose in terms of evangelism—as a witness to what Christ has done for members and can do for others.

Outreach is all-important, although relatively little is directed to the immediate neighborhood. Through the years Grace Assembly has learned that its message "doesn't sell" among its West End neighbors. As a result, Grace's efforts are focused elsewhere, and it shows relatively little interest in neighborhood needs and activities, although it is mindful of community sensitivities.

Grace is not, nor does it have any pretentions about being, the community church it once was. Through its evangelism efforts and the movement of lifelong members to the suburbs, Grace has become a "commuter" congregation. Perhaps as a result of this it spends little effort on defining a specific service area or parish. According to the members, they are called to witness "everywhere we live," "at our places of work," and "throughout the city of Hartford."

Neither the senior pastor nor the associate pastor live in the immediate area. The senior pastor lives a good fifteen miles and three suburbs to the east. The associate pastor lives in West Hartford; he and his wife recently have made an effort to make friends in that community but report little success in bringing other young couples into the life of the church.

The pastors and members do not think the people of the neighborhood know much about Grace Assembly. They are correct. A few members believe that the church has a positive image among neighbors; the majority, however, are not so sure. "They think we're off the wall," said one. "Neighbors don't like all the cars on the street," said another. And one member who is involved in the youth program admitted that the group tries to keep a low profile in the neighborhood: "We keep the programs and children inside the building so we won't disturb the neighbors."

Neighbors do comment about the cars on the street and about the mix of races they see coming and going. They also say they know no one who attends the church and expect they will never go there. As many of the

Grace members fear, the neighbors are leery of "those Pentecostals" with "lots of no-no's" and "all those tongues."

As far as the members are concerned, the Assembly exists to be a beacon to the city and to let people know that God is at work in Hartford. This task is accomplished "through evangelism," and if the neighborhood does not have ears to hear, it's a big city.

Expectations of Members

Few, if any, new members just "drop in" to Grace Assembly. Most are attracted through the witness and invitation of its members. Once they are taken enough by that witness to visit the church, there is a definite and deliberate process for receiving new members, and those who join accept clear and stringent expectations. Each Sunday visitors are greeted from the pulpit and immediately receive from an usher a visitor's packet, which includes a visitor's address and information card and a pen, so the visitor "can fill out the card on the spot." During the next week visitors are sent a letter inviting them to attend three Sunday morning membership classes with the pastor. After completing the classes the names of those who express interest in joining are submitted to the Executive Board for approval. Applicants also sign a card that states:

> *Having personally experienced the New Birth, through faith in the atoning blood of the Lord Jesus Christ; and having considered favorably the doctrines and practices of the Assemblies of God, and being in complete agreement with them; and desiring to be associated with those of life and precious faith in Christian fellowship, I hereby apply for church membership.*
>
> *I agree to be governed by the rules of the church, to attend the means of grace regularly as I have opportunity, and to support its ministries with my tithes and offerings as God shall prosper me.*

Other expectations are set forth in a publication entitled "Service Through Membership":

> *Persons seeking membership and service in the church should experience the New Birth and have received or be seeking the baptism of the Holy Spirit.*
>
> *It is also expected that applicants be baptized by immersion.*
>
> *Association with the church should indicate cessation of worldly practices, such as the use of alcoholic beverages, tobacco, narcotics, the practices of gambling, dancing, and attendance at theaters and other places of questionable amusements.*
>
> *He should develop the practice of daily prayer, Bible study, personal witnessing, and faithful attendance at worship and observance of the sacraments.*

Membership is demanding and discipline is strict. But for most it is rewarding and transforming. Commitment and loyalty are high at Grace, and membership becomes a matter of central importance in the lives of those who join. Many report that Grace Assembly has literally become their family. Several others testify emphatically that membership has enabled them to get off and stay off drugs. Just about all say that membership has made a decided difference in how they relate to their families and to work. Few will miss the weekly contact with those who believe as they do.

Given Grace's expectations and the commitment that its discipline fosters, it is not surprising that the church's average attendance at worship is much higher than its formal membership. In 1980 the church had 158 voting members, 24 of whom were new within the year. Affiliation, however, is not measured entirely in terms of formal members. Average attendance at worship in 1980 was 250, and more than 400 visitors were counted. Over the past five years the budget has doubled.

The church's Executive Board reviews the membership roll annually, and those who have not attended worship for three months or who have fallen "into sinful practices" are notified by letter that they are being dropped from the rolls. Those being dropped have the right to petition for a hearing. Reinstatement is at the discretion of the pastor and the board.

Only members who are eighteen or older may vote at Grace Assembly business meetings. The expectation that members will attend such meetings is thought to be one reason that the formal membership roll is low compared with average attendance. In the week-to-week activities of the church, however, no distinction seems to be made between members and nonmembers.

The median age of the congregation has declined over the past few years and educational levels have increased, according to the pastor. Services seem to be attended in the main by young families and older people, with only a scattering of men and women in the forty-five-to-sixty age bracket. By and large the members are blue-collar workers, with a few educators, social workers, and middle-management executives. There are no company presidents or other members with direct links to Hartford's or the surrounding communities' power structures. Blacks and Hispanics in the congregation are, in the estimation of the pastor, better educated than their brothers and sisters in the area.

Members spend a good deal of time interacting socially outside of regular church programs. Much of this is programmed: a jogging group, prayer groups for young mothers, Bible studies, and "Acts"—groups of young couples that meet on Saturday nights. There are many more informal groups and most members tend to find their friendships among other members. These formal and informal networks provide not only spiritual support, but also a ready-made network through which members can attend to the material needs of one another.

Divisions within the membership, to the extent that they exist at all, tend to run along age lines rather than along racial or economic lines. The older members tend to be more restrained in worship and less engulfed in the Pentecostal and evangelistic fervor so evident in the younger members.

The racial diversity of the congregation is a source of pride among the members, especially the pastor. A college major in sociology, he says, helped him understand and lead the church in a ministry to all people.

Theology

Grace's theology is summarized in the Statement of Fundamental Truths, which is issued by the General Council of the Assemblies of God. These fundamentals, derived from a conservative reading of scripture, include belief that the Bible is the infallible rule of faith and conduct, an emphasis on the baptism of the Holy Spirit, the practice of divine healing, and expectation of the Second Coming of Christ.

The purpose of the church is to worship God, to convert the unsaved, and to train believers in Christian living and service. Asked about the church's purpose, many Grace Assembly members unhesitatingly answer, "To win the lost for Christ." Both pastors add the dimensions of nurture, education, and training. The associate pastor sees the church as "strengthening members so they can fulfill the second purpose, which is to go out and win the world to Christ." The senior pastor described the church as "a place where we come to celebrate and be strengthened, encouraged, and admonished so we can step back into the world."

The members of Grace Assembly reflect a virtual consensus on the broad contours of their beliefs and on the purposes of their church. The Statement of Fundamental Truths is part of the congregation's constitution and is alluded to on the card signed by new members. This statement is found in pamphlet form on the literature tables throughout the church building, and the fundamental doctrines are recognizable in sermons, announcements, and conversation. People speak of "God's plan" for them. The healing power of God is taken for granted. An expectation that the Second Coming will occur soon puts more emphasis on the present than on the future, more on individual preparation for the Lord than on efforts to change social situations. However, some little hint that the Second Coming may not be tomorrow showed up in the fiftieth anniversary theme: "If Jesus should tarry for another fifty years."

Organization and Program

The senior pastor is president of the Grace Assembly Corporation, chairs the Executive Board (which oversees finances and administration), and presides at periodic business meetings of the church. Six deacons elected by the members serve as advisers to the pastor and make up the board. Each deacon is given a portfolio responsibility, such as membership or education, and may have the aid of a committee. The congregation meets at least once a year, has the right to call the minister, and elects the officers. The polity is somewhat presbyterian in form.

The pastor exerts, and is expected to exert, a major role in decision making. He has been called by God to lead, not only in spiritual matters, but also in the general programmatic and administrative decisions of the church. However, in the pastor's words, "to lead is not to dictate," and although neither he nor his congregation consider his style overly direct, they do consider him a strong leader—and are quite comfortable with this fact, although a few people wish he would delegate more responsibility, "for his own sake."

Perhaps in response to his congregation's desire that he "delegate more responsibility," the pastor recently has established an ad hoc planning committee to examine thoroughly the congregation's current situation and to help focus its future direction through the proposal of goals and objectives.

The Long-range Planning Committee may also have been constituted because of the complexity of several problems that Grace faces. Foremost among these problems, in the eyes of several members, is the seeming limitation of Grace's present location for membership growth. Many factors are involved. As already noted, few, if any, of Grace's members live in the immediate neighborhood, nor does the kind of person to which Grace tends to appeal; yet the church is relatively centrally located for the scattered congregation. Grace has extremely limited parking; because most cars have to be parked on the streets nearby the church, latecomers often have to walk two blocks or more from their cars to the church. There is awareness that several of the small Assembly of God satellite churches in the area's suburbs have grown up and now offer large, modern facilities with plenty of parking. According to the pastor, Grace has lost about twenty members a year over the past few years to these new churches. At the same time the identity of Grace as a "beacon to the city of Hartford," "the salt of its urban earth," is important to many members, including the pastor. If Grace should move to the suburbs, this central piece of its identity would be weakened, if not lost.

Above all, at its core, Grace's evangelistic purpose is to win the lost for *Christ,* not necessarily for Grace Assembly. Accordingly, Grace should find joy in every conversion to which it contributes, even if the converted happen to join another church. Finally, Grace's membership has continued to grow over the past few years but just barely; and its financial situation remains strong. Yet Grace does not exhibit the strong membership growth pattern that was established in the first years of the current pastor's ten-year tenure, despite an increasingly active evangelism program. Neither the pastor nor members of the planning committee have any clear sense of where the Spirit may lead them in responding to their dilemma, but they are confident that guidance will come.

The pastor is a strong leader who has a sense that the vitality of his church is related in part to his personality and style. He is also aware that such personality-centered leadership always runs the risk of insensitivity to the needs and desires of those he is called to lead. He worries about suppressing their creativity and initiative. Grace's pastor thinks he has struck "a pretty good balance." Nevertheless, he views the planning committee as added protection against losing touch with his members' needs.

The pastor is clearly the pivotal decision maker at Grace, but neither the Executive Board nor the membership rubber-stamps his ideas. For example, two years ago the pastor proposed a new board of elders to share with him the "conduct of spiritual matters," a function previously assigned to the Executive Board. The elders were needed, argued the pastor, because the Executive Board had more than enough to do taking care of financial matters and property maintenance. The pastor's proposal was voted down at a business meeting of the congregation. Still wanting the elders, the pastor commenced an adult education program on the role of elders in the early church and looked forward to winning the vote at the next annual business meeting. He did.

Such a process is indicative of how major decisions are made at Grace and of the pastor's style. Most often the idea originates with the pastor; then an educational program firmly grounding the idea in its biblical context is put together to inform and "inspire" the congregation; and finally, the matter is voted at the annual business meeting.

The same process is being followed in regard to starting a prison ministry. For many years Grace had a teaching and prayer ministry in several Hartford-area prisons. It still has a cooperative arrangement with the Gideons for distributing Bibles to inmates, but the more intensive and personal contact with prisoners has lapsed. The pastor thinks that the time is right for reinstituting the prison ministry. An adult education program on prison ministry will be highlighted, and the pastor hopes that the congregation will be motivated enough by the experience to launch a prison ministry.

Grace Assembly is in a strong financial position, operating on a "faith budget" (undisclosed to outsiders) raised primarily through tithing. Individual-giving records apparently are not kept. The church believes that when money is needed it will appear. So far it has.

Church programming is done with an explicit awareness that members are scattered. Programs and meetings at the church are limited, as much as possible, to Sundays and to Wednesday evenings; much programming is done in small groups that meet in members' homes.

Services of worship are held on Sunday morning and Sunday evening, with a family service on Wednesday night. These services are long—about two hours—and somewhat unstructured. The Sunday bulletin carries few directions for worship because those who lead "must feel free to follow the guidance of the Holy Spirit." People wander about greeting one another, singing, clapping, and shouting "Amen." Soloists make their selections under the guidance of the Holy Spirit. Singing is a major part of worship, but hymnals are seldom used; the people know the songs by heart. During prayers, which are offered by laypeople chosen by the pastor, a background chorus is audible as all take part in various "tongues." Loud interruptions by those who are seized by the Spirit are common.

Sermons at Grace Assembly are long, forceful, seemingly spontaneous and Bible-centered, and point to the need for salvation and the presence of God's grace. There is no doubt that the preacher is convinced of the truth of what he propounds. Sermons always include calls for "decisions," either in one's pew or at the altar. The invitation to come forward evokes a contagious response.

Christian education for all ages takes place before Sunday morning worship and is strictly biblical. Nursery care is available, but toddlers are sent to a class as soon as they can pay attention to instruction. The adult class has about sixty members and is taught—lecture style—by a layperson who has taken correspondence courses from an Assemblies of God Bible college. A "youth church" for those in the sixth grade and below is held during regular worship. This program combines arts and crafts, recreation, Bible stories, and refreshments. The children seem excited about their church and do not seem to mind spending hours there on Sundays.

The emphasis on the Bible in worship and education is in keeping with both the Statement of Fundamental Truths and with the pastors' understanding that they must "feed the sheep so they can convert the world."

Activities for all age-groups take place on Wednesday evening. The pastor teaches an adult course; the choir rehearses. The Royal Rangers, a scouting program for boys, meets, as do various other clubs. Occasionally, outside speakers are brought in or films are shown.

Members are serious about carrying their faith into their places of work. Several mentioned participation in prayer groups with fellow workers, some who are also members of Grace but most like-minded people who are not of the fellowship. One woman reported that she met with a group twice a week for forty-five minutes before work. Another member said that his boss asked him to pray with a fellow employee who was having emotional problems. According to this member, "my boss recognized that my faith made a difference."

"Acts 82," a series of young couples' groups started by the associate pastor, is an enthusiastically attended program that attempts to re-create the spirit and understanding of the early Christian church. The Acts groups meet on Saturday nights in homes. Each member has a turn at being the leader and teacher. In addition to prayer, Bible study, and fellowship, Acts has a common fund—a jar—into which couples put money and from which those in need can take money. Special projects are also undertaken, such as a recent summer program of personal witnessing in Bushnell Park. Acts has become a vital network of support groups for members and an example for the rest of the congregation.

Grace is attempting to devise a plan that would divide its membership into small study and support groups, perhaps using zip codes. The plan is for these groups to meet for prayer, study, and mutual support. Grace Assembly is not overly concerned that such units might split off into separate churches; if that happens, it will be seen as part of God's plan.

Beyond the Congregation

As indicated earlier, Grace Assembly does not often look beyond its fellowship except in its task of winning converts to Christ. It is not involved in any social-service-type programs and has no organized social action ministries. Socially and materially, it cares for its own. Spiritually, it hungers to convert the world, not totally unaware that conversion is one means of dealing with many of the personal perversions of the world, such as drugs, alcohol, gambling, dishonesty, and pornography. And it is in this individualistic sense of not following the world's ways that Grace understands St. Paul's admonition to "be not of this world."

To be so set apart from the world's ways, however, does not mean not being present in it. Rather, Grace understands itself as being called into the world to evangelize through the witness of individual members. The world is perceived as an evil place, devoid of Christian values and therefore in need of salvation. The world is the place where the media, books, and schools bombard people with base values, where marriages and families fall apart. Christians seeking sanctification or holiness must separate themselves from what is evil by dedication to God. The ensuing relationship of church to world is that of the church being God's agent for evangelizing the world and bringing individuals to Christ.

Members of Grace Assembly seek their primary human relationships with those who share their beliefs. A few members identify a need for contact with other kinds of people and churches, but most do not want extensive interaction with those who are "different," except to evangelize. Most members think that their church offers a unique presence in the world and has a unique—spiritual—answer to the world's problems. They see themselves as models of the true Christian life, as witnesses who do not smoke, drink, dance, or go to movies and who are ever ready to share their faith experience.

Organized outreach, always intended to bring the lost to Christ, includes (1) the distribution of Bibles and other religious literature in public places, such as shopping centers and parks; (2) visitation ministries to convalescent homes and hospitals; (3) preaching and healing crusades held at the church; and (4) occasionally cosponsoring the Hartford appearance of national crusade organizations, such as Grace's recent invitation to host a week-long children's crusade and involvement with the Billy Graham Crusade's appearance at the Hartford Civic Center.

Grace's crusade work, as well as some of its special adult education programs, are always preceded by heavy advertising. Newspaper ads and radio spots are used most often and are specifically targeted as to geographic distribution and time slot. Occasionally, posters are tacked up at strategic public locations—usually shopping centers and parks; sometimes groups of members pass out leaflets. Thus far Grace has not ventured into television advertising because of the cost of both production and air time.

Personal witnessing at shopping centers—the Hartford Civic Center is a favorite spot—and in parks is primarily a lay activity. When the time seems appropriate—particularly around religious holidays, "when people are thinking about God"—small groups of volunteers are recruited and, always accompanied by one or both of the pastors—to show their support and sense of evangelism's importance—may spend anywhere from a few hours to an entire day distributing Bibles and literature and sharing their faith with all who will listen. Recruitment of skilled volunteers is seldom a problem. As one member put it, "testifying about the experience of God in one's life is a way of life at Grace, interwoven in all we do—prayer, study, education, and fellowship."

Sometimes the witnessing done in the parks, particularly that done by and targeted for youth and young adults, is accompanied by "attention-getters," such as music, drama, or puppet shows. The recent children's crusade held in a nearby park, for example, used members dressed in animal costumes and a magician. Building on models suggested by national crusade groups, Grace has a drama group writing its own scripts to dramatize Bible stories and is just beginning a puppetry program intended for use in its visitation ministry to children's hospitals.

Does all this public witnessing pay off in new members for Grace? Yes and no. "It's not really thought of as a way to make our church grow," says the pastor; "rather it's a general opportunity to share 'out there,' to raise interest, to draw attention to the gospel." Perhaps this explains the pastor's lack of discouragement over the fact that the Billy Graham Crusade did not eventuate in any new members for Grace, nor for that matter, as far as the pastor could tell from his conversations with other pastors, many new members for most churches.

"I wish we could say with certainty that such and such number of new members resulted from such and such a crusade or from a day of witnessing here or there," says a lay leader, "but I can't. Occasionally, however, we hear of a direct connection."

One such "connection" at Grace is a middle-aged divorcée. "I was in the hospital," she relates,

> and had just been visited by the pastor. Of course I didn't know him then. He just dropped in to say, "Hi," to see how I was doin'. Before he left we prayed together. I thought that was that, but the name of his church kept turning over in my mind. Then I remembered. I had been at the Civic Center one day and someone had given me a Bible. It was someone from his church. The next time the pastor came by the hospital—I was in for two and a half weeks—I told him about it, and we prayed again. Then a few laypersons from the church visited. And visited again—full of the Holy Spirit. And here I am today, a member of that church, healed and doing my best to share with others what this church has shared with me. Amen and Amen.

Reflecting on this story, the pastor reiterated his sense that the public witnessing and crusades create an interest, plant a seed, create a receptivity or hunger, but that the majority of new-member growth at Grace comes through the gradual experience of God's healing and wholeness between a member and someone seeking a place of nurture and expression for his or her kindling faith.

Grace Assembly has no organized charity programs, but in individual cases it will respond to the hungry and the unemployed. It also supports financially a number of evangelically oriented mission programs.

Public issues of greatest importance to Grace Assembly more often than not have to do with personal morality rather than social justice. Pornography, homosexuality, abortion, and the "secular humanism" taught in the public schools are seen as contrary to biblical teachings and are interpreted as important signs of the breakdown of moral values in society. But except as individual sins to be avoided or from which one "needs beg God's mercy," such concerns are not addressed in sermons. Public efforts to combat them are primarily a matter of individual choice. Prolife films have, however, been shown at the church, and occasionally, petitions are circulated or made available at the church's literature tables for individuals to sign.

The fact that most church members commute may explain why the church has not developed any community-based programs, but few Assemblies of God are community centers in terms of social services. That is not their nature. They are spiritual centers.

Grace Assembly's theology is conservative and its people are on a religious pilgrimage that begins with "being saved" and anticipates the culmination of God's promises in the Second Coming—always near. The time is short; the fundamental truths are known and the rules of waiting are strict. The "saved" go into the world to recruit more converts, but they do not linger.

MOUNTAINVIEW EVANGELICAL BAPTIST CHURCH

MOUNTAINVIEW EVANGELICAL BAPTIST CHURCH, only six years old and in its own building less than a year, draws an expanding membership from the hills and dales of the affluent suburb of Rockfield.

> We were Southern Baptists, and when we moved to Connecticut we looked around for a church. We found Mountainview to be the best place for a believer in Jesus Christ who is born again to receive biblically based instruction and be strengthened in the vision to reach out to people in the name of Jesus.
>
> We were attending a Methodist church in the area but were unhappy. We looked for one that offered biblical preaching and was Christ-centered. We found Mountainview.
>
> We were Baptists where we lived before, and when we moved to Connecticut we looked for a church to help us grow in Christ and use our resources wisely for the church and Christ. We were looking for a church with a conservative viewpoint. Mountainview had this, it was near us, and it had a youth program.
>
> We were Catholic originally but had been attending an evangelical church in a town near Rockfield. It had an older congregation, however, and when we got married we looked around for a place with more young couples like us and found lots of them at Mountainview.
>
> We decided to break off ties with the Congregational church in Rockfield because we liked the scripture-oriented preaching at Mountainview and the warmth and love among the people.

Within a five-mile radius of Mountainview Evangelical Baptist Church are several areas of recent residential development, clusters of single-family homes costing more than $100,000 each and owned by business executives and professionals. A few farmhouses remain, their elderly occupants reminders of Rockfield's character before it became another of Hartford's fashionable suburban havens for upwardly mobile families with young children. More than 40 percent of the Rockfield population is under twenty-one years of age. Although some of the children attend local private schools, a large percentage go to the beautifully maintained public schools within a short bicycle ride from Mountainview Evangelical. The rolling greens and recreational facilities of the town park are only a stroll from the church. The area also has other churches, Catholic and Protestant, as well as a convalescent home, all built in the understated but expensive style of most recent construction in Rockfield.

Although the town is not considered especially religious—in fact, many people are unchurched—its residents, public officials, and institutions are friendly toward organized religion. For example, meeting space in public schools is made available to developing congregations. During its first five years Mountainview Evangelical held its services in a school cafeteria and used public classrooms for Bible study groups.

Mountainview's new brick building, set in attractively landscaped grounds, is functional but not fancy. Folding partitions are found throughout; space can be divided or opened up as needed. A large entrance foyer leads into the chapel, which, when all partitions are open, can seat 450 persons. The chapel has natural lighting from windows on two sides. The impression conveyed inside and out is of simplicity, warmth, and comfort. In this setting Mountainview Evangelical Church pursues its publicly stated goal of "winning a lost world to Christ."

Historical Factors

The church was started in 1976 by five families meeting in homes for weekday prayer and Bible study. Disenchanted with the churches they had attended, these families decided to form their own congregation. The regional organization of the Baptist General Conference offered consultation on how to organize a church and provided financial assistance for several years. The founders called their first pastor—a young man fresh out of seminary—in November 1976.

The thirty to forty persons meeting in the cafeteria at the end of 1976 had increased to 100 a year later. By 1982 almost 400 persons were attending Sunday morning worship. Lay leaders at Mountainview attribute the fast growth to pastoral effectiveness in evangelical and family-oriented programs and to biblical preaching.

The pastor offers the following reflections on the rapid growth:

> *I think part of the growth happened because the demographics were right. . . . I suspect every church in this area is growing some. . . . Another factor is our belief system as an evangelical church. People are looking for the assured word of God, and the evangelical church deeply believes that it has one to give. . . . Another factor was, from day one, the decision-making capacity of the leadership. . . . Sitting around the first governing board was a vice president of United Technologies, a vice president of Connecticut General, the president of a community college and a plant manager. Each of them had twenty years of church experience. . . . And then another attraction was the style of ministry we quickly settled on. For some reason the*

church always had a warm, friendly personality—even before I came. People come, they feel warmth, they feel the friendliness.*

These factors, together with an effective evangelism program, contributed not only to a burgeoning membership, but also to a healthy budget. Four years after it was begun the church was able to build its building, although the congregation was fortunate to include architects, landscapers, lawyers, business executives, and engineers who could handle the details of design, financing, and construction.

Along with wanting a home of its own, the congregation realized that a building would be appealing to new, unaffiliated, or religiously marginal residents. As one member put it:

> *One of the reasons we built was to increase our ability to attract church-going non-Christians . . . that is, people who go to church but don't really believe, have not developed a personal relationship with Jesus Christ. In building the new church to be attractive, one of our goals was to have church-going non-Christians who move into Rockfield consider going here . . . to look at us and say, "I ought to give that church a try; just look at the size of that building . . . something is going on there." Americans are attracted to success. Let's face it. They like to be where something's happening. And this is the church where something is happening.*

Once the building was completed, attendance and membership did continue to increase. Within a year the new building and the parking lot were being pushed to their limits. An associate pastor was called and a committee named to seek a third minister. And growth also raised the challenge of finding ways to retain a close-knit church community.

Recruitment and Image of the Church

The pastor and lay leaders believe that their building has helped create a favorable image of Mountainview Evangelical Baptist Church in Rockfield. Although the town, as indicated, is friendly toward religious bodies, "Baptists" are not well known in the area. The pastor explains: "To attend a Baptist church on a Sunday morning, people have got to be awfully interested. Baptist is a very bad word in New England. A very negative term. It has to be overcome. People expect us to yell and scream and pound the pulpit and to be Jerry Falwell."

This, indeed, was the perception held by several of the church's lay

---

*The pastor's perception that "every church in this area is growing" is not quite accurate. Most are, but at least two of the area's established mainline Protestant churches' membership has remained virtually unchanged in the past five years and another's has actually declined.

leaders when they heard of Mountainview. One man said that it took years of regular attendance and participation before he applied for membership. "I am originally from Boston and 'Baptist,' in my mind, was shouting and rolling in the aisles," he said. Even after he discovered that there were no aisle-rollers at Mountainview, he was apprehensive over the reactions of neighbors and professional colleagues if he became Baptist. Positive attitudes toward the church within the broader community helped him to overcome his reluctance to join. No doubt the aura of prosperity and respectability generated by the building dispelled doubts about the religious legitimacy of a "Baptist church meeting in a school cafeteria."

One indicator of the local acceptance of Mountainview is the increasing number of non-Baptists who are coming into the fellowship. They include both newcomers to Rockfield and established residents who are dissatisfied with another church. A telephone survey of Mountainview's elected lay leaders found an almost even percentage of those who were originally Baptist and those who were not.

The founders of Mountainview were business or professional people, and most of the newer members fit this mold, except that they tend to be younger. "Five years ago," said a lay leader, "about a third of the church was over fifty, a third between thirty-five and fifty, and a third under thirty-five. Now people are mostly in the last two categories, and there are very few people over sixty-five."

The increasing youth of Mountainview's membership has been accompanied by an increasingly active program of evangelism aimed at families with young children and teenagers. Certain community service initiatives—such as a film series on the family and counseling about drug problems in local schools—have underscored the evangelistic effort and increased visibility and community acceptance.

Church leaders say they would like to attract more of the relatively small elderly population. However, they do not expect to be as successful with that age-group as with the younger families. Their reasoning for this conclusion is probably correct: The elderly in the area are either not mobile (confined to hospitals or nursing homes) or they are content with the churches they have attended for years. Older people in Rockfield are not likely to be newcomers and are not shopping for a church; therefore, as one of few seniors in Mountainview Baptist said, "I don't feel there is anything here that would attract our age-group." The pastor would like to change that but isn't sure how.

The willingness of Mountainview to evangelize among the churched as well as the unchurched has caused tensions with some of the other churches in the area, including a few that had assisted the Evangelical Baptists in earlier years. The pastor described the situation from his perspective:

> *When we first began, the other churches were very cooperative . . .*
> *and they have continued to be cooperative. Their understanding is*
> *that they are "liberal Protestant" churches and that we are not. But*
> *their attitude was, "We need a church of your style and flavor in*
> *Rockfield." Now, since we have grown, things have changed a bit. . . .*
> *What has happened is that several of the other churches have had*
> *enclaves of evangelicals who have been attempting to bring about*
> *changes in these mainline liberal churches, but they have not been*
> *too successful. Eventually, these evangelicals give up and come to us,*
> *usually about the time their kids start puberty. We really hadn't*
> *sought it, and it is a little embarrassing. At times, although they have*
> *been gracious about it, the other churches struggle with it emotion-*
> *ally.*

Although the pastor, who belongs to the local clergy association, seems genuinely concerned about relationships with other churches, the laity at Mountainview apparently give the matter little thought. "You can't steal well-fed sheep," one layman quipped. The members are more concerned about internal relationships and about what growth may do to the valued component of a warm, intimate fellowship. Some worry that growth has negative as well as positive consequences:

> *Four years ago the church was much smaller; we knew everyone. It*
> *was very family oriented and it was not difficult for the whole church*
> *to get together for a picnic. As the church has grown, so has the*
> *complexity in interpersonal relationships. Although I know more peo-*
> *ple now, I don't know them as well as I knew the first sixty.*

Mountainview's lay leaders doubt that the church is as successful now as it was initially in attracting visitors to become regular attenders and eventual members. Although the outreach program attracts a larger number of new faces, the leaders are concerned that not all who visit come back. "Growth is normal and good," a layman observed. "We have had a lot of new people come. Our biggest problem is trying to keep the new people who visit."

Motivated by its theological convictions constantly to seek new converts for Christ—and for the congregation—membership growth is expected to continue. In a very real sense Mountainview does not believe that it has the choice of reaching an optimum size and staying there; hence it must struggle to find ways to continue growing, while maintaining the intimacy critical to its growth and its theology. One course of action would be to divide the congregation, establishing a second church in some locale with a concentration of members. Mountainview is not ready for that option and thus tries harder to improve the way it incorporates newcomers and to strengthen fellowship by means of small groups.

Conception of Membership

Mountainview Evangelical Baptist, like most congregations of its theology, understands church membership as a formal relationship that is established at some point after a believer is "saved." Regular attendance and membership are not synonymous. Of the almost 400 active, regular participants, only 215 are members and therefore qualified to vote and hold church office. At the same time the "regular" nonmembers are afforded all the ministries and services and are quietly urged to prepare themselves for membership. The regulars are visited at intervals by deacons, but they are not given a hard sell; on the contrary, membership is not necessarily easy to achieve. Christian commitment must be verified by the Board of Deacons. The "new birth" must be evident in both motivation and behavior.

When a person desires to become a member, as outlined in the Mountainview constitution, he or she notifies the pastor or deacons. Often such individuals have been active in Sunday school or weekly Bible classes for a year or longer. The applicant appears before the Board of Deacons to be tested on knowledge of and commitment to the theological precepts of Mountainview, on whether he or she intends to participate actively in worship and church work, and on the degree of seriousness about living "an exemplary life fittingly representing the Lord and His Church in the community." The applicant is expected to give a brief testimonial to a personal relationship with Jesus Christ.

Once a person is accepted the procedure for formal membership touches first on baptism, specifically the mode of baptism by immersion. No one can belong to Mountainview Baptist who has not been totally immersed. Among other things, this requirement provides assurance, according to the pastor, that applicants are sincere in desiring membership:

> Immersion is a barrier to some. So the people wait and think and make sure that they really want to be a part before they join. So, for many people joining is a very deep statement of commitment. For many, it means being baptized as an adult, and there are significant social barriers to that, so they really have to be determined.

Those who were baptized by immersion elsewhere are not rebaptized but must satisfy the deacons as to their commitment to Christ and the church.

Mountainview has few written guidelines on what members are expected to do, other than to observe Christian obligations and virtues and show "regular participation in the public services of the Church, faithful stewardship of time, talents and possessions in the ministry of the Church." These obligations are interpreted to mean that members neither smoke nor drink alcohol and that they attend worship on Sundays, volunteer their services as needed, and support the church financially. The range of participation and contribution varies greatly. Members who are heavily involved in community activities, such as schools and charitable organizations, are not expected to devote as much time to the church as do others. New members are expected to attend one spiritual growth group during the week, especially if they are "new to Christ." Those who are maturer in faith are expected to engage in evangelistic ministries under the jurisdiction of the deacons.

The church's constitution contains a section on the conditions under which a member will be asked to resign voluntarily and quietly. One is no longer welcome if he or she becomes "opposed to the fundamental doctrine of this Church and Baptist denomination to which we belong." Members may also be dismissed by means of a "disciplinary discharge . . . to be considered only in extreme cases where the neglect of Christian obligations or the gross violation of Christian virtues makes it reasonable to doubt the reality of a member's union with Christ," and only after attempts are made to restore the wayward "to the path of duty."

All elected lay leaders—elders and deacons—must be members for a year before selection. This requirement can be waived if a person has the requisite skills and personal qualifications for the position and had been a regular attender before becoming a member. Elders have general oversight of the church's business affairs and program; deacons screen new members, organize parish ministries, and assist with worship.

The qualifications for an elder, according to the constitution, are set forth in 1 Timothy 3:1-7 and Titus 1:6-9, passages often held up as describing the ideal church members. To qualify under the rubrics of Timothy and Titus, an elder must be "blameless, the husband of one wife, vigilant, sober, of good behavior" and "one that rules well his own house." One who drinks or has marriage problems is not likely to be considered: "If a man knows not how to rule his own house, how shall he take care of the church of God?" (1 Tim. 3:5). Also, the person should be "not a novice" to the faith.

The stated requirements for a deacon are from 1 Timothy 3:8-13 and are similar to those for an elder. A deacon must be a sober, ungreedy man, giving sufficient evidence of having lived a good life, of being a husband of a faithful wife, and of having managed his own house well.

Being a *man* is an implicit condition for elders and deacons but is not formally stated in the Mountainview Evangelical constitution.

Members and leaders "don't smoke or drink," but the congregation does not discourage sinners of those faults from attending. Rather, they hope that involvement will produce change. Smokers and drinkers are welcomed and loved for the sake of their potential; however, Mountainview subtly, if not explicitly, "cools out" charismatics who are inclined to speak in tongues.

The pastor believes that charismatics may be good people, but that Mountainview is not for them; the congregation has no desire to accommodate charismatics or to incorporate their beliefs and practices. Said the pastor:

> The church has attracted a lot of people from charismatic backgrounds. Wonderful people. So we have developed a rather clear-cut policy that we communicate up front, and that is: "If you talk in tongues in your private life, wonderful, go right ahead. We are not going to ask you to deny that you do it; that is not fair. If you want to meet in a small group of people who speak in tongues for private worship, great; go right ahead. But if you feel you want to speak in tongues in a Sunday morning service . . . or you want to hold a small prayer group and invite other people who don't speak . . . God is guiding you to a different church. . . . Churches have different personalities and styles and attract different kinds of people. . . . We are seeking to attract the cerebral corporate executives.

Theological Self-understanding

Basic to Mountainview's theology are the beliefs that the Bible alone constitutes religious authority and that a worthy life is not possible without a personal relationship with Jesus Christ. "We believe that people who are outside a personal relationship with Christ are lost," said the pastor. "That is very biblical; it is what Jesus taught." Trying to save the "lost" is what makes the congregation evangelical. Members have the duty to introduce others to the possibility of salvation. They see this responsibility as larger than expanding the role of their church. "Our pastor doesn't want us to be concerned only with bringing people to this church, but rather with bringing people to Christ, wherever they choose to go to church." All church programs are devoted either to evangelizing outside the community or to nurturing the "evangelists," that is, the members.

Sunday morning activities (worship and Sunday school) serve the purposes of both evangelism and strengthening the faithful, but the pastor sees his primary Sunday role as that of "feeding and nurturing those who have already accepted the lordship of Jesus Christ." At the same time, visitors are given a basic introduction to the church and to the fellowship that might be provided to them.

Weekday programs are directed primarily to the unsaved, with the nurturing of "evangelists" as a by-product. "Jesus didn't say, 'Come and be disciples,'" the pastor remarked. "He said, 'Go and make disciples,' take the message outside. So we take it outside. We encourage members thoroughly to share Jesus Christ and we train them to do that."

Biblical precepts, as understood from the evangelical point of view, underlie every part of the structure and program of Mountainview Bap-

237

tist, including stewardship. Their theology rules out rummage sales, bake sales, and the like to raise money.

> We believe that the Bible teaches that a church is to be supported by freewill offerings. . . . We believe that the Bible teaches that the way to raise money for ministry is just to present the needs, teach people what the Bible says about giving and life-styles, and let them go home and prayerfully decide what they will pledge to the church.

The freewill offering, prayerfully decided, works for this congregation. The 1983 budget of $135,000 was oversubscribed by $19,000 after straightforward sessions on the Bible and giving.

The church's preaching is Bible-centered and considered a major drawing card. Yet the sermons are not notably revivalistic. The pastor characterizes his preaching as "warm" and "friendly," without an "unhealthy emphasis on guilt." His aim is to use contemporary illustrations to underscore the timeless relevance of the Bible to modern issues and daily life. This is not to say that the sermons are not at times dramatic. The pastor recalled one of his favorites:

> I brought from home a beautiful caramel roll and began to eat it while I was preaching. I described . . . what it tasted like and got them hungry. I then asked, "Do you sense what we are talking about? That is what our relationship with Christ is like. People ought to see how it really works, make them hungry for what we have in Christ."

Services of worship frequently include testimonies from members on how God has worked in their lives or accounts of experiences while they were engaged as lay evangelists.

Social action, as understood in much of mainline Protestantism, does not figure in the preaching, but the pastor says he is free to talk about anything so long as what he says is rooted in biblical authority. The congregation apparently is not of one mind on how Christians or the church relates to political institutions. Members with a strong Baptist legacy tend to see a sharp line of demarcation between church and state and disapprove of political discussions in a religious context. Others take a more flexible position. One layman commented: "We have a responsibility as Christians to support government officials but also to see that government officials are ethical. We pray a lot for the government." And another:

> Our church encourages us to be good citizens. At the same time we need to be aware in our voting of what our elected officials are doing. Also, if the state or nation goes in a direction totally opposed to our

beliefs, then we should speak out as a body about it. I believe the church would do this if it saw the need.

The pastor noted that he never tells people how to vote, but he does present biblical principles that may inform political decisions. "For example," he said,

I will show them that God makes it very clear in the Old Testament that his people are to make sure that other people do not get locked into abject poverty. I can say, "Now, come on folks. Look at the North End of Hartford. Let's face it, we need some changes. I am not going to tell you how to do it because that is a political *statement, only that it must happen—that is a* Christian *statement."*

Concern for political and social issues in the congregation does not come close to the emphasis on winning souls for Christ. Like most evangelical churches, Mountainview Baptist believes that people are better helped by a personal relationship with Christ than by making social changes aimed at feeding, housing, and educating the disadvantaged. Of the poor and hungry, a lay leader said, "You feed them today, but they will be hungry the day after. Unless they change in their hearts so they will be able to feed themselves, they will always be hungry." The clear theology here is that genuinely converted people will change their own situations with the direct assistance of God. It could be called "pulling yourself up by God's bootstraps."

Structure and Organization

In 1982 the church had a senior pastor and a youth pastor and was searching for a person to fill the newly created post of pastor of family care and counseling. The clergy and the lay elders and deacons provide leadership and determine program. Pastors are called and elders and deacons elected by the voting members of the congregation.

The eleven elders, including the senior pastor, are charged with the responsibility for all decisions related to spiritual or business affairs. Each is assigned responsibility for a different area within this purview, such as missions, finance, evangelism, facilities, youth, Christian education, and "social communications." On average, excluding the pastor, elders report devoting between five and ten hours each week to the church's business.

Eight deacons, chaired by an elder, assist with spiritual matters and conduct ministries of caring. Each keeps in touch with about twenty families, checking on spiritual and personal welfare, hearing complaints or suggestions, and reporting to the elders. Deacons give from two to ten hours a week to their tasks.

The terms of elders and deacons are limited to three years to "facilitate the incorporation of new people into leadership roles." Only six years old, Mountainview Baptist has already experienced some tension between long-time members and newcomers. Questions arise about the fairness of the rule that elders and deacons must have been members for a year before election. Some people oppose the policy, arguing that an "old guard" is too entrenched and that newcomers should be allowed into leadership positions sooner.

By and large, relations between the governing board and the membership in general are harmonious. This is important because both elders and deacons must depend on volunteers to help them with assigned areas of ministries. Most elders have encountered little difficulty in recruiting assistance, with the exception of the elder for facilities. The executives and professionals of Rockfield do not seem as eager to volunteer for manual labor as for other aspects of church life.

At least three reasons are given for the relative ease of recruiting members to volunteer their time to the church: (1) The theology anticipates and expects members to work; (2) the elders are mostly corporate managers with experience in involving others in tasks; (3) Mountainview has a computerized data bank on members' interests and skills. Information is fed into the computer from forms voluntarily filled out by members and visitors. When "people power" is needed the computer provides the names of individuals who may be interested. "Our computer system is part of the caring ministry of this church," an elder said. The computer also tabulates attendance and giving records.

The boards of elders and deacons each meet monthly with the pastor. In addition, the pastor tries to hold individual sessions with each elder every other month. He sees the chairman of the deacons every other week. Democratic is the term the pastor uses to describe his style of leadership in church administration, and his assessment is shared by most of the elders and deacons. It was a style assumed when Mountainview was much smaller and that it has so far been able to maintain.

However, the pastor finds the rapid growth nudging him toward a more direct role in decision making. Bright and inquisitive, the pastor has studied the impact of growth on church administration. He reports:

> As the church grows there is the sociological reality that the people look to me for leadership. In a church under a hundred members, the key leaders are laypersons. But in a church that approaches three hundred fifty–four hundred fifty–five hundred, the pastor has to take a more central position in the decision making and planning. It is a sociological reality having nothing to do with theology. . . . It is simply that under these conditions the senior pastor has to be chief administrator or the church is not going to grow. . . . So there are

changes. I now take more initiative in the general programs and I contribute many of the ideas. But I need to bring the leaders on board. In fact, I would be an idiot not to listen to them because they have a higher level of organizational knowledge than I do. I have a strong leadership role, but in no sense is it my church.

Elders and deacons are, on the whole, pleased with the pastor's leadership style—democratic in the way he elicits the opinions of others but able to make a direct decision. The pastor is called "a marvelously good persuader."

The youth pastor was added in the church's fifth year, not because the congregation had so many young people, but in anticipation and expectation of getting them. Census figures showed that more than 40 percent of the area's population was under age twenty-one. The job description of the youth pastor includes work within the congregation and with the middle- and high-school youngsters of Rockfield and neighboring towns.

One recent debate in the governing board involved the job definition of a third staff position. An original proposal envisioned an ordained "Ph.D. counselor" who could provide psychological services not only to members, but also to outsiders who were open to religiously grounded counseling. Discussion refined and somewhat redirected the responsibilities of what came to be called the "pastor of family and congregation life." This person will be expected to spend 25 percent of his time in direct counseling, 25 percent in training members to visit as evangelists, and 50 percent in organizing and overseeing the program designed to hold the attention of visitors and nurture the membership.

Program and Activities

Virtually all programs and activities are geared to bring people to Christ, to bring them inside Mountainview Evangelical, and to feed them once they are there. Major emphases include:

1. *Sunday worship.* Mountainview has one Sunday morning service and another in the evening. Worship in the A.M. is similar to that common in New England Congregational, Presbyterian, or Methodist churches. The format includes prayers, hymns, the sermon, offering, and special seasonal observances. The Lord's Supper, served to worshipers in the pews, is observed once a month.

Because visitors are always present, the pastor provides helpful instructions on procedures, such as for communion, and the flow of the service. Average Sunday morning attendance is beginning to exceed the capacity of the 450-seat chapel. Mountainview will likely go to two Sunday services, but with misgivings.

The Sunday evening service is less formal and often has a strong emphasis on music, including concerts by Mountainview's choirs or by choral groups from other congregations. When there are no concerts the program generally takes the form of a discussion on a particular theme.

2. *Visitation and deacons' programs.* Although they may undergo changes in form when the pastor of family life arrives, the visitation and deacons' programs currently are directed toward incorporating people into the church community. They are particularly important because the church's growth has strained the cohesiveness of former days.

The visitation program is targeted to new faces on Sunday morning. Visitors are encouraged to remain after worship for an informal coffee hour (there is none for members) at which they chat with hosts and hostesses. Telephone calls are made to the visitors during the following week and invitations to return are extended. As people begin to attend regularly, they are assigned to a deacon.

The deacon's program, in distinction from the visitors' program, is explained by one of the deacons in this way:

> We have grown to such a size that the pastor cannot maintain contact with every member. Therefore, we have divided the congregation into eight groups, or twenty-one families per deacon. We visit in each home twice a year and keep in telephone communication regularly, and if we don't see them a couple of Sundays in a row, we call up to find out what is happening. We pray for each family, and generally try to keep contact between members and deacons. If they have some problems with the church, they will tell us, and we will try to straighten it out. Or if they have some personal difficulty we will try to help. We have a deacons' fund that can be used for material needs; we can help them find transportation and generally support them in difficult times.

3. *Classes and groups for parishioners.* The church's leaders are aware that they must create "community"—or, better, "communities"—among the members, to, as one put it, "provide a small-group experience within the larger church." Partly toward that end, and partly to advance general Christian education, a variety of classes and groups meet on Sundays and during the week.

Sunday school for children and adults provides small-group experience before the morning worship. The Sunday school is typical of those found in evangelical Protestant churches. It is Bible-centered and happy. Four adult classes are available: one for young singles, one for couples with young children, and two general Bible studies. One of the Bible groups, which has a particularly popular teacher, draws seventy-five people weekly.

An initial plan to use the Sunday school structure for weekday group meetings did not work out. The church is still looking for an arrangement that will get every member and regular attender into a group where they will form primary friendships. The youth pastor puts much of his energy into this effort.

For teenagers, Mountainview has both a Sunday morning group and a Tuesday evening group. Although some crossover exists between the two, each group attracts a large percentage of youths who do not attend the other group. Most who come on Sunday are part of the Mountainview community; by contrast, many who attend on Tuesday are relatively un-churched or sporadically go to other churches. Two reasons for selecting Tuesday was to avoid competition with Wednesday youth-night activities at another church and to attract athletes who often have Wednesday night games. The youth ministry is considered comparatively successful; never-theless, participation in both youth groups fluctuates, partly because young people in affluent suburbs have many options to choose from and are generally serious about their schoolwork.

Every week Mountainview has study/discussion groups for working and nonworking members. Different groups are geared to young adults with careers, young mothers, mothers with teenaged children, and busi-nessmen. These sessions do not require a high level of preparation or firm commitment to attend every meeting.

Recently introduced "growth groups" entail both advance preparation and a pledge of participation. Established with the aid of a professional consultant, growth groups, which are limited to fourteen persons each, are led by members with special training in outreach evangelism and personal spiritual growth. Leaders report weekly to the pastor on what is happening in their groups.

To take part in a growth group a person must agree to attend a two-hour session every week (except in emergencies) for two years and to do at least a half hour of homework in Bible study before each meeting. One fourth of each session is devoted to the Bible, one fourth to personal concerns, and the remainder to prayer and pointers on evangelism. After five months the time given to "outreach" is gradually increased and includes, among other things, "communicating with those who are hurting" outside the church. For example, one group learned of a local waitress whose son was dying of cancer. The woman was not pleased that a clergyman (not from Mountainview) who visited did not seem to know how to pray *with* her and her son. So a member of the Mountainview growth group went as prayer agent. Four growth groups are functioning and two are being organized.

Mountainview's Discovery Class is for those who are "new to Christ." It also meets during the week.

4. *Classes, groups, and events for nonmembers.* Two types of pro-grams, operating under the pastor and elders, are primarily for adults who do not attend Mountainview. One is organized around home Bible studies; the other focuses on family life. Lay leaders are proud of these

two programs, believing that they are successful in bringing people into a personal relationship with Christ. They are especially proud of the home Bible studies.

The home Bible studies are led by members who exhibit a gift for teaching. These members are specially trained and helped to set up a weekly or bimonthly group in their homes, to which they invite friends, neighbors, and co-workers. The Bible groups—primarily for non-parishioners—are *never* held at the church, and leaders are told explicitly not to mention the name of the church they attend unless asked directly. "The purpose of the Bible study is to bring people to Christ."

A typical evening begins with supper, followed by study. Describing the latter, one leader explained:

> *We will, say, open the Gospel of John and just begin to discuss as we go what it has to say about a personal relationship with Christ. Then we will share with one another through answering questions like "How can Christianity have meaning for our daily lives?" "How are Christ's teachings relevant to the decisions of a businessman today?"*

Although the point of these home Bible studies may be to "enhance people's relationship with God," as a leader noted, "some do come to decide that our church is the best place to realize that relationship." Indeed, a recent study of new members disclosed that of those who were newly baptized at Mountainview (not transferred from another Baptist church), 75 percent were drawn into the congregation through home Bible study.

Somewhat different, but no less evangelical in intent, are Mountainview's family ministries to the community at large. One of these takes the form of six-week film series on family living and other topics of general interest. The films in any given series are shown morning and evening, one day a week. They draw, on average, 100 persons to the morning showing and 75 in the evening. Only about 15 percent of these people are members of Mountainview. Few of the nonmembers who attend appear to have any interest in joining the church, but they are exposed to subject matter that is consistent with its theology and thereby obtain a better understanding and perhaps appreciation of the church.

Another dimension of Mountainview's family-oriented outreach program is conducted by the associate pastor and aimed primarily at youth. He teaches classes—for example, hygiene—and is a guest lecturer in the public high school, where he also counsels students who have drug and family problems—all without fee. His activities serve the double purpose of creating a good image for the church in the community and of recruiting young people for Mountainview programs. Although he never "pushes" the church, the rapport established with some of the young people draws them to Mountainview. As an added benefit, as one layman noted, the church can sometimes make contact through the youth with parents "in homes we would never have gotten into otherwise."

Beyond the Community

Mountainview Church was one of the host congregations for the recent Billy Graham Crusade in Hartford; it works closely with the Hartford-area network of Young Life; it supports Baptist foreign missionaries and one summer permitted a group of its teenagers to take part in a Methodist project among the poor in Tennessee—"a good experience for the young-sters," according to one parent. But at present the central focus of Moun-tainview's outreach is on Rockfield. In addition to the home Bible studies, film series, visitation, and youth pastor's work in the local school system, Mountainview has cooperative musical programs and holiday services with other churches in Rockfield. Lay leaders and members make a spe-cial effort to patronize local businesses and restaurants. And deacons conduct services at a convalescent home every other week.

Building on the Tennessee experience, the youth pastor and several lay leaders hope to interest the church's youth in helping the needy in the general area. Rockfield is affluent, but "down the road are plenty of poor," a layman said. "Although working in this area is not as glamorous as going off to Tennessee, we would like them to think about service in *this* com-munity." A current proposal is exploring the possibility of interested teen-agers working in one of the area hospitals.

Such initiatives mature slowly. The prevailing theology does not place great emphasis on social service. Most members would agree that provid-ing food, shelter, and medical services to the poor is good and necessary. But they also think it is more important, and more to the church's unique purpose, to save souls. The congregation, in fact, does not really—at least yet in practice—draw any distinction between acts of charity and evange-lism. The youth pastor's counseling activities are a case in point. Another is the church's sponsorship of a refugee family. The church provided housing and work. It also recruited the new Americans as parishioners.

The majority of the congregation would not want Mountainview to become involved in social issues, much less direct efforts at social change. The same majority, however, would allow individuals to be active in civic and political affairs, "as their consciences dictate." Mountainview Evangelical explicitly does not advocate Christian withdrawal from the world. Both the church and individuals should be active in order to exemplify Christian faith in everyday life. Christian living can be outreach only when it is in the world.

The business executives and professionals who are the breadwinners in the church are encouraged to use their skills and expertise on behalf of the congregation. At the same time they are exhorted to project their Christian values into business life. Many leaders indicated that they are more honest in their business dealings because they are born-again believers, that they make a greater effort to be fair to employees. They reported a few instances of experiencing discriminatory treatment because of their evangelical Christianity, but most believe that their faith is respected in the workplace. Some are asked to pray for colleagues.

"Having this congregation as a backup system helps me follow Christianity a lot better in my business," one corporate executive said. And another corporation man commented: "I do think about what scripture says about business decisions. In making a particular decision, I sometimes ask, 'Is this what Christ would do?' That is what we are taught at church to ask."

Mountainview Evangelical Baptist is only six years old, and although it may not be the largest or wealthiest church in Rockfield, it has people taking notice. Its evangelical presence is helping to change the religious map of Hartford's western suburbs.

CHAPTER 10
THE MISSION ORIENTATIONS REVISITED

The case studies of chapters 6 to 9 have put "flesh and blood" on the "skeleton" provided by the four mission orientations. However, such a wealth of descriptive material can make it difficult to see subtle and not-so-subtle differences that the mission orientations make in congregational presence in public life. In this chapter we look comparatively at the cases in an effort to generalize about these differences. What can be said by way of summary about the diversity of religion's public presence that the orientations enable us to grasp? In the second part of the chapter we try to answer the questions "Why the differing orientations? How do we account for the differences?"

A COMPARISON OF THE CASE STUDY CONGREGATIONS

1. *The congregation as activist.* The two activist congregations (and activist-oriented individuals and para-congregational organizations as well) are the most manifestly concerned to seek justice in public life and public policies.*

The two activist churches illustrate the critical importance of pastoral

---

*An exception is the Citizens' Voice group (see chapter 4), the unofficial Catholic organization that demonstrates on occasion in opposition to legislation or programs deemed inimical to traditional Catholic teachings about morality.

leadership in shaping a congregation's mission orientation. Regardless of the degree to which a congregation emphasizes shared ministry of clergy and laity, the pastor is of key importance in shaping the ethos and mission orientation of a congregation. This is true generally because of several sources of pastoral authority: The pastor is the symbolic representative of the sacred within the congregation; he or she is viewed as having special expertise for leading the congregation; and he or she is the only (or one of a few) paid person in what is otherwise a voluntary organization. These factors give pastoral leaders considerable opportunity to shape a congregation's mission orientation; this is especially important in activist congregations. Because activism often leads to controversy, it is a difficult orientation to sustain, and it would be difficult for either St. Margaret's or Downtown Baptist (although less so for Downtown) to continue as an activist church without strong clergy support.

Ironically, the two activist congregations represent extremes in polity—one strongly emphasizing congregational autonomy, the other a hierarchical tradition—and these differences affect the exercise of pastoral leadership. In Catholic parishes the pastor has considerable formal authority and the laity tend toward passivity—albeit less so since Vatican II. St. Margaret's activism is, to a considerable extent, the result of its pastor's leadership. If a pastor with a sanctuary orientation, for example, were sent to the parish, the congregation would be likely to follow his lead—such is the importance of pastoral leadership in the Catholic tradition. This is especially likely in a predominantly Puerto Rican parish like St. Margaret's, where traditional patterns of respect for priestly authority and an individualistic spirituality remain strong, particularly among older members. It is the youth, primarily, who join the pastor in engaging in social action. In contrast, at Downtown Baptist the lay leaders of the congregation made commitment to justice issues a high priority for the kind of pastor they were seeking. Thus there is among the laity a broad base of support for an activist ministry that is less evident at St. Margaret's; at Downtown it would be more difficult for a pastor with a different orientation to shift the congregation's orientation. This suggests that churches with hierarchical polities can more quickly effect a change in a congregation's mission orientation by the choice of pastors appointed to the congregation than is the case in churches with more congregational polities. In the latter a change of orientation, especially a change to an activist orientation, is more likely to develop slowly through nurturing a body of lay leadership who shape the ethos and orientation of a congregation, including the selection of pastoral leadership.

Despite the polity differences, the two activist congregations have several things in common in addition to strong pastoral leadership. First, for both, the activist orientation is grounded in a theology that makes commitment to social justice an explicit and central priority. In the Baptist case a number of members describe their theology as "old-fashioned So-cial Gospel liberalism," that is, an emphasis on Christian responsibility for working for change in society as a means of serving God. For them, God meets a person in his or her spiritual pilgrimage, not simply in the privacy of his or her interior life, but in the world, in the struggle for love and justice. In the words of the signboard, "What Can We Do Besides Pray?"

A similar theme, grounded in Catholic sacramental theology, is sounded at St. Margaret's. To recall the pastor's statement: "The Mass is the center of everything. The eucharist is the living presence of Christ. In sharing that presence the call is to go out to make that presence opera-tional, living in the world. . . . The Mass is part of the world and the world is part of the Lord." Although the two theologies are quite different in their formal aspects, they both issue in a commitment to justice that is, in effect, nondebatable. When compared with the three civic congregations, which also emphasize responsibility for life in this world but with a much less clear theological center, the activist congregations present a striking contrast. Although the theology differs considerably, the two activist con-gregations are much more like the evangelistic congregations in being clear where they stand theologically.

Second, the two churches' activist emphasis is complemented by care-ful attention to pastoral care and nurture of the members. In other words, the personal needs of the members are not neglected in the emphasis on justice (although some St. Margaret's members grumbled that the pastor was often unavailable to them because of his social involvements). For the Catholic congregation, meeting personal needs is also grounded in the Mass, which contains the "spiritual food" that "gives me the strength to keep on fighting," as one member put it. The pastor speaks of the rhythm of being both "pushed out" and "drawn back" by the Mass. The church is also the center of many social and cultural activities for the members. At Downtown Baptist the pastoral emphasis is sounded in the balance be-tween "in-house" and "out-house" concerns. Its pastoral staffing pattern also reflects these two emphases in its division of labor, with the senior pastor taking primary, although not exclusive, responsibility for the pas-toral care and nurture of the members and an associate giving primary pastoral leadership to the congregation's various community ministries. At St. Margaret's the roles are reversed, perhaps accounting for the grumblings.

The balance between justice-oriented ministries and the pastoral needs of members is a critical one, we believe, for the success of an activist congregation. Congregations, as do other organizations, not only have to come to terms with their social context—either as the arena in which they try to accomplish their mission or as a reality whose influence is to be neutralized—but they also have to deal with needs arising internally in the lives of members and in members' relationships with one another.

Unless pastoral and integrative needs are met, and unless internal tensions and conflicts are managed, a congregation is unlikely to be effective in its external mission, whether of social activism or evangelism. Without attention to inner renewal, members of activist congregations are likely to experience burnout. Indeed, being an effective mediating structure, as Peter Berger and Richard Neuhaus point out, involves giving a measure of stability to private life, while at the same time transferring meaning and value to structures of public life.[1] The relative success of our two activist congregations in achieving a balance between inner renewal and outward action stands in contrast to a congregation described by sociologists Jeffrey Hadden and Charles Longino.[2] That congregation, an experimental one established to give priority to social action, especially in behalf of racial justice, ran into difficulty largely because of its neglect of its internal life. Not only was there lack of a clear theological center binding members together, but also pastoral needs and internal conflicts were often ignored in the congregation's "instant plunge into social action projects."[3]

A third point of similarity between the two activist congregations is in the resources on which they are able to draw for both their social action and social service ministries. Neither the essentially suburban, moderately affluent, but relatively small membership of Downtown Baptist, nor the large, but predominantly poor Puerto Rican membership of St. Margaret's has sufficient financial resources within itself for the activities in which each engages. For Downtown Baptist, the resources are in the form of a substantial endowment and highly desirable property surrounding the church building that assist it in its multiple ministries. For St. Margaret's, the resources come primarily as funding from the archdiocese and, for much of its more purely social welfare work, from governmental sources. In both instances the additional resources free the congregations from being overly concerned with survival needs.

Most congregations (and other organizations as well) tend to give priority to survival needs, especially if survival is in any way threatened.[4] Freed by their resources from threats to their survival, these two congregations can express their belief in the necessity to seek justice. Having adequate resources is not, in itself, a necessary and sufficient condition for an activist missional stance; nor do such resources need always to come from the outside (or from the past, as in the case of Downtown's endowment). But having adequate resources does appear to free a congregation to give active expression to seeking justice if that search is central to the congregation's self-understanding.

A fourth similarity in the two congregations is typical of most of the congregations we have studied. Their members are hardly unanimous in holding an activist orientation. Many of St. Margaret's members, especially the older ones, view the church as a sanctuary. It is also a vehicle for maintenance of Hispanic culture (which the pastor recognizes and affirms along with his activist leanings). This relatively strong sanctuary bent among some of the members is part of the reason that the congregation's orientation could well change if the bishop were to assign a different pastor. Downtown Baptist, however, is mainly a mixture of activist and civic types, with the latter preferring a less activist, more educational stance toward social issues, leaving more of the decisions about action to individual members.

2. *The congregation as citizen.* As is evident from the case studies, civic congregations share much in common with activist ones, especially in the importance attributed to this world as the arena in which members are called to be responsible. But there are significant differences, especially in what responsibility within this world means and how it is to be exercised.

Like the activist churches, each of the three civic congregations reveals a concern for the realization of social justice. For the civic congregations, this concern manifests itself primarily in the variety of social issues that are considered within the congregation. This is particularly evident both at First Church, East Town and Carmel Baptist, but it is also a factor at River Plain Jewish. There, it will be recalled, members criticized the rabbi for not dealing enough with social issues.

Although the civic congregations' concern to explore the ethical dimensions of issues only rarely leads to direct congregational action, it is nevertheless an important service that they render their members, and one that is welcomed. In fact, one source of disappointment for some community leaders we interviewed was the lack of such exploration in their own congregations. The implications of religious beliefs and values for public issues faced by men and women in their daily lives are rarely self-evident. One of the strengths of civic congregations is their presentation of a forum in which such exploration can occur.

But unlike the activist congregations, in which commitment to justice is nondebatable, concern for justice takes a more tentative expression in civic congregations. An ethic of individual responsibility is typically encouraged. Each member is left to make up his or her own mind on what justice means and how it is to be applied. Ethical commitments, like beliefs, are generally viewed as private matters. Recall, for example, the controversy that ensued in First Church, East Town when the pastor announced an openness to draft resistance and called for amnesty for those who had left the country to avoid the draft. In seeking to involve members in this controversial action, which some feared might be interpreted as the position of the congregation, he overstepped the line between personal opinion and corporate action, or so it seemed to many members. But when he owns his positions on justice issues as his personal opinion rather than as *the* Christian position or that of the congregation, such behavior is not only tolerated, but also deeply appreciated for helping members clarify their own positions.

The line between corporate action and individual decision making reflects, on the one hand, a much less clear theological center in civic congregations. In First Church it is a vague theological liberalism—love of God and love of neighbor—but there is lack of consensus as to how love is to be applied. Rather, this is viewed as a matter of individual responsibility and discretion. Because Judaism is much more a religion of practice than of belief, the lack of a clear theological center in the River Plain congregation is perhaps more understandable. Yet even the commitment to affirming their Jewishness as a central theme of belonging has to be broadened and compromised in order to accommodate the diversity of interpretations of Jewishness in the congregation. There is also considerable latitude in the matter of ritual observance. This lack of a clear center—whether of belief or of ritual observance—is one factor reflected in the civic orientation's emphasis on individual decision making rather than corporate congregational action.

On the other hand, it reflects what is generally the overriding commitment of civic congregations—tolerance and respect for diversity. We are tempted to say that there is probably only one issue over which civic congregations would likely take corporate action, and that would be to fight an attack on pluralism and tolerance. Jews and Christians seem united on this. Thus congregational social action or official positions of the congregation on social issues are generally ruled out for fear of dividing the congregation and alienating the community. The latter fear is understandably stronger for members of River Plain Jewish, who do not wish to make themselves vulnerable to anti-Semitic attacks. They want to be Jewish but not so distinctively that they are not accepted as good citizens and as part of East Town's interfaith religious community. At Carmel Baptist the same tension is present between identity with the black community and with the corporate and public leadership structures within which the pastor and many members are well placed. Similarly, civic-oriented para-congregational organizations generally avoid taking stands on issues that will alienate their members or the broader community. Sociologist John Murray Cuddihy says that such concerns are the result of the corrosive effects both of the pluralistic situation of American society and of American civil religion.

> *Civil religion manages, in the end, to convince the traditional believer that to make specific allusions in public places to, say, the saving Gospel of Jesus Christ (should he be an evangelical Protestant) or to the chosen-people doctrine (should he be an observant Jew) is to*

> *commit a social impropriety that is at the same time a religious her-*
> *esy.*[5]

We would add to Cuddihy's list of "improprieties" taking a congregational stand on a controversial social issue.

The emphasis on pluralism and tolerance makes the job of pastor or rabbi of a civic congregation a difficult one indeed. As we have seen in the cases, such pastors and rabbis must walk the tightrope between dealing with social issues in light of Judeo-Christian beliefs and values—which their members expect them to do—and doing this in such a way that members are left to make up their own minds. It is important that social issues be addressed, but they must be addressed in ways that avoid giving offense. Conflict management is an increasingly valued ministerial skill and is especially valuable for the civic pastor if he or she, or an activist group within the congregation, crosses the boundaries of civility. The relatively long tenure of the pastors of First Church and Carmel Baptist is in part a testimony to their ability to walk the tightrope.

Tolerance of diversity often leads civic congregations to downplay public issues in favor of private concerns—family life, personal growth, personal morality, and so forth. Nevertheless, civic congregations do escape being totally captive to the private sphere by their involvement in social service programs and by providing opportunities for members to reflect on personal and social issues in light of religious beliefs and values. In the latter, especially, the congregations play the important role of mediating structures, linking members and public life. Yet in refraining from taking stands and by leaving action to the discretion of individual members, civic congregations do implicitly, if not explicitly, support the status quo.

Members acting individually out of an ethic of individual responsibility frequently find themselves caught between various cross-pressuring interests—those of family, neighborhood, job, racial or ethnic identity, and other organizational involvements—that make it difficult for them to challenge the status quo in terms of their faith commitments. In the three civic congregations we studied, these cross-pressuring elements spring rather consistently from the involvements of their generally upper-middle-class members. This is true not only of First Church members, who historically have been the "establishment," but also of members at River Plain Jewish and Carmel Baptist. They too, for the most part, have made it to upper-middle-class status, and being rather newly arrived at this position, they are even less likely to want to jeopardize it by challenges to the status quo. Thus in many instances no challenge gets made; no questions get raised about the implications of one's faith for particular situations; no alternatives get proposed when action is left to individual discretion. Although a congregation or a group within it taking a public stand or action on an issue of social justice may not be able to "move mountains," it frequently introduces a transcendent element into the situation that cannot forever be ignored. And it does so as a group, not as an isolated individual.

The cross-pressures felt by upper-middle-class congregations, extenuated by a commitment to tolerate diversity and norms of civility, also work against any strong evangelistic thrust. Tensions in this regard are most evident at Carmel Baptist, whose periodic "revivals" maintain at least some tie to this central element of its black heritage. First Church, East Town, in contrast, is so thoroughly and historically civic that the matter of evangelism is rarely an issue.

Finally, we note that for both River Plain Jewish and Carmel Baptist, strong sanctuary overtones are combined with the civic orientation. The synagogue and the congregation provide safe havens, respectively, for Jews and blacks who live most of their lives in a majority gentile and white environment. This is also the role, it will be remembered, that St. Margaret's plays for its Hispanic members. In a less manifest and less encompassing way, this is also the role First Church, East Town has played for East Town's "Yankee" establishment. The function of religion as a way of affirming and maintaining ethnic identity is an important one. It is similar to, indeed part of, the role that religion plays more generally in personal integration, which was noted earlier as a necessary counterpoint to the activist commitment to justice. Nevertheless, the emphasis on maintaining ethnic identity often creates severe tensions between ethnic particularism and a more universalistic perspective, whether it is the "universalism of tolerance" of American civil religion or the more demanding, justice-oriented universalism of the Judeo-Christian prophetic tradition. Although our personal sympathies lie with the latter, we believe that it is important not to ignore or underestimate the significance of the identity-maintenance function of religion—a mistake often made by those who criticize churches and synagogues for their failure to be more aggressive in seeking justice.[6]

3. *The congregation as sanctuary.* Identity maintenance is also very much at issue in the three congregations representing the sanctuary orientation: Cristo Pentecostal, St. Felix, and Faith Episcopal. For Cristo, ethnic identity is an explicit concern. This is also true to some extent for Faith, where "Anglo-Catholic" and "American" (as contrasted with "Hispanic" and "Portuguese") are important sources of group identification. For St. Felix, identity maintenance is important, but it is less explicitly linked to ethnicity, at least in the parish's corporate life, partly because St. Felix's membership represents the dominant social-cultural ethos of its suburban community.

In addition to their strong emphasis on the identity maintenance function of religion, the three congregations share at least one other trait: They place little, if any, emphasis on action in the world as a priority for Christian ministry. The reasons for this shared attribute differ among the congregations; however, even the physical appearance of their buildings and grounds symbolizes separation from the world: Recall the fences around Cristo and Faith and the hedge that almost hides St. Felix from public view.

Unlike Cristo, with its premillenarian theology of individual salvation, which defines the world as evil, both Faith and St. Felix share a decidedly sacramental theological emphasis that, at least in principle, does not devalue the world; so too, it will be recalled, does St. Margaret's, the activist Catholic parish. But whereas sacramental theology at St. Margaret's is interpreted as emphasizing sacramental involvement of Christians in the world in seeking social change, it has a different significance in the two sanctuary congregations. At St. Felix this seems intentional. The pastor, who plays a powerful role in shaping the congregation's ethos and orientation, defines what happens at the altar as primarily *individual* reconciliation to God, which is, secondarily, expressed by the *individual* in his or her daily life through doing good and being an exemplary citizen. In contrast, at Faith there is an explicit acknowledgment, at least by the rector, that what happens at the altar should flow into both a corporate and an individual concern for the world. Although many of the members agree, there is little evidence that this happens. Indeed, we are struck by the ambivalence about community involvement at Faith. To recall but one example, the sign in front of the church building is in English and in Portuguese, but members do not reach out to the Portuguese, nor do they seem to know how to do so; and the one thing they know would help— learning to speak Portuguese—they are not interested in doing. They are in Holtville but no longer of it.

At St. Felix the pastor sets the tone of the parish and is primarily responsible for the strong, inward-looking sanctuary orientation that exists. Most of the members seem to acquiesce to his leadership—in part because of its affinity with their own expectations—finding satisfaction in the well-done liturgies for which the parish is noted and taking pride in their building. It is here that the congregation's identity seems to be focused. Not much is demanded of members either by way of financial contributions or in outreach to the community. Furthermore, the lack of facilities and additional staff precludes many nonliturgical kinds of parish activities that could lead to a stronger bonding and experience of community among the members, which might, in turn, issue in greater concern for the broader community. As a mediating structure, it truncates its "public face" in favor of its "private face," except for the rather vague

255

emphasis on good citizenship. In so doing the congregation generally reinforces the split between the public and private sectors and supports the status quo.

Faith fails to give expression to the public thrust of its sacramental theology for quite different reasons. These seem to be the combination of a complex community setting and, especially, a lack of resources and will to reach out to it. Although the congregation has adequate financial resources for the limited ministry in which it engages, it has (or at least perceives it has) no surplus on which to draw, as was true for the two activist congregations. More important, members do not perceive themselves to have adequate human resources to carry out ministry in the community. They are not only mostly elderly, but also are generally nonresident in the community around the church. Furthermore, as "Americans," they are different from those who now inhabit the community— Hispanics and Portuguese. Efforts to reach out to the community have not been particularly successful, and lacking successes on which to build, it becomes even more difficult for them to continue to try. Thus they have come increasingly to define their presence and identity primarily in noncommunity terms as offering an Anglo-Catholic "sanctuary" in the Greater Hartford region. Also working against a greater involvement with the world is the awareness that if they were to be successful, substantial changes in the nature of the congregation would probably result; and the risk of "losing ourselves" is not one the current members are willing to take.

Cristo Pentecostal is a very different sanctuary-oriented congregation from either of the others. The difference results partly from the fact that it is Hispanic and Spanish speaking, but it goes much deeper. Its theology stresses individual conversion out of the world, which, in keeping with Cristo's premillenarian theology, is itself devalued and defined as evil. There is no concern at all for a change-oriented ministry within society; rather, the Christian is to live in the world insofar as that is necessary but keep herself or himself as free as possible from its corrupting influences (the theological embodiment of Faith's fear of "losing oneself"). Its theology provides a definition of the situation that encourages its members to separate themselves from the world. Its intense congregational life, which involves members at Cristo for much of their waking, nonwork time, ensures that they will not have much opportunity to be corrupted.

The intensity of congregational life at Cristo may be contrasted with what happens at both St. Felix and Faith. We have already noted how St. Felix's lack of adequate physical facilities beyond its sanctuary forecloses other kinds of programs and social interaction among members. The widely dispersed congregation of Faith, the lack of much program beyond the Sunday Masses, and the division of the small congregation by the two Sunday services also weaken the bonding and sense of community of its members. If a congregation wishes to maintain a distinctive theological identity or a distinctive orientation to mission, it must develop a strong social base in which its orientation is rehearsed and the bonding of its members strengthened. In this regard Cristo has the strength for a much more publicly proactive ministry. However, its theology generally precludes an activist orientation, and limitations of language generally preclude a more widespread emphasis on evangelism.

"Withdrawal" themes are more pronounced at Cristo than at the other two congregations. Nonetheless the congregation illustrates a distinctive form of mediation between members and the wider society. The case illustrates clearly this church's role in reinforcing values of personal discipline, family life, hard work, and patriotism—all of which serve Cristo members well in the very world the church devalues. Although the church is otherworldly in its theology, it encourages values and traits that often lead to worldly success.[7]

Will Cristo help its members move into the mainstream of American life? And if so, will they remain at Cristo? And with what effects: possibly pushing it toward a more civic (witness Carmel Baptist) or evangelistic (as Grace Assembly) orientation? We cannot answer these questions here, but they are among the more fascinating ones emerging from the cases themselves. Speculation about the role religion has played in the mainstreaming of other ethnic groups that have moved into, up, and out of Hartford has led some local commentators to draw rather pointed conclusions about the appropriate role of religion among the disenfranchised in the city.[8]

4. *The congregation as evangelist.* The two evangelical congregations are characterized by their commitment to proclaiming salvation in Christ to others. Both churches know what they believe, have a clear sense of their mission in the world, and are organized to carry out that mission. They have a stronger and more unified sense of purpose than is found in any of the other cases, and their program is more consistently expressive of that purpose. Strong pastoral leadership is evident, as is true of most of the other cases; but at Mountainview Baptist and Grace Assembly it is supported by a distinctively high level of lay involvement, both in the congregations' internal programs and in their outreach ministries.

Both Mountainview Baptist and Grace Assembly of God, like the two activist cases, have a good grasp of their environment but with very different consequences. Grace, located in Hartford's most affluent neighborhood, finds itself both sociologically and religiously removed from its immediate community. Correctly perceiving that this distance makes the neighborhood generally unreceptive to its ministry, it turns its attention elsewhere—to public parks and shopping areas. It remains a "city church," but one that sees its ministry directed toward the entire metropolitan area. Unlike Faith Episcopal, which is both perplexed and uncomfortable with its Holtville neighborhood, Grace seems to have ceased worrying about it; through broadening its target service area it goes on with its business of "winning the lost for Christ." Mountainview, however, has a more complex relationship to its wealthy suburban community. It lives with the realization that Mountainview Church is "different" and that its presence is regarded ambiguously by neighboring congregations, who waver between seeing Mountainview as an ecumenical and civic partner and as an unwelcome, competitive intrusion prone to improprieties. Mountainview's pastor and members want cordial relations with the community, but they are unwilling to accept fully the rules of mutual toleration that make the relationship between River Plain Jewish and First Church, East Town, for example, a comfortable one.

The uneasy relationship between Mountainview and its community grows out of the community's suspicion of "Baptists," on the one hand, and the church's conviction that its way is "*the* way," on the other. The laity are clear that their purpose is to bring people to Christ, and for at least some, that includes, in one member's words, "church-going non-Christians."

Whereas Grace Assembly's biracial membership stands out in Hartford's predominantly white West End, Mountainview's members fit very well in Rockfield. Like most of the community's residents, its members are affluent, white family members. Many commute to white-collar professional jobs in the city and are above average in educational background. If Mountainview's members are different from their neighbors, it is because they live "redeemed" lives, marked by abstaining from alcohol and tobacco, by devoting significant portions of their time to the work of the church, by holding to exemplary standards of personal behavior, and by standing ready to share their faith with others.

Evangelism occupies a central place in the life of Grace and Mountainview churches, but it takes different shapes. At Grace, members "take to the streets" with their promise of salvation. Leafleting at the convention center, visiting at the hospital and prison, distributing Bibles at shopping centers, and witnessing to co-workers and family members are very much public activities. Mountainview takes a more relational and program-based approach that better suits its "sophisticated" suburban community. The church knows that "street-corner evangelism" will have little appeal in Rockfield, but home Bible study, informal counseling for those facing life crises, a strong youth program with a presence in the public schools, and aggressive home visitation efforts serve the church well.

The two evangelical congregations are somewhat more intentional about the social dimensions of their community role than the three sanctuary cases. Although neither sees advocacy on behalf of social change as important to its mission, contemporary issues do receive attention from the pulpit and in group study. The choice of issues centers almost exclusively on matters of personal moral concerns, with abortion, homosexuality, drug abuse, and family life being of special concern. Both pastors are careful to distinguish between the "moral" and the "political" aspects of public issues and define their responsibility as exclusively directed toward the former. Thus Mountainview's pastor can speak of Hartford's poverty and the need to address it but is quick to add, "I am not going to tell you how to do it because that is a *political* statement, only that it must happen—that is a *Christian* statement."

This approach to community and regional concerns is different from that of the civic congregations, in which the distinction between the moral and the political is not made so sharply and one finds openness to diverse moral and political answers; in most cases there is resistance to the thought that a *single* morally or politically correct position exists. The two evangelical congregations are more open to the possibility that scripture and tradition do provide moral absolutes but carefully avoid the "politics" of public issues.

As was true for the two activist cases, the two evangelistic cases complement their strong outreach ministries with an equally strong concern for the pastoral and spiritual needs of members. Also similarly to the activist cases, both Mountainview and Grace Assembly appear to draw on extraordinary financial resources. However, in the evangelistic cases this is due to the unusually high level of giving of members rather than to the endowments or outside sources drawn on by the two activist cases.

Pluralism and tolerance of diversity are not major concerns of Mountainview or, especially, Grace. Their theology is clear and unequivocal, discipline is strict and demanding. To the extent that "other points of view" are taken into consideration, it is largely in terms of combating or co-opting them, rather than embracing them. Yet it must also be noted that Grace is one of the few truly ethnically integrated congregations in the Hartford area. Like activist-oriented Downtown Baptist, this stems in part from the conscious attempt to embody the theological tenet that all are one in Christ. Combined with this, it is also due in part—more so at Grace than at Downtown Baptist—to a clear and passionate focus on religious matters. That is, like-mindedness may be the norm, but it takes the form of religious conviction rather than racial distinctiveness. At the same time neither church is able totally to transcend social homogeneity. At both Grace and Downtown Baptist socioeconomic affinities are evident with the working class at Grace and with the middle class at Downtown Baptist. This may be more a matter of style or practice than of belief or intention, but it nevertheless appears as a sociological factor that works against either congregation's ability to mediate across the social divisions of public life.

Why the Different Orientations?

To this point we have avoided speculation on the sources or "causes" of the four mission orientations around which we have organized much of our discussion of religious presence. We have tried to tell the story of Hartford religion in terms its key actors would recognize and understand and have tried to restrain our own "sociological imaginations" in the interest of fair and accurate description. One cannot leave the congregational case studies, however, without some reflections on the sources of the diversity we have seen. Why do these ten congregations—nine of which share a common Christian background—understand their relationship to their community so differently?

We have earlier expressed our point of view that a congregation's mission orientation grows out of interaction between its social context, the social worlds of its members, and the history, internal structures, processes, and programs of the congregation itself. This perspective has informed the presentation of the congregational cases; it also helps us understand the diversity we see in them.

1. *Social context.* Chapters 3 and 4 look at the historical and contemporary social context in which Hartford's religious bodies minister. Individual congregations live within that general context but experience particular pieces of it more directly than others. First Church, River Plain Jewish, and Mountainview Evangelical Baptist, for example, share a comfortable suburban environment in which the separation of the public and private spheres of life is especially pronounced, in which norms of civility prevail, in which the future looks fairly bright, and in which significant social problems are generally "hushed up." The problems of the central city seem very abstract and far away. Given such a community setting, the prevalence of civic themes in these congregations is not surprising; the notion of the congregation as informed but free citizen fits the environment. Even Mountainview, whose evangelistic orientation is unmistakable, has adopted a "no offense" style. To do otherwise would establish clearer boundaries between the church and its community than the church itself desires. It is also evident in the cases that the "comfort" of suburban life contributes to the more casual and self-centered nature of many suburban congregations' identities, a relationship certainly not missed by many of the church's more staunch critics of decades past (see, for example, the discussions of chapters 1 and 2).

For the city congregations—notably Carmel and Downtown Baptist, St. Margaret's, and the two Holtville neighborhood churches—the problems of poverty and of racial and economic injustice that from a suburban standpoint seem distant are real and immediate. How they are to be approached remains at issue, but even for congregations whose members live elsewhere, the problems are inescapable. Not only are city congregations more immediately confronted with the social problems and dilemmas of modern-day urban existence, but they are also more directly confronted with the diversity of urban life. As commentators on urban life have argued for generations, the city—in contrast to smaller, less complex communities—provides and indeed forces choices on individuals and institutions. Perhaps this explains in part why in both the cases and in the survey of congregations we find that city congregations are more likely to have strong identities than are their suburban counterparts, and that there tends to be more diversity between congregational identities in the city than elsewhere.

Such diversity in the orientations of city congregations is not new; our historical overview of religious presence in Hartford showed that the variety of religious responses to changes in the city dates almost to its founding. Even within denominational traditions, churches and synagogues have defined their relationship to neighborhoods and communities in different ways. That process of definition and redefinition continues, with the range of choices and possibilities being perhaps greater than ever before; it is especially evident in the heart of the city. Peter Berger writes of individuals when he speaks of modernization's disruption of traditional patterns of ordering human life. "What previously was self-evident fact," he asserts, "now becomes an occasion to choose."[9] His point applies to institutions as well. As the "outer world" of contemporary urban society becomes more diverse, the "inner world" of individuals and institutions becomes more complex; part of this "inner complexity" is a growing awareness that choices have been and must continue to be made. The social context, therefore, has an impact not only at the point of *what* choice might be made. It also, and perhaps more important, has an impact on the realization *that* a choice must be made.

2. *Social worlds.* A second important source of the diversity we have observed in mission orientations comes from the varying values, interests, and backgrounds that members bring to their congregations. Contrast, for example, the immigrant backgrounds of Cristo and St. Margaret's members with those of the members of nearby Faith Episcopal or suburban First Church of Christ in East Town. The fact that the members of River Plain Jewish are a generation removed from the Holocaust, that Carmel Baptist's members are descendants of slaves, that St. Felix's parishioners are mostly blue-collar factory workers, that Grace Assembly of God and Downtown Baptist attract mostly Jamaican but fewer American-born blacks all suggest the variety of social worlds that church and synagogue members bring to their religious participation.

John Michael Cuddihy has noted that for most Americans, church membership is but one of several sources of individual identity that pull members in different directions; being part of several groups subjects individuals to cross-pressuring. Cuddihy calls this "crisscrossing." Increasingly, lines of social cleavage come to be drawn not only among institutions and groups, but also *within individuals themselves.* If any of the East Town congregations, for example, were to address urban issues or economic injustice in a forceful manner (as St. Margaret's does), they would likely put members into conflict with themselves in the other roles in which they are engaged. Thus the civic strategy of leaving application of ethical understandings to individuals becomes a way of dealing with cross-pressuring, without undue prejudice to any of the conflicting sources of pressure. Carmel Baptist illustrates one common consequence: a "softening" of the church's activist and evangelical instincts. The same dynamic is evident in the more sanctuary-oriented St. Felix and Faith Episcopal. Other congregations handle the problem differently. Downtown Baptist, the example, while taking risks in speaking and acting corporately on controversial matters, leaves most of the implementation of its action to its staff; St. Margaret's manages a compromise by permitting different groups to involve themselves differently, unity being maintained through the shared experience of the Mass. In each case, nevertheless, there is evidence of the limiting effect of members' social worlds on the degree to which the congregation is publicly proactive. It seems too that whatever the nature of the compromise involved it arises in large part out of a conscious commitment to an inclusive conception of membership.

Grace Assembly and Cristo, however, take a different approach. Rather than presenting members with some sort of compromise between "religious" and "secular" cross-pressures, these congregations, in effect, force a choice. Either one becomes "transformed" in line with church teachings or one is removed; or, as is more often the case, one removes oneself from active involvement in the congregation. For those who become transformed, cross-pressuring is reduced not only by a singular and intensely salient adherence to belief, but also by increasingly limiting one's social interactions to church-related activities. More and more one's social world and one's religious world become one.[10]

3. *Theology.* At several points in the previous section in which we reflected on the cases, we noted the significance of polity, organizational structure, program, leadership roles and behavior, financial and human resources, member bonding and expectations, and other internal features of congregational life in contributing to the definition of mission orientations and their working out in congregational praxis. Here we simply reaffirm their importance without further commentary. There is, however, one aspect of congregational life that we believe is critical in shaping its mission orientation and accounting for the diversity that exists in those orientations. We refer to the importance of a congregation's theological stance.

We believe that it is impossible to read the congregational cases and fail to conclude that, in fundamental ways, each congregation's mission orientation is grounded in its understanding of the action of God in history. The mission orientations mirror the congregations' core theological assumptions that are drawn from the various strands of their faith traditions. As important as the social context, members' social worlds, the internal processes and programs are to the church or synagogue's understanding of mission, its theological self-understanding remains critical. The pluralism we have witnessed as we looked at congregations from the standpoint of their community presence reflects a deeper diversity in the ways congregations see themselves before God.

At the risk of repeating what may now be obvious, we recall that the activist orientation reflects a theology grounded in beliefs about God's purposes to realize a realm of justice and peace in the world. The church exists as a means of redemption for individuals and the world, not as a haven in which individuals can escape the world. What happens in the fellowship and worship of the congregation or in the celebration of the eucharist leads not only to individual renewal, but also to active participation by the congregation in work for God's kingdom of justice and peace in the world. As we have seen, the civic orientation is grounded in a somewhat similar theological understanding of the world; however, it is more individualistic in its understanding of how Christian (or Jewish) responsibility is to be exercised, and it makes seeking peace—understood to a large extent as harmony and respect for differences—more central than justice. In contrast, both sanctuary and evangelistic orientations stem from a theological understanding of the world as transient, essentially evil, and to be tolerated, if not avoided altogether. The premillenarian theology of both Cristo and Grace Assembly, looking to the soon-to-be-experienced "end times," is a basic theological foundation of their mission orientations. For Cristo, it leads to the creation of an alternative community that consumes much of the time and energy of its members; for Grace, it sends members out into the highways and byways of the city to fulfill Jesus' Great Commission and save individuals from the cataclysms that are to come. Although the other sanctuary and evangelistic congregations do not ascribe to the same premillenarian theology, their orientations also seem grounded in a belief that God's purposes are to be realized in the church, not in the world. For the sanctuary orientation, this means withdrawing to experience the means of grace through the Sacraments, through the preached Word, and through the fellowship of like-minded believers; for the evangelistic orientation, it means also a compulsion to call others to share in this new life apart from the world. And while Jesus' command to love and serve one's neighbor leads to acts of charity and service, there is no corresponding expression of a mission that seeks to realize justice and peace. The kingdom of God is to be realized within the *redeemed individual*, not within society.

Although more could be said about the theological grounding of the four mission orientations—especially their historical roots in different strands of the religious tradition—our basic point is that the orientations cannot be understood solely as a function of the social context or the social worlds of the members; they must also be understood as the working out of theological assumptions about God and God's purposes for the world and the role of the church or synagogue in it.

At the same time that we stress the theological grounding evident in all the cases, we do not want to suggest that theological considerations are given equal valence in all the congregations we have studied. The case studies suggest that the centrality and clarity of a theological base are directly related to the urgency of choice felt by a congregation and are indirectly related to commitment to tolerance of diversity. The former, as argued above, is itself related to being located in the city, whereas the latter has a decided affinity with the social worlds of higher socioeconomic status groups.

These reflections confirm for us the importance of an interactionist perspective for understanding congregations, including their mission orientation. In their normative concern with theology, religious leaders sometimes forget the major role that social factors—context and social worlds—play in shaping orientations in congregational "earthen vessels." Others, however, including many social scientists, tend to downplay or disregard the role of theological factors and see social class or context as determinative. As a more adequate perspective, we repeat the two propositions about congregations stated in chapter 2:

> 1. A congregation—its theology and ethics, its worship, its programs, its style of operation, and what it does or does not do with reference to mission—is profoundly shaped by its social context and the social class of its members.
> 2. A congregation, by virtue of its relationship to a religious or faith tradition, has the capacity, in a limited way, to transcend the determinative power of its context and the values and interests of its members, so that it influences them as well as being influenced by them.

Max Weber expressed this interaction especially helpfully as reflecting an "elective affinity" between certain constellations of ideas—theological beliefs, for example—and such social factors as class interests. Neither completely determines the other. Rather, to use his image, ideas (or beliefs) serve analogously to railroad switchmen, directing the tracks along which interests are pushed.[11] Weber's point is clearly made in several of the cases. Sometimes class interests and theology seem to be harmonious, as in the case of the members of St. Margaret's. Again there are times when a congregation's theology seems to push its members in directions counter to their class interests, as at Downtown Baptist. We have also seen how the pull of interests deflects and weakens theological influences, as in several of the civic congregations.

Acknowledging both the importance of theology in shaping the orientations and the interaction of theological and social factors, however, does not solve the more basic normative question of which is the *right* or *true* mission orientation. As important as it is, this question has not been our primary concern. Rather, our purpose has been to describe and analyze the pluralism that exists and the contributions that each of the various orientations make to public life in an urban region like Hartford. It is important that this diversity be recognized and that the variety of contributions to public life of religious groups be taken seriously, however positive or negative these contributions are judged to be from a normative perspective. Nevertheless, there are normative implications to such description and analysis. It could imply a totally relativistic position that ignores differences to the point that it cuts the nerve of commitment, as it sometimes seemed to do in several of the case studies. But this need not be the result. Rather, it can lead to what H. Richard Niebuhr called *historical* relativism, which is quite different from a totally relativistic stance. Historical relativism recognizes the limitation imposed on our ability to see truth whole and without distortion by virtue of our situation in the midst of history. In Niebuhr's words:

> [It] does not imply subjectivism and skepticism. It is not evident that the man who is forced to confess that his view of things is conditioned by the standpoint he occupies must doubt the reality of what he sees. It is not apparent that one who knows that his concepts are not universal must also doubt that they are concepts of the universal, or that one who understands his experience is historically mediated must believe that nothing is mediated through history.[12]

The response to revelation (and here we speak more theologically than sociologically) must be confessional and provisional, made from within the limited point of view of personal history and the community of faith. "Religious response to revelation," as Niebuhr puts it, "is made quite as much in a confession of sin as in a confession of faith."[13] Such a position would probably be unacceptable to several of the congregations we have analyzed, but to us it seems virtually inevitable in a pluralistic society, and in a more positive sense, it prevents the idolatry that comes from absolutizing one's historically limited perspective—without, we would add, cutting the nerve of commitment.

CHAPTER 11

RELIGIOUS PRESENCE: CONCLUDING REFLECTIONS

Beyond the comparisons and generalizations about the congregations and their mission orientations of chapter 10, what can be said by way of conclusion about religious presence and its consequences for public life? What, additionally, has been learned about the possibilities for a more effective religious presence that may be helpful to those who are concerned with urban ministry? Each of these questions is addressesd briefly in this chapter.

RELIGION'S CONTINUING CONTRIBUTIONS TO PUBLIC LIFE

During the course of our research someone asked us what difference it would make if Hartford's churches and synagogues were suddenly to disappear? Would their absence have any effect on the quality of life in the city?

Taking a broad historical perspective we acknowledge that we cannot say with any certainty that religion is more effective or less effective in public life at the present time than it has been in the past. Clearly, its social role is different from what it was in the days of Thomas Hooker, when religious presence was equivalent to Congregationalist presence; or of Horace Bushnell, when the dominant presence was still primarily Protestant; or even in the 1950s, when people could look to a "triumvirate" of religious leaders who represented a recognized interfaith presence as they spoke to public issues in the name of religion. Institutionally, many religious organizations face problems. The steady membership and financial growth of the years after World War II appears to be over; as we saw in chapters 1 and 3, the problems facing city neighborhoods and suburban towns are complex and do not lend themselves to simple solutions, and there is little consensus, either within the churches and synagogues or outside, on religion's public role. Certainly the various types of data we have analyzed during the course of this project bear out each of these generalizations.

For all the differences between the present and past and the changes in religious institutions, much of our data shows that religion remains an important and broadly appreciated positive presence in the life of the region. This presence takes diverse forms. Church buildings occupy prominent locations at the center of most of the region's communities, their steeples rising above the region's "Main Streets" as silent reminders of the presence of the transcendent in the middle of life. People gather in churches and synagogues, communicating to outsiders a corporate dimension of their religious faith that transcends individualism and isolation. Religious communities provide rites of passage that help individuals pass through personally and socially disruptive transitional experiences—birth, puberty, marriage, death. Fellowship and solidarity are offered in the face of the loneliness and isolation of a mobile society. Congregations—some more effectively than others—help members develop values that provide guidance in their private and public lives. Both congregations and para-congregational organizations provide many needed social services in all the region's communities. Individuals, acting out of religious commitment, witness to their faith as they serve the region and its people in countless ways. Indeed, if the various religious organizations of Greater Hartford ceased to exist, if nothing else, their absence would mean the loss of the estimated $5.5 million that they contribute annually to meeting human need, plus the uncalculated worth of volunteer time that members contribute in human service programs, and the use made of synagogue and church buildings by community organizations and agencies. These and many other positive contributions of religion to the life of the Greater Hartford community are important and should be affirmed. Their absence would create a considerable void in the life of the region far beyond the dollar value of the services provided.

Some Issues and Implications

To rest the matter with a summary of the positive contributions is not enough. Our data also reveal potential not yet realized and suggest to us several issues that must be confronted if that potential is to be realized. Five issues in particular bear mentioning.

1. *Religious pluralism and moral discourse.* One thing should be quite obvious by now: Religious presence in the public life of Hartford is plural rather than singular, polychrome rather than monochrome. Although pluralism is so obvious a reality, we are struck by the way in which people often speak or write about "*the* church," "*the* synagogue," or "religion," as if each were a single, undifferentiated whole with a character and mission that is the same in all places and all times. We found this perception common to many of Hartford's leaders, who seemed to assume considerably more homogeneity and shared values within the religious community than actually exist. There may be some transcendent values shared by the various faith communities in Hartford that, if pursued with sufficient diligence, could be identified, but these do not translate easily into a shared conception of the common good nor a unified stance with regard to public life.

The most obvious consequence of this is a sense, frequently expressed, of the lack of a compelling moral framework, grounded in religion, in terms of which public life and various public issues in the region can be understood and purposes defined for the city and region. People we interviewed put this in different ways. They reminisced about earlier times in which key religious leaders could "bring moral force into government" or "make the community do what it should do." They spoke of a desire for the religious community to "frame issues in a moral tone," to "take care of the whole body politic," to "capture the hearts, not just the pocketbook." Many community leaders and average citizens continue, therefore, to look to denominations, local churches, synagogues, and, specifically, religious leaders to take the lead in articulating a moral framework, but they sense with some disappointment that this is not being done. Given both the complexity of the issues and especially the pluralism that exists religiously, it is unrealistic and naive to think that anything approximating a consensus could possibly be attained that would satisfy the expressed desire for such a framework as is thought rightly or wrongly to have been a reality in some past time.

At the same time this does not preclude efforts to stimulate moral discourse that take a more confessional, historically relative form analogous to that we advocated with reference to theology in chapter 10. For example, one important contribution might be careful, thoughtful analyses of public issues and various aspects of public life undertaken by representatives of the religious community (clergy and lay), perhaps working together with leaders and others from the community. To do so would require taking the time and making the effort to listen to one another, to understand the issues in depth, and to ask what insights their particular faith tradition has to offer on the issues. The recent pastoral letter on disarmament by America's Catholic bishops is an example at the national level of what is possible, perhaps on a less grand scale, at the local community level. Such analyses obviously would not take the place of other kinds of public activity on the part of religious organizations, but they would be one important way of providing religious and moral guidance on public issues that seems presently to be seriously lacking. Also important in this regard is the kind of religious and moral reflection on public issues that some congregations—notably ones representing civic orientations—engage in within the congregation. Insofar as they provide this kind of reflection and, equally important, provide support and encouragement for members who seek to incorporate these insights into their thought and behavior in the public sphere, congregations themselves can play an important role in fostering a religiously grounded moral framework for public life and issues.

2. *Religion and the "public."* Reflection on our data suggests a second, closely related issue. It is not only a sense of a religiously grounded moral framework for understanding public life that is absent, but also a sense of the "public" itself, and it is terribly difficult to articulate a religious and moral basis for public life when there is no real awareness of what that public is. The "public" is "all the people" in an area—black, white, brown, yellow, male, female, rich, poor, middle class, old, young, Republican, Democrat, Italian, Lithuanian, Puerto Rican, Irish, WASP, city dweller, suburbanite, and so on and on. The lack of a sense of the "public" in its diversity and commonality is at the root of enclave politics and privatization. People think in terms of group or individual interests, with little or no concern for that which makes for the common good.

In times past, when communities were smaller and admittedly more homogeneous, the parish church, along with the market and other public places, provided settings in which the "public" could be experienced in its diversity, and in which one would be aware of both diversity and commonality. Religious ceremonies were also particularly important in this regard. Historian Peter Brown describes one consequence of the regular pilgrimages that Christians in late antiquity made to the tombs of the saints, which typically were located outside the city walls. In the pilgrimages were women and men, slave and free, upper and lower classes. In this experience they could look back at the city from which they had come and gain new perspective on it, its structures, and the distinctions and divisions that were part of its life. The pilgrimages provided new insight into the character of public life. In Brown's words:

> As Victor Turner has pointed out, the abandonment of known structures for a situation where such structures are absent, and the consequent release of spontaneous fellow feeling, are part of the enduring appeal of the experience of pilgrimage in settled societies. The accustomed social world looks very different from even a short walk outside the town. William Christian has described the effect of

processions to nearby shrines of the saints in northern Spain: "As images of social wholeness, the processions have an added significance. The villagers for once in the year see the village as a social unit, abstracted from the buildings and location that make it a geographical unit."[1]

Today's churches and synagogues—or at least most of them that we have studied—are relatively homogeneous enclaves, rarely providing such experiences of the public in all its diversity. Partly this reflects the "captivity" of congregations to particular geographic settings that are homogeneous in class, race, or ethnicity. Also working against the experience of wholeness is the particularistic role that religion plays in affirming and maintaining ethnic identity that we noted in the discussion of the cases. Important exceptions among the case studies include Downtown Baptist and Grace Assembly of God. With their racially diverse memberships, these congregations exemplify Christianity's universalistic thrust that transcends the barriers of race, gender, and class. Unfortunately, these are exceptions and not the rule; thus the important potential contribution that churches and synagogues could make in sustaining a sense of the public is seriously weakened. A continuing effort must be made by congregational leaders to counter the "walls of separation" that geography and particularism create so that members can have that sense of involvement in a public that is broader than "our kind of folk." Some ways of doing this are suggested in the following sections.[2]

3. *Identification with the community.* In the interviews with community leaders and in the cases of particular congregations, there was evidence that some congregations have little real identification with the community immediately around them, much less the Greater Hartford community. Rather, they have created physical, social, or psychological walls between the congregation and the local or regional community. To be sure, this is somewhat consistent with the theology and mission orientation of some of the congregations; nevertheless its consequences for public life are negative.

Meaningful presence in public life, including fostering a sense of the public good, calls for evidence that congregational leaders and members identify with the community and genuinely care about it. This begins with the immediate community but does not end there. In a very practical sense it means coming to know the community, its structures, and, above all, its people. It means having a visible presence on the streets, at city and town council meetings, in union halls and the homes of welfare recipients—not to deliver pronouncements, but to listen and communicate the congregation's role as full participant in community life. Such "being there" in identification with the community is the kind of presence implied in what was called "milieu transformation" in earlier uses of the language of religious presence.*

Identification with the larger community of which neighborhoods and towns are a part is perhaps even more crucial but also quite difficult. As we have already noted, dominant residential patterns contribute to a lack of significant social interaction across ethnic and economic lines for both city and suburban congregations, and both geographic separation and the fierce autonomy of Hartford's suburban towns create additional barriers for suburban congregations in focusing their concerns beyond their town's borders. Such boundaries will not be crossed without intentional efforts by congregational leadership. Several Hartford-area suburban and inner-city congregations have formed partnerships to address particular regional concerns and to increase identification of each type of congregation with the region as a whole. Quite important too in this connection is the assistance of denominations and ecumenical agencies that are organizationally better situated to provide opportunities for identification with the larger community. Even these organizations, however, are sometimes trapped by boundaries that make identification with the broader community difficult. We noted earlier that at least one Protestant denomination uses the Connecticut River as an ecclesiastical boundary. To be sure, this boundary generally respects town lines; nevertheless, it has the consequence of dividing the larger natural community of Greater Hartford into two artificial parts. Although the division may make some sense from an organizational standpoint, it makes little sense as far as the identification of the denomination and its congregations with the public life of the larger Hartford community is concerned.

4. *Structures.* The matter of organizational structures deserves additional comment. We have focused heavily on congregations in our belief that they are the critical starting point for understanding religious presence in a community like Hartford. But existing structural patterns, both congregations and denominational and ecumenical organizations, are not sacrosanct. In his book *Encounter with Modern Society*[3] Bishop E.R. Wickham makes the point that the church and civil structures in the Middle Ages developed parallel or coincidental structures along a hierarchical and territorial principle. This made church and civil authorities organizational counterparts; they operated at the same levels, had access to each other, shared comparable geographic "turf," and shared many concerns within their respective areas of responsibility. Wickham's point is that this model is often dysfunctional in modern industrial society, and that appropriate new structures need to be developed to engage public issues and problems.

*See chapter 1.

If by this Wickham implies the abandonment of the congregation in a search for "new missionary structures," as was popular in the 1960s, we disagree for reasons expressed in chapter 2. To the degree, however, that he means recognizing the limits of current structures—whether congregations or existing para-congregational organizations—for some kinds of religious presence in public life, we strongly agree. We have seen in the case studies that congregations can do a great deal in meeting human needs and in contributing to a more vital sense of public life. But we have also seen their limits. Some public issues and community problems lend themselves to specialized forms of religious organization as congregations and individuals join together to meet their public interests and responsibilities across territorial, class, ethnic, and religious lines. Hartford's Center City Churches, which brings together ten churches for a wide range of community-based ministries, is but one of several examples of ways of overcoming the structural limits of congregational forms of presence in addressing issues of human need. Coalitions of congregations and other organizations combining study and action around specific issues—housing, peace, racism, or hunger, for example—are other possibilities. Such structures, more radically ecumenical than is the case for most existing interdenominational and interfaith organizations, are needed if an effective witness is to be made in public life to the unity that transcends our various particularities.

5. *Leadership.* In much that we have said we have highlighted the importance of the role played by the clergy—ministers, priests, and rabbis—in religion's relationship to public life. One way of understanding this role is as managing the interface between the religious group and the community. As we have seen, religious groups mediate not only religiously, between individuals and God, but also sociologically, between individuals and public life. Clergy, who play an assisting role in the first form of mediation, also are important bridge figures in the latter. This is especially true in the perceptions of many in the community, especially leaders. Religion is heavily identified with religious professionals. Unless ministers, priests, or rabbis are present and visible in public affairs, religion is thought to be absent. We acknowledge this as an important finding, even if we have some difficulty with it otherwise, as we note below.

But first, what can be said about clergy effectiveness in public ministry? Too often religious leaders approach public issues in a cavalier fashion, fail to prepare themselves adequately, and do not sustain their own interest and concern over time. Greater effectiveness will come as those representing the religious community are able to demonstrate concern about community problems, adopt strategies that are sensitive to political and economic realities, build relationships with those who make and are affected by public policy decisions, and distinguish between their own roles as representatives of specific constituencies and carriers of religious "truth." Without these abilities, religious leaders carry no more credibility than other interest groups in the community. With them, the potential for being taken seriously in the public arena is considerable. To do this, however, the risk of setting priorities, of choosing a few focal issues to the exclusion of others, must be made.

There are implications here for the recruitment and training of religious professionals. Suffice it to say that we question what seems to be an excessively narrow emphasis in much seminary training and continuing education for clergy on ministries to individuals and institutional management. As important as these emphases are, they leave clergy ill-prepared to function effectively as managers of the interface between the congregation and public life.

Let us return to the perceptions of the relative importance of clergy and lay roles that were expressed by a number of community residents and leaders, including many, we would add, who are lay members of religious groups. Over the centuries, clericalism has been a problem in religious communities as clergy have abused their power, either in the church or in the secular realm. Current perceptions about clergy and laity are in fact a form of clericalism, in which clergy are thought to be the only authoritative spokespersons for the religious community. Although we continue to affirm the important bridging role that clergy play in relating religious communities to public life, it is nevertheless the laity, not clergy, who are daily inhabitants—often key decision makers—of the institutions of the public world. That laity do not perceive themselves, or are not perceived by others, as credible spokespersons regarding religious and moral dimensions of public issues represents a serious failure. For both Jew and Christian, a concern for justice is regarded as a priority for the entire religious community, not simply for ordained leadership; nevertheless, too often—at least within the Protestant churches that we know best—the "ministry of the laity" seems to mean laity assuming responsibility *within* the religious community.

In the historical overview of the use of the concept, religious presence, in chapter 1, it will be recalled that the first efforts at exercising Christian presence in France were "combative" efforts by the hierarchy to reestablish the church—not entirely unlike more recent efforts by the leaders of the Moral Majority to reestablish a (Protestant) Christian America. But the focus soon shifted away from reestablishment of Christendom to an exercise of presence in the secular world through evangelism and milieu transformation. Significantly, that movement was essentially a *lay movement* through Catholic action, and when priests joined them it was as *worker*-priests, working alongside laity with no special privileges.

We are not advocating worker-priests—at least not ordained ones—but laity who are encouraged and supported by the congregations to exercise their ministries of presence in the day-to-day issues of public life, where they, not the ordained clergy, are the experts. For this to happen will take more than wishing it were so; there are any number of examples of things that can help it to happen in the case studies.

One thing, however, does deserve repeating, and it is critical for clergy as well as laity. It is the need to be able to articulate one's faith in relation to the complex issues of public life. As we have seen, both pluralism and the limits that come from our location in history mean that this articulation must be done confessionally, not dogmatically. Nevertheless, one of the common contributions of the great faith traditions present in Hartford and throughout the nation is a sense of the possibility that exists beyond the realities we now know. Although that possibility includes hope for a world to come beyond this present one, it also speaks to possibilities for life in this world: the chance for the poor to live in decent homes; for minority youth to find jobs; for an end to sexism, racism, and the other "isms" that oppress human beings; and for the community to discover a sense of itself as something more than an arena for interest groups to compete in for their share of economic and social rewards. The realization of these and other possibilities will be pushed forward as laity and clergy have the capacity to articulate clearly their belief in a God whose presence in this world expects more of them than they expect of themselves, and who can give expression to the implications of that belief in the issues of public life.

NOTES

CHAPTER 1   RELIGIOUS PRESENCE: AN INTRODUCTION

1. Lisa Alther, *Original Sin* (New York: Alfred A. Knopf, 1981), p. 238.
2. See, for example, *Handbook of Contemporary Urban Life,* ed. David Street and associates (San Francisco: Jossey-Bass Publishers, 1978).
3. "What the Next 50 Years Will Bring," *U.S. News and World Report,* May 9, 1983, p. A15.
4. W. Neenan, "The Suburban-Central City Exploitation Theses: One City's Tale," *National Tax Journal* 23 (1970): 117–39. Cited by John D. Kasarda, "Urbanization, Community and the Metropolitan Problem," in *Handbook of Contemporary Urban Life,* op. cit., pp. 53–54.
5. Parker Palmer, *The Gathering of Strangers* (New York: Crossroad, 1981), p. 18.
6. See, for example, Daniel Yankelovich, *New Rules* (New York: Random House, 1981).
7. There is in fact no real contradiction between enclave politics and privatization. The former provides a way of promoting one's private interests through collective action.
8. Ellen Goodman, "Moving from Community," *The Hartford Courant,* April 18, 1981.
9. See William Severini Kowinski, "Suburbia: End of the Golden Age," *New York Times Magazine,* March 16, 1980.
10. Martin Marty, *Righteous Empire* (New York: Dial Press, 1970), p. 179.
11. The distinction between "public" and "private" Protestants has affinity with another distinction important for understanding Protestant Evangelicalism— that between "pre- and post-millennial" thinking. For a discussion of this distinction and its implications for Christian social concern, see Donald W. Dayton, *Discovering an Evangelical Heritage* (New York: Harper & Row, 1976), pp. 121–35.
12. C. Kirk Hadaway, "The Church in the Urban Setting," in *The Urban Chal-*

lenge, ed. Larry L. Rose and C. Kirk Hadaway (Nashville: Broadman Press, 1982).

13. Sidney E. Ahlstrom, *A Religious History of the American People* (New Haven: Yale University Press, 1972), p. 741.

14. Ibid., p. 738.

15. For a discussion of some of these developments, see Sister Marie Augusta Neal, "Catholicism in America," in *Religion in America,* ed. William G. McLoughlin and Robert N. Bellah (Boston: Houghton Mifflin, 1968).

16. Nathan Glazer, *American Judaism* (Chicago: University of Chicago Press, 1956), p. 136.

17. For an example of this and the tension between identity maintenance and exercising a public religious presence, see chapter 6.

18. John Murray Cuddihy, *No Offense: Civil Religion and Protestant Taste* (New York: Seabury Press, 1978), p. 7.

19. James Davidson Hunter, *American Evangelicalism* (New Brunswick, NJ: Rutgers University Press, 1983), p. 87.

20. George W. Webber, "The Struggle for Integrity," *Review of Religious Research* 23 (September 1981): 7.

21. Gibson Winter, *The New Creation as Metropolis* (New York: Macmillan, 1963), p. 33.

22. For a description of many of these efforts, see Rudiger Reitz, *The Church in Experiment* (Nashville: Abingdon Press, 1968).

23. "Ghostly and Monstrous Churches," *The Christian Century,* June 2, 1982, pp. 663–65.

24. Arnold Toynbee, *Cities of Destiny* (New York: McGraw-Hill, 1967), p. 28.

25. Bruce Reed, *The Dynamics of Religion* (London: Darton, Longman and Todd, 1978), pp. 55–56.

26. For discussions of the presence of the sacred in various religions and in Old and New Testament perspectives, see G. Van der Leeuw, *Religion in Essence and Manifestation* (New York: Harper & Row, 1963), and Alan Richardson, ed., *A Theological Word Book of the Bible* (New York: Macmillan, 1953).

27. Peter Brown (*The Cult of the Saints* [Chicago: University of Chicago Press, 1981], pp. 86–105) suggests that the spread of relics of the saints to widely scattered shrines and congregations in late antiquity played an important role in promoting a sense of belonging and solidarity throughout the Roman Empire.

28. Calvin was more radical in this regard than Luther was. For Calvin, *finitum non capax infiniti,* the finite cannot contain the infinite; whereas for Luther, *finitum capax infiniti,* the finite can contain the infinite. But for Luther, the infinite was known only to faith in the mystery of the baby in the manger, in the crucified Christ, and in Word and Sacrament.

29. Max Weber, *The Protestant Ethic and the Spirit of Capitalism,* trans. Talcott Parsons (New York: Charles Scribner's Sons, 1958), pp. 181–82.

30. Here we are especially indebted to a summary of these developments by Jean Dimnet, "Towards the Discovery of a Genuine Presence," *Student World* (1965), pp. 223–32, and to our colleague at Hartford Seminary, Willem Bijlefeld for insights into the adoption of "presence" language by some in the Christian missionary movement.

31. Quoted in Dimnet, "Towards the Discovery of a Genuine Presence," op. cit., p. 227.
32. Ibid.
33. M.A.C. Warren, "General Introduction," in John V. Taylor, *The Primal Vision: Christian Presence Amid African Religion* (London: SCM Press, 1963), pp. 10–11.
34. Harvey Cox, *The Secular City* (New York: Macmillan, 1965), p. 36.
35. Winter, *The New Creation as Metropolis*, op. cit., pp. 5–6.
36. "The Christian Community in the Academic World," *Student World* (1965), p. 234.
37. Peter Berger, *The Noise of Solemn Assemblies* (Garden City, NY: Doubleday, 1961), pp. 148–49.

CHAPTER 2   RELIGIOUS PRESENCE: A CONGREGATIONAL PERSPECTIVE

1. Sidney Ahlstrom, "Theology and the Present-Day Revival," in *The Annals* 332 (November 1960), pp. 20–36.
2. Sidney Ahlstrom, "The 1960's: Radicalism in Theology and Ethics," *The Annals* 387 (January 1970), p. 5.
3. From "Tho' Our Hearts Dwell Lovingly," a sermon preached by Abraham J. Feldman, Temple Beth Israel, Hartford, October 18, 1968.
4. Martin Marty, *The Public Church* (New York: Crossroad, 1981), p. 45.
5. Ibid., pp. 53–54.
6. Jurgen Moltmann, *Hope for the Church* (Nashville: Abingdon Press, 1979) pp. 21, 40–42.
7. David O. Moberg, *The Church as a Social Institution* (Englewood Cliffs, NJ: Prentice-Hall, 1962), chap. 6.
8. Peter Berger and Richard Neuhaus, *To Empower People* (Washington, DC: American Enterprise Institute for Public Policy Research, 1977), pp. 2–4.
9. Ibid., pp. 26–33.
10. Parker J. Palmer, "Going Public," *New Conversations* 5 (Spring 1980):15.
11. Browne Barr, *The Well Church Book* (New York: Seabury Press, 1976), p. 7.
12. Carl S. Dudley, ed., *Building Effective Ministry* (San Francisco: Harper & Row, 1983).
13. H. Paul Douglass and Edmund deS. Brunner, *The Protestant Church as a Social Institution* (New York: Russell & Russell, 1935), p. 237.
14. Max Weber, *The Sociology of Religion*, trans. Ephraim Fischoff (Boston: Beacon Press, 1963).
15. Ernst Troeltsch, *The Social Teachings of the Churches*, trans. Olive Wyon (New York: Harper Torchbooks, 1960), esp. pp. 331–43.
16. H. Richard Niebuhr, *The Social Sources of Denominationalism* (New York: Henry Holt & Co., 1929).
17. See especially his *Religious Sects: A Sociological Study* (London: Weidenfeld and Nicholson, 1970).
18. Douglass and Brunner, *The Protestant Church as a Social Institution*, op. cit.
19. H. Richard Niebuhr, *Christ and Culture* (New York: Harper & Bros., 1951).
20. Avery Dulles, *Models of the Church* (Garden City, NY: Doubleday, 1974).
21. The questionnaire by which we classified Hartford-area congregations was

slightly different for synagogues than for churches, although the general meaning of the orientations remained the same.

22. See Robert N. Bellah and Phillip E. Hammond, *Varieties of Civil Religion* (San Francisco: Harper & Row, 1982), p. 191.

CHAPTER 3   A SOCIAL HISTORY OF RELIGIOUS PRESENCE IN HARTFORD

1. For anecdotal material we are especially indebted to two "popular" histories of Hartford: Glenn Weaver, *Hartford: An Illustrated History* (Woodland Hills, CA: Windsor Publications, 1982), and Ellsworth S. and Marion H. Grant, *Passbook to a Proud Past and a Promising Future* (Hartford: The Society for Savings, 1969).

2. Robert Handy, *A History of the Churches in the United States and Canada* (New York: Oxford University Press, 1977), pp. 77–78.

3. Sidney Ahlstrom, *A Religious History of the American People* (New Haven: Yale University Press, 1972), p. 288.

4. Patricia Tracy, *Jonathan Edwards, Pastor* (New York: Hill and Wang, 1980), p. 189.

5. Weaver, *Hartford,* op. cit., p. 66.

6. Milton Rugoff, *The Beechers* (New York: Harper & Row, 1981), p. 31.

7. Morris Silverman, *Hartford Jews: 1659–1970* (Hartford: Connecticut Historical Society, 1970), pp. 19–21.

8. Weaver, *Hartford,* op. cit., p. 96.

9. Louise C. Wade, *Graham Taylor* (Chicago: University of Chicago Press, 1964), pp. 25–26.

10. Ibid., p. 37.

11. Andrew J. Gold, "Economic Interdependence in the Greater Hartford Region—City and Suburbs." Prepared for the Capitol Region Council of Governments by Greater Hartford Process, Inc., October 1976.

12. William McKinney, David A. Roozen, and Jackson W. Carroll, *Religion's Public Presence* (Washington, DC: Alban Institute, 1983), p. 13.

13. Ella Friedman Norwood, *Not Bad for an Immigrant Boy* (New Haven: Oz Publications, 1979), pp. 51–52.

CHAPTER 4   HARTFORD TODAY

1. The four indexes measure different dimensions of religious commitment but are correlated highly. $R = .50$ or higher.

2. We looked at relationships between various demographic characteristics and the four religiosity indexes. Women, people over age fifty-five, minority group members, and people with lower educational levels are consistently more "religious" than are other sample members. Age has the strongest overall relationship to each index, followed by education. Education is most strongly related to orthodoxy ($R = .30$). Family income and city-suburban residence are not related significantly to any of the indicators.

3. The items were adaptations of those used in the mail survey of Hartford-area congregations discussed in chapter 5 and used in constructing the mission orientation scales introduced in chapter 2.

CHAPTER 5 AN OVERVIEW OF CONGREGATIONAL PRESENCE

1. See James H. Smylie, "Church Growth and Decline in Historical Perspective," in Dean R. Hoge and David A. Roozen, *Understanding Church Growth and Decline* (New York: The Pilgrim Press, 1979).

2. See, for example, Dean M. Kelley, *Why Conservative Churches Are Growing* (New York: Harper & Row, 1972).

3. The informing methodological model was ethnographic, although we entered the "culture" of the congregations with more structured conception of the questions we wanted to answer and the observation was of considerably shorter duration than is normally the case in ethnographic analysis. For an extended discussion of the ethnographic approach to studying congregations, see Melvin D. Williams, "The Conflict of Corporate Church and Spiritual Community," in Carl S. Dudley, ed., *Building Effective Ministry* (San Francisco: Harper & Row, 1983).

4. The team of case researchers consisted of nine persons of diverse ethnic and religious backgrounds, all with graduate-level training in social research. Members participated in a day's orientation conducted by the authors, and consulted with the authors no fewer than three times during the course of their individual field work.

CHAPTER 7 THE CONGREGATION AS ACTIVIST

1. "K of C Welcomes Reagan, Policies," by John P. Tarpey, August 4, 1982.

CHAPTER 10 THE MISSION ORIENTATIONS REVISITED

1. Peter Berger and Richard Neuhaus, *To Empower People* (Washington, DC: American Enterprise Institute for Public Policy Research, 1977), pp. 26–33.

2. Jeffrey Hadden and Charles Longino, *Gideon's Gang: A Case Study of the Church in Social Action* (New York: The Pilgrim Press, 1974).

3. Ibid., p. 153.

4. See Donald L. Metz, *New Congregations: Security and Mission in Conflict* (Philadelphia: Westminster Press, 1964). What Metz found for new congregations seems true for older ones as well.

5. John Murray Cuddihy, *No Offense: Civil Religion and Protestant Taste* (New York: Seabury Press, 1978), p. 27.

6. For a discussion of this problem, see Hans Mol, *Identity and the Sacred* (New York: The Free Press, 1976), pp. 82–84.

7. See Benton Johnson's classic essay on this theme, "Do Holiness Sects Socialize in Dominant Values?" *Social Forces* 39 (May 1961):309–16; and Robert Moore's insightful analysis of the broader social implications of this phenomenon in an English mining community, *Pit-Men, Preachers, and Politics: The Effects of Methodism in a Durham Mining Community* (New York: Cambridge University Press, 1974), pp. 9ff.

8. For example, Marion Hepburn Grant, in a speech delivered to the Society of the Descendants of the Founders of Hartford, not only applauds the current effectiveness of congregations like Cristo for advancing their members "steadily up the economic ladder to middle-class status," but also contends that it reflects the very same process "of grass-roots empowerment—spiritual, eco-

nomic and political"—first brought to Hartford by the Rev. Thomas Hooker in 1636. ("The REAL Hartford Process," photocopied ms., May 1982).

9. Peter Berger, *The Heretical Imperative* (Garden City, NY: Doubleday, 1979).
10. See Douglas McGaw, *A Tale of Two Congregations: A Comparative Study of Religious Meaning and Belonging* (Hartford Seminary, 1980), for an insightful discussion of the empowering and mutually reinforcing nature of strong social bonding and high salience of belief.
11. Max Weber, "The Social Psychology of the World's Religions," in *From Max Weber, Essays in Sociology,* ed. H.H. Gerth and C. Wright Mills (New York: Oxford University Press, 1946), p. 280.
12. H. Richard Niebuhr, *The Meaning of Revelation* (New York: Macmillan, 1941), p. 19.
13. Ibid., p. 42.

CHAPTER 11   RELIGIOUS PRESENCE: CONCLUDING REFLECTIONS

1. Peter Brown, *The Cult of the Saints* (Chicago: University of Chicago Press, 1981), p. 42.
2. For a much fuller discussion of the role of religion in creating a sense of the "public," see Parker J. Palmer, *The Gathering of Strangers* (New York: Crossroad, 1981).
3. E.R. Wickham, *Encounter with Modern Society* (New York: Seabury Press, 1964), pp. 36–38.